From the Banks of the Rhine to the Banks of the Mississippi:

The History of Jewish Immigrants and Their Individual Stories

Anny Bloch-Raymond

Translated from the French by Catherine Temerson

Janaway Publishing
Santa Maria, California

Copyright © 2014, Anny Bloch-Raymond

ALL RIGHTS RESERVED.
No part of this publication may be reproduced, stored in a retrieval system, or transmitted in any form or by any means whatsoever, whether electronic, mechanical, magnetic recording, or photocopying, without the prior written approval of the Copyright holder or Publisher, excepting brief quotations for inclusion in book reviews.

Originally published in France by:
Michel Houdiard Éditeur
Des Berges du Rhin aux rives du Mississippi . Histoire et récits de migrants juifs
2009, 2010

Published by:

Janaway Publishing, Inc.
732 Kelsey Ct.
Santa Maria, California 93454
(805) 925-1038
www.janawaygenealogy.com

2014

ISBN: 978-1-59641-342-9

Cover design by Anthony Nelzin/Zinzolin

Made in the United States of America

In memory of my parents

Contents

List of Illustrations vi

Acknowledgements vii

Preface ix

Introduction xvii

Chapter I: The Departure, the Crossing and the Promised Land 1

Chapter II: The Paths to Success 23

Chapter III: The Emergence of Communities 51

Chapter IV: The New Configurations of Judaism 67

Chapter V: Dwellings, Languages and Cooking 91

Chapter VI: Pledges of Fidelity to the New Country 137

Chapter VII: The Relation to the Other 165

Conclusion 201

Endnotes 209

Appendix I: Tables 233

Appendix II: Louis Geismar Letter With Store Letterhead 245

Appendix III: Maps 247

Bibliography 251

General Index 275

List of Illustrations

Flo Geismar Residence, New Orleans, Louisiana 123

Portrait of Isidore Newman 124

Portrait of Rebecca Kiefer Newman 125

Alice Wilson with Fraenkel Children 126

Grave of Felix Fraenkel, Baton Rouge, Louisiana 126

Felix, Jules, and Émile Dreyfous 127

Four Generations of Franco-German Women 128

Leon Fischel 129

Philip and Sophie Roos Sartorius 130

Page of Autobiography of Philip Sartorius 131

Picard & Geismar General Store 132

Geismar Plantation, New River Landing, Louisiana................132

Grave of Louis Geismar, New Orleans, Louisiana..................133

Lemann General Store, Donaldsonville, Louisiana.................134

Marriage Certificate of Moïse Waldhorn 135

Acknowledgements

I should like to express my deep gratitude to Freddy Raphaël who followed every stage of this work. I would also like to thank all my colleagues and friends in Strasbourg, Toulouse, Louisiana and Mississippi who agreed to read my manuscript.

This book could not have been written without the warm welcome of many individuals in the United States. I would like to particularly thank the people who extended their hospitality to me and helped me make important contacts. First and foremost Roberta and Neil Tepel, Stephanie Golden and Ellen Fine, thanks to whom I discovered a vast number of resources in New York. Rabbi Stanley Dreyfus and his wife gave me invaluable information as did Philippe Baumann and the members of the *Société Israélite Française de New York*.

In New Orleans, Flo Geismar was my hostess throughout all these years and a fascinating storyteller; Jackie and Benny Toledano initiated me to the life of the *Vieux Carré*. Cathy Kahn made the archives of the Touro Infirmary available to me and disclosed some of the city's secrets. Carolyn, Will Lazarus and their children were always present when needed. Herman and Nancy Kohlmeyer graciously spent entire days with me. Joel and Bert Myers were charming hosts. Oscar Lévy was my musical and Creole culinary guide. In Baton Rouge, Metz Kahn was the most patient and loyal of hosts, answering all my many questions over the years. In Jackson Marcie Cohen Ferris, Macy Hart and Mark Greenberg from the *Museum of the Southern Jewish Experience* guided my research work in Mississippi. I should like to thank all my hosts in Dallas and Cincinnati. In Montgomery, Babette and Charles Wampold were infinitely patient in welcoming me. In San

Francisco, I was received by Ellie and Albert Fraenkel, who did everything they could to facilitate my work. It would be impossible to thank everyone I met and spoke with; I hope they will accept my apologies. Special thoughts for those who are no longer with us: Moise Dennery, Ruth Dreyfous, Ruth First, Gaston Hirsch, Georges Simonnot, Benny Toledano, Fred Kahn, Gerald Posner, Rabbi Stanley Dreyfus, Aaron Steeg, and my dear cousin Flo Geismar.

I was very touched by the welcome I received at the Center of Jewish Archives in Cincinnati, both from the center's personnel and its directors, Abraham J. Peck and Rabbi Zola, as well as at Tulane University's Howard-Tifton Library and at the New Orleans Historical Collection. I would particularly like to mention the *Southern Jewish History* journal, and thank Mark Bauman and Rachel B. Heimovics.

The English-language version of this book would never have seen the light of day if not for the support of *La Fondation du Judaïsme français* and its director, Nelly Hansson, and the *Centre d'anthropologie sociale* and its director, Jean-Pierre Albert, as well as the generous grant from the Southern Jewish Historical Society. I should like to express my gratitude to my generous donors and thank them for their faith in me: Herman and Nancy Kohlmeyer, Ellie and Albert Fraenkel, Joan Loeb, Minette and Charles Cooper and Sera Segal. My thanks, as well, to my translator, Catherine Temerson, for her warmth, patience and insight.

Preface

The urge to travel, to immigrate to America, the desire for a better life, the longing for a promised land-these are sentiments that were shared by many population groups. Among them, the French and German Jews who made the decision to leave the banks of the Rhine and settle along the shores of the Mississippi.

Why emigrate?

A chance meeting, an article, an advertisement...

How did my research begin?

Chance, a series of encounters, broken threads woven together again little by little?

Shortly after my visit to the Société israélite française de New York in mid-September, 1991, one of its members sent me an article that appeared on the front page of *The New York Times* on September 29, 1991. I found myself riveted: "South's Small Towns Lose their Communities but Cling to Jewish History." The article described how a Methodist inhabitant of Port Gibson, Mississippi, had restored the town's old synagogue. The article gave the names of Jewish families originally from Germany and Alsace who had settled in the South of the United States.

I wanted to know more. I contacted the Jackson, Mississippi offices of the Utica Museum of the Southern Jewish Experience, referred to in the article. One of the administrators, Marcie Cohen, kindly ran a small ad appealing to Jewish families of French origin. I received over twenty responses. This is how my research began: a first meeting, an article, and an advertisement.

A few family correspondences had been maintained for several generations from continent to continent. They were small in number, but they allowed me to forge ties and build networks. This book, therefore, is the fruit of circumstance, of prior knowledge of the United States, and of a reciprocal trust established with the families I met. It examines the reality and the imagined perception of Jewish emigration from eastern France and southern Germany to the banks of the Mississippi during the nineteenth and early twentieth centuries, from the point of view of an outsider, a French sociologist. Exploring the South from another perspective, differently from the academics presently living in the South or in the United States can bring a valuable contribution to the knowledge of this fascinating and complex area. The new life in America often started in New Orleans, the port of arrival for many of these immigrant families.

New Orleans

I landed in New Orleans for the first time in June 1992. I was immediately struck at the airport by a tropical atmosphere: the predominant colors were blue and green. A group of visitors in shorts and bright-colored shirts, wearing panamas and Texan hats, filed past me. Gumbo, crayfish, shrimp; the dishes and menus attracted my eye. I sensed the influence of South America. The fragrance of fresh roasted coffee and chicory hung in the air. Both English and Spanish were displayed on the billboards welcoming travelers.

Before reaching New Orleans, or "the Crescent City," my friends and I drove down bumpy roads cracked by flooding. We crossed through Metairie, where a segment of the younger population lives, those who prefer the suburbs for their more spacious accommodations, their modern, more reasonable houses, and their upscale environment. Many businesses and companies have their headquarters there. Though they don't say it explicitly, people hesitate to live near the predominantly "black" neighborhoods of the city center.

The urbanization is chaotic: small shopping centers, factories, funeral homes, cemeteries, small companies, and a few strips of land protected by palm trees. Magnolia trees have been planted around savings banks. We stopped to sample dishes of fried fish, shrimp, crab, catfish and fried oysters. Keith, a young Creole whose skin is almost white, was accompanying my friend Flo Geismar, a Southerner of Alsatian origin. Flo Geismar's father left Alsace in 1909 to join his uncle on the banks of the Mississippi, in New River Landing-Geismar. This is a place where the river bends and meanders, making it easy for steamboats to dock. The little city took on the Geismar family name when it acquired a railroad track, in the beginning of the twentieth century. Geismar is about sixty-two miles from New Orleans and close to the capital, Baton Rouge. Since the 1960s, private plots of land have been purchased by the petrochemical industry, and the physical layout of the area has changed completely. The little towns used to be dotted with dry goods stores selling a wide range of products, and general stores and warehouses facing the landing piers. The towns consisted of several streets-Main Street, Commerce Street-with churches and synagogues built between 1879 and 1890. The train station stood at the heart of the city, an important landmark, the railroad being the primary means of communication after river transport. The plantations were spread out along the river, usually not far from one another. Since the discovery of oil and natural gas, the landscape has become industrialized; some of the plantations no longer exist.

Léon Geismar, Flo's father, never left the area, not even when his sugar cane plantation felt the impact of the Great Depression of 1929. His children moved to New Orleans after 1945 and adopted a completely different lifestyle, though they never gave up the motto "Let the good times roll." In the evening, in the garden of their house on Washington Avenue, when the family comes together, they enjoy several pounds of crawfish as their meal, or else they reheat a dish of steamed bisque. They purchase the dish, which takes hours to prepare, in the city of Gonzales, near Geismar. It combines lobster, crab, spices, pepper, paprika, Tabasco, onion, lemon and brandy.

Keith, the young boy with Flo Geismar, is fourteen years old. He lives in a little wooden house on the edge of the affluent Garden District, long the exclusive neighborhood of Anglo-Americans. As for many of the houses close to the levees, air conditioning consists in sitting in rocking chairs on the veranda and enjoying the cool evening breeze. These little houses are similar to the wood cabins of the West Indies, but they are larger and painted in bright colors, blue or yellow, and they shine in the sun. The most beautiful avenues uptown are lined with enormous oak trees laden with Spanish moss. Their roots split the sidewalks open but the shade of the giant trees protect against the harsh sunlight.

The French Quarter, originally Spanish, reflects the many influences that the city has undergone. Its history is French and Spanish, as explained in the Louisiana State Museum, The Cabildo, a late eighteenth-century Spanish building. But the city could really be likened to a gumbo, the first course served in every restaurant in New Orleans, whatever the price range. This dish consists of vegetables imported from Africa, such as okra, a variety of refined spices from the Caribbean, and rice, shrimp, crab and onion, attributed to both the French and the Spanish. The city's highly diverse immigrant population also includes Italians, Irish and Germans, though they came to the region more recently, in the course of the nineteenth century.

In the Company of Families of Franco-German Origin

Time was short and I had so much to see. With Carolyn and Will Lazarus, whose ancestors came from Duppigheim (Bas-Rhin, Alsace), I discovered the working-class restaurants where you eat "po boys," sandwiches stuffed with shrimp, ham or crab. This used to be the staple diet of the impecunious employees in the French market. Oscar Levy, who worked in the import-export coffee business in Panama, was my guide in the Vieux Carré. He made a point of telling me that the city was built below sea level: when there are heavy downpours, a pumping system transfers surplus water from the canal into Lake Pontchartrain. He showed me the remains of the first synagogues on North Rampart Street. We walked past the Opera, the cathedral on Jackson Square, the street where the cotton exchange, painted by Degas, was located (Degas' family lived in New Orleans). Then we made our way through the French market with its mounds of fruits, vegetables and traditional spices. Some of the produce is imported from South America.

Le Café du Monde, reputed for its sweet beignets and *café au lait*, gives out on the river. We watched the barges being towed along the Mississippi…

Oscar mentioned the *bayous*, (from the Choctaw bayuk, "river") the stagnant expanses of water formed by of the Mississippi's former anabranches and meanders. The river and marshland are rich in fish, birds and cypress trees. The river, navigable for thousands of miles, spreads out in southern Louisiana.

We stop in front of a row of narrow rectangular buildings: "shotgun" cottages dating from the 1900s, so-called because theoretically a shot could travel from one end of the house to the other, straight through its three consecutive rooms. The residences in the French Quarter are permanently lit by gas street lamps. Gas and oil are provided by the North of the State since the beginning of the century. In the rear, you can make out the houses of the mulatto Creole woman and, here and there, former slave cabins.

Canal Street, a major shopping street, serves as a dividing line between the Franco-Spanish Vieux Carré, and the Anglo Garden District, on the west side of city. The former is characterized by two-story buildings with wrought-iron Spanish balconies, and the latter by neo-classical *ante-bellum* mansions (belonging to plantation owners, industrialists, or artists). A trolley links the uptown, residential St. Charles Avenue to the Canal Street business district.

Knowing that I was in New Orleans, many people came to see me. They brought me their genealogical tree, usually the work of the youngest member of the family, and told me their family history. Sometimes they found information inscribed inside their prayer book: a list of births and deaths. In one of the houses I visited, I noticed, hanging on the wall, a slave contract that had belonged to an ancestor.

Furtively, I entered into the family geography of the South.

My hosts asked me scores of questions on their family origins, and wanted to know the locations of different villages. Fortunately I had brought maps of Alsace and Germany. We retraced the journey of the first immigrants. The frontiers between France and Germany were sometimes ill-defined. My interlocutors situated German villages in Alsace and vice-versa.

"Could you go to the archives and find so-and-so's birth certificate?" Sociologist, genealogist: seen from afar it's all the same. Then I received more elaborate requests: "Help us to get to know of our family history." Exchanges began, and little by little trust was established. My cousins offered me hospitality. Then I stayed with friends I had made by exchanging letters — in Baton Rouge, Louisiana, in Jackson, Vicksburg and Natchez, Mississippi, and at later on, in Montgomery, Alabama, Martin Luther King's city. I was given books on the South as welcome gifts: cookbooks, as well as books on architecture, history, and literature. I had the privilege of living through some unforgettable experiences. Several families entrusted me with the writings or correspondences of their ancestors. Ruth Dreyfous gave me the correspondence of her grandfather Abel with his French family (1849-1890). The Scharffs presented me with the Memoirs written by their ancestor Philip Sartorius in 1910. Thanks to French contacts in New York I was able to find the diary of Isaac Levy written in 1890-1892 in German. On my last day in Cincinnati, at The Jacob Rader Marcus Center of the American Jewish Archives, I discovered the voluminous correspondence of Benoît Fromenthal, an immigrant from Alsace, dating from the period when he lived in New York, from 1865 to 1872; the archive consists of one hundred and forty-seven letters. Finally, the Memoirs of Rosalie Weil Cahn (1837-1909) were given to me by Jonathan Parker, one of her descendants, thanks to a demographer friend who interceded on my behalf. It reflects her trials and tribulations as she journeyed from Bischwiller to Paris, and then on to New Orleans, and San Francisco.

Handed down from generation to generation and sometimes

forgotten, diaries, correspondences, memoirs, suddenly turn up unexpectedly: when people move, or as part of the family archives donated to, or purchased by, the special collections of libraries.

Abel, Philip, Julius, Rosine, Benoît, Isaac, and later Clara, these are the names of those who crossed frontiers and sailed the ocean, becoming emblematic actresses and actors in the long history of migrations in the nineteenth and twentieth centuries; from small villages in the Palatinate, Baden, Alsace, and Lorraine, they journeyed to the cities in Louisiana and Mississippi, New York and California.

Introduction

Who were the Jewish Immigrants from the Rhine valley?

The immigrants from the Rhine valley[1] can be described in different ways. First as a population that crossed national frontiers and chose to settle in the South of the United States. But they were also a religious minority and, in adapting to their new environment, distant geographically and mentally, they adopted new values and invented new ways of being. Observing how new ways of life were set up over a long period of time in a world that was sometimes open, sometimes hostile, is the object of the present book.

Every emigration is an uncertain and risky gamble, but based on the thought that life in the new environment will be better. It includes its share of dream and its share of temerity. It implies a long preparation, confronting the unknown, and not looking back on the past. It requires leaving a part of oneself behind and tapping into a new world that will have to be deciphered. The narrators of these experiences stress their successes; setbacks and obstacles are scarcely outlined. Leaving home is like a wonderful epic tale, full of pitfalls, but victorious in the end. Few families returned to their country of origin. Somehow, they adapted, settled in, became established and in the end chose to make their life in the new land. They rarely departed alone. They left in groups belonging to the same generation, and entire families met in ports and ships, including friends and neighbors who lived on the other side of the border.

In studying the migrations of French and German Jews we were able to compare the two countries and found that frontiers, far from separating people, brought them together. The wave of immigrants from both banks of the Rhine took place more or less in the same years: 1830-1869, 1880-1930. Though the reasons for departure are not identical they are similar economically, demographically and religiously. The term "frontier culture" could apply to German and French Jews, for they had much in common. They shared the same religion and professions, had Yiddish as a common language, and intermarried. The Rhine frontier was porous in the 1850s, and even more so after the Second Reich's annexation of Alsace-Lorraine in 1870. It allowed for commerce, the development of communications, and exchanges. When they wanted to emigrate, the frontier populations used the same agencies and the same transportation routes. They met and mingled on the same ships.

This book deals only incidentally with the post Second World War period. Indeed emigration after the Holocaust is very specific, involving families of victims and displaced persons welcomed in the United States. In the course of my research I met several concentration camp survivors or former prisoners who had come to America after the Second World War, but their immigration falls within the province of the history of the Holocaust and its consequences on the American continent, raising issues that are different from those of immigration in general.

Who Were the Pioneers: Community, Diaspora, Ethnic Group?

The first question is one of numbers: can the number of Jewish immigrants in this region be calculated? How many were there? A few answers can be provided, though they cannot be exhaustive. While remaining cautious I can give an approximate idea of the size of these departures. The total number of Jewish immigrants from the Rhine region is hard to assess. Based on the prior research of historians Vicki Caron and Nicole Fouché and on consulting the lists of immigrants and of requests for passports, I estimate that slightly over 10,000 Jews from Alsace and Lorraine left for America between 1830 and 1914.

Ten to twelve percent chose to live in the South of the United States, primarily in Louisiana. On the German side of the Rhine, according Avraham Barkaï, over 200,000 Jews left their country during the same period. In 1850 in New Orleans, the second port of entry into the United States, the count comes to 11,531 French and 11,425 Germans, of which approximately 12% to 20% are Jews.[2] Immigrants from rural backgrounds quite naturally chose a rapidly expanding rural environment. Indeed, small Southern towns were valued places in which to settle. But settling did not necessarily mean settling for good. Newcomers chose to live in small towns at first. Later on, they moved to urban centers or migrated out west in the 1850s during the gold rush. Families moved to the big cities only after prospering in the small towns where they had first settled.

The aim of this study is to make the words of the immigrants heard through the stories of their descendants and their own personal reminiscences. I wish to give prominence to the narrative and personal experiences of French and German families who have been living in the United States for four or five generations and shed light on the ways in which individuals explore and remember the lives of their pioneering ancestors. This book does not attempt to render an accurate or comprehensive history; I am not a historian and the book should not be regarded as the history book. It should be read as a suggestive collection of family memoirs. Its substance lies in the way the characters talk about themselves, highlight their adventures, picture their lives and stage their experiences. My interlocutors are the actors in their own lives and they intend to remain so. That is the underlying principle I have culled from their testimonies.

Contrary to what is commonly thought, immigrants were not illiterate, quite the opposite. Their prior education was not insignificant. They acquired German and French in school and some among them received training in professional trade schools or schools of arts and crafts. These qualifications greatly facilitated their adaptation in the new country. French was the majority language in Louisiana, while German was spoken in churches and synagogues and was the language of many immigrants of German and French descent. Even before the creation of The Hebrew Immigrant Aid Society (HIAS), the Hebrew Benevolent Societies and later the Ladies Hebrew Aid Association played an important role in giving support to immigrants. As charitable institutions they operated just like the region's Catholic and Protestant associations. Other institutions, like the Howard Association in New Orleans, were multi-denominational and assisted patients in the city hospitals. Indeed, Jewish immigrants did not form a self-enclosed isolated group. Immigrants belonged to a social group, but did they form an ethnic group?

In France, the term "ethnic" is used cautiously and has been the object of much questioning, stemming from the fear of dividing and fracturing the unity of the French Republic and ministering to the interests of community groups. The term is just beginning to be used in the press in reference to Black, Rom, and North-African minority groups. In the United States, the concept has been defined in many works by sociologists and historians and is used extensively to identify groups, on the social, cultural or religious levels. The status of communities, which could be called intermediary bodies — religious communities, school communities, community associations — is fully recognized, whereas in France it is the individual and not the group that constitutes the French nation. Religious communities in France are associations of worship; they are not recognized politically and as such are not entitled to financial support from the State. But ethnicity was defined very progressively in the United States, dating back to the Chicago school of sociology in the 1940s. In attempting to define ethnicity, the sociologist Everett C. Hughes makes a completely valid point in emphasizing not so much the importance of the content of an ethnic group as the role of the relationships among different groups. In the meeting of ethnic groups and cultures, "The relations, however are never studied. Since it is generally true that members of a minority have a more lively experience of the dominant group than members of the latter have of the minority, more can perhaps be learned about the inter-group relations by studying the minority than by studying the dominant group.[...] Much is to be learned about the inter-group relations by probing to the depths of personal experience, by discovering through what experiences the individual learns both the realities and the fictions of his position as a member of an ethnic group."[3]

Does this minority constitute a Diaspora? This opens to interpretation. The works of researchers are invaluable in analyzing Diasporas using various approaches — literary, political, sociological — and from the points of view of authors in different continents, American, European and African.[4]

These studies also allow us to define how cultural groups born of the same transnational history are confronted with national questions. Though we commonly refer to a Jewish "Diaspora", wouldn't it be more accurate to speak of a variety of Diasporas within the Jewish Diaspora, divided, as the case might be, into Western and Eastern Diasporas, Ashkenazic and Sephardic Diasporas?[5]

The French sociologist Dominique Schnapper emphasizes phenomena of acculturation that occur between the Diasporas and the host territories also called "settlement" territories, a notion that implies the permanent settling of the immigrant population.[6] National frontiers are stronger than the transnational cultural identities. However, for every Diaspora, national conflicts, rivalries, and hostilities can die out in the course of a new transplantation. Different alliances come to light in the host country, with priorities of integration prevailing over national identities. A new Diaspora is formed. Former national cleavages fade away into a new national entity. Richard Marienstras analyzes the patterns of Jewish life with acuity and claims to be an ardent champion of the Jewish Diaspora. Indeed, for him, the Jewish experience has always been transnational: "Rather than see it from the perspective of narrow-minded and limited chauvinistic nationalisms, it should be seen from a new perspective that makes each culture an irreplaceable worldly possession, and the participation in several cultures should be seen not as treason, but as an enrichment. Diaspora

Jews are doubly rooted: on the one hand in their respective Diasporas — and these are genuine, deep roots (...) — but also, beyond these first geographic, cultural roots-they have other roots which makes them participate in a historical space — that of the Jews — a second space that does not intersect with the ethnic groups of the majority."[7]

His thoughts on the Diaspora contributed in developing a model: a group of exiled immigrants, some of whom remain aware of their origin, maintain a collective memory of the history of their dispersal and a loyalty to their original country. The group splits up into communities and establishes transnational networks. The possibility of returning is omnipresent: "Maintenance and reestablishment of the country of origin, Diaspora populations retain contact with their country of origin in a variety of ways." A relationship with the lost area, dispersion, a relationship with the Nation-State are constituent elements in the concept of Diaspora.[8]

The term "rooted" can seem problematic and contradict the notion of Diaspora that assumes the idea of mobility and dispersion. I would more readily talk of settling, or of sojourn, a term that seems more suitable and appropriate to the mobility of Diasporas. The term "sojourn" assumes the possibility of leaving or going elsewhere. It combines two ideas, the idea of a compulsory departure from the country of origin, exile, and the idea of a reinvented, imagined, country of origin.

The Jews from the Rhine valley whom I met in the Southern states wholeheartedly support the existence of Israel since 1967.[9] Yet their country of origin is neither overshadowed nor dismissed. That country is an asset; it is part of the group's identity. They become interested in it in particular circumstances: when they return to the ancestral country or, better yet, when writing their memoirs. That's when the birth country cannot be ignored.

Is it possible to stay somewhere for a sojourn and, as the writer and sociologist Nicole Lapierre puts it, "Think elsewhere"?[10]

Disquietude

This idea comes from the fact of having a stake in a country combined with the possibility of an elsewhere, the ubiquity of the place of sojourn: "disquiet". This way of being from one place and from elsewhere at the same time seems to be one of the permanent traits of Diasporas. This includes not just the ability to wander and be nomadic, but also Judaism's characteristic internal duality of being both "here and elsewhere," of being able to stop and settle, and still think of leaving. The image of the immigrant and his suitcase or the immigrant asleep on his trunk runs through literature and cinema. To borrow the term used by the writer Pessoa, Diasporas are made of "disquiet" in their very essence, made of the desire to belong and be foreign both at once. Diasporas know that they are on the margins and precarious because they are "on the border of the page," on the edge of the frontier. From one day to the next, they can become objects of suspicion, rejection, not to say exclusion, and thus put in the position of experiencing frontiers, of crossing them, of being "frontier prowlers" or, more seriously, of being exiled.[11]

Yet it is possible to settle permanently. It is possible to belong to a dispersed people while being, for a time, permanently settled or "liable to become so" and being rooted in this way can also be creative and dynamic.[12] The distinctive feature of Diasporas is to organize networks that provide the possibility of maintaining family identities, as well as religious, cultural, and economic ones, across different countries. These relationships, essential elements in the dynamic of identities, empower the group to find its place in the social, economic, and political world, to have an influence on the host country and to fight for it, as in 1917-1918 or 1942-1945.

But in it is not sufficient to view the Diaspora on the social, cultural and political levels alone. The correspondences of immigrants show that banking and businesses organized economic and financial exchanges at a very early date both internally within the United States, and externally, between America and the European continent.

Immigrants, a Heterogeneous Group

The concept of "social class" is rarely explicitly referred to in the survey conducted between 1992 and 2000. Religious and community feelings prevail over social inequality. Distinctions are made according to the criteria of success and create disparities, hierarchies of power and influence. There are few workers included in the group concerned. Indeed, the majority of the people in the group are small business owners, employees, artisans, members of the upper classes. The more impecunious include peddlers, traveling, non-nomadic peddlers whose greatest wish is to settle.

Thus the concept of social class does not seem adequate in analyzing groups of immigrant Jews. Wealth and poverty are the categories that make a difference, however they are too vague to be effective. Though the distinctions between different social strata do not constitute pre-established dividing lines, they exist nonetheless. They stem from a multiplicity of phenomena. Indeed, the dividing lines take into account length of time in the new country, economic success, and prominence gauged by commitment to Jewish and civil institutions. Hence eminence is acquired thanks to the recognition of moral values, an interest in preserving the Jewish heritage, a philanthropic bent, and local economic influence.

Respectability, eminence, and wealth are the emblematic values. They represent the markers of integration. The same hierarchy can often be found in private social or religious organizations that solicit financial support. Indeed titles are revealing: honorary members, benefactors, ordinary members. They reflect the importance of donations. Hence cleavages appear very starkly between the upper classes, a kind of Jewish aristocracy, and the other social categories. In the South the former are often connected to plantations, to the various professions and speculation involving cotton and sugar, to finance, and capital invested in department stores. A clear distinction is made between the venerable aristocracies of the old

South and the recent newcomers, who are certainly respected but have less prestige.

The earning of money is a sign of success and an important factor in social recognition: it changed the status of first-generation immigrants from Poland and Russia as well. The financial success of immigrants from Eastern Europe allowed them to acquire respectability, following in the footsteps of the French and German immigrants. This new wave of immigrants at the end of the nineteenth century was initially disparaged by Franco-German Jews, but a generation later, in the 1920s and 1930s, they were seen as "prosperous and respectable families or generous donors," to use the words of my interlocutors.

It is impossible to speak of dividing lines without including a genuine racial order that differentiates Whites from other groups.

Dealing with the "Racial Order" and the Color of the Immigrant
In the South, there are still traces of segregation in the way society functions; you are still defined as either white or black. Elites meet in a few clubs or philanthropic associations. Though workers of both races rub shoulders in the work place, they do not mix socially. In Montgomery, Alabama, entire neighborhoods are populated solely by African-Americans, and this is also the case in the poorest neighborhoods of New Orleans. The public schools, with the exception of the magnet schools and semi-private public schools, are in majority black. Whites and African-Americans do not attend the same private schools, except for the Catholic parish schools.[13] Clubs are selective. Some only recruit powerful African-Americans from the middle and upper classes. "Within the black community, some classes discriminate against others," remarks Babette Wampold, one of my interlocutors in Montgomery. Segregation and separation can in fact be likened to a colonial situation. Indeed it seems possible to draw a parallel between colonial situations and the "racial order" in the Deep South. In her book on sociological understanding, Dominique Schnapper writes: "In colonial society, the relationships between individuals, regardless of personal intentions or "good will" on either side, could never escape the effect of belonging to the group of colonizers or the group of colonized. Nor could the relationships

between Black and White individuals in the South of the United States develop outside the constraints and violence imposed by the racial order. [...] The political condition-the colonial society or the society born of slavery- imposed its logic inexorably on all the exchanges between individuals and gave rise to particular social types."[14]

Indeed it is interesting to examine the position and color of immigrants, as historians and sociologists have done. In 1957, the historian of immigration Oscar Handlin emphasized that beyond the ethnic mobility and inclusion of immigrants, the history of European immigration seemed to him not so much proof of America's democratic opening and of American capitalism's capacity for absorption, but that it was the racial status of Europeans, seen as free and white, that constituted their entry ticket. This analysis of the boundary between the white and the black worlds has been reconsidered since the 1990s. In *Whiteness of a Different Color* (1990), about European immigrants, the historian Matthew Frye Jacobson suggests that immigrants, including Jewish immigrants, only attained a white status very gradually. David R. Roediger makes the same argument in *Whiteness, a Wayward Construction* and *Working toward Whiteness: How America's Immigrants Became White*. The historians of immigration and of Judaism have revisited the question of the immigrants' cycle of assimilation and of the relations between the races. Let us note Leonard Rogoff's *Is the Jew White? The Racial Place of the Southern Jew* (1997) which raises the question of the color of the Southern Jew: from 1850 to 1910 Jewish immigrants were not really seen as belonging to the white race; they could be regarded as white, black, or of mixed race. In 2006, Eric L. Goldstein studied the cost of whiteness in *The Price of Whiteness. Jews, Race and American Identity*.

Historians and sociologists have shed light on the social and religious evolution of the Jewish identity and on the social and cultural status of Jewish immigrants living in the Southern States. Beyond the observation of places, groups, and individuals, personal and collective identities are affected by movement — geographical movement and movement towards the other —

complex permutations occur involving an attachment to the new country, sporadic fidelity to the former one, the invention of new religiosities, the synergy and conflict between the majority and minority populations.

What are the characteristics of the Jewish immigrant from the Rhine as opposed to other Jewish immigrants, or other immigrant minority groups? How do their adventures first start, what are their reasons for leaving and choosing to settle in the South?

I will attempt to answer these questions by studying the groups and pioneers in their transatlantic journey to the banks of the Mississippi.

CHAPTER I-

The Departure, the Crossing and the Promised Land

A Young, Adventurous and Well-Educated Franco-German Immigrant Group

Some facts and figures will help give an idea of the size of our emigrant group. The Jewish population made up about 1 to 1.5 % of the population in the German and French provinces; the immigrant population is estimated to have been close to 4% of the total population, with Jewish immigrants constituting about 12 % of the total number of immigrants. These figures are based on the lists of people leaving.[15] Whereas the peak years of emigration for the population of Alsace-Lorraine as a whole are 1840-1850, the peak years for Jewish emigration occur later, between 1847 and 1857.[16] The time lag in the Jewish emigration can be explained by professional reasons. Most of the professions listed are in the business sector, with a small number in industry and agriculture, as opposed to the immigrants as a whole, the majority of whom are farmers and craftsmen. The Jews are less affected by the agricultural crises of the 1830s and 1840s that strike these regions and lead to heavy emigration. However they are more affected by economic transformations and overpopulation. The development of capitalism, industrialization, and progressive urbanization lead to the disappearance of professions traditionally held by Jews.

Added to these general economic causes are factors that concern Jews more specifically, namely their precarious status during crises and social upheavals. The anti-Semitic riots of 1830 and 1848, and later, in the 1880s and 1890s, in the midst of a renaissance of nationalism, are confirmation of this. However, the historians of transatlantic immigrations, Camille Maire for the Moselle, Avraham Barkaï and Hans G. Reissner for Germany, see no proof of direct links between the anti-Semitic riots and the departure of this minority.[17]

I think it may be useful to provide a more detailed picture, based on the information collected from the lists of requests for passports and departures from small towns. These lists allow us to tally the dates of departure, the professions of those leaving and to know the destination places of the immigrants. From consulting the lists I was able to count the number of Jewish immigrants from the Bas-Rhin, Alsace, who left for America during the first wave of emigration, from 1828 to 1837.[18] From the fifteen towns in the Bas-Rhin, Alsace, there were 71 Jewish immigrants out of a total of 615 immigrants, in other words, 12 % of the total were Jews. Other periods are representative of the migratory flow of the Jewish population. Between 1857 and 1867, French and foreigners leave from the Wissembourg train station: among the 764 French immigrants, there are 97 Jews, in other words, Jews make up 12.6 %.

The list of immigrants from the Haut-Rhin, Alsace between 1800 and 1870, established by Daniel Dreyer based on requests for passports, are another source of knowledge about the departures. Though it does not claim to be complete, it provides some important clues. Starting in 1827, the date of the first request for passports by Jewish immigrants, to 1870, I counted 134 Jewish immigrants bound for America. The greatest number of departures date from between 1850 and 1870. The choice of France for residents of Alsace-Lorraine, as provided in the Frankfort Treaty after 1871, required a certain cultural level, knowledge of French, and contacts in France. Rural Jews living in towns of less than 2,000 inhabitants often had no choice but to try their luck in America or Algeria.

On the list of young people from Mulhouse who left for America between 1874 and 1897, giving up their Alsatian nationality, we count 118 Jews out of 1,100 immigrants, in other words, they make up slightly more than 10 %. Though I researched the registers of ships arriving in New Orleans at the Williams Research Center of the Historic New Orleans Collection, I did not find the families bound for New Orleans. Indeed the lists are incomplete.

According to the data provided by the historian Avraham Barkaï, who studied the Jewish population more specifically, 140,000 Jews left the territory of the German Reich for the United States between 1840 and 1870. The greatest number were from Bavaria, particularly the Bavarian Palatinate and the region of

Baden, which are in the Rhine valley. On the whole, from 1830 to 1914, over 200,000 Jewish immigrants came to the United States from Germany. If you take the example of the Bavarian Palatinate, you note that the migratory peak from that province was between 1852, with 18,956 immigrants, and 1855, with 21,897.[19]

The emigration of Jewish populations in Germany occurred during the same period as in Alsace: the 1850s. In 1900 the Jewish population in the region of Baden — a region with a high rate of Jewish emigration — maintained its numbers thanks to a high fertility rate-in other words, 26,492 inhabitants-but now representing only 1.4 % of the total population as opposed to 1.7 % in 1852.[20] In 1881, prior to the massive emigration of Jews from Eastern Europe, the Jewish population in the United States is estimated at 280,000 persons.[21]

In spite of the quantitative differences between the two banks of the Rhine, the way of emigrating is identical. French and German immigrants end up on the same ships, and use the same travel agents-there are seventy-two offices in the small towns of Switzerland, Germany and Alsace, organizing the same journey to Le Havre. This is applies to the border areas in the region of Baden and the Palatinate. In fact, American historians readily put Alsatians and Mosellans in the same category as Germans.[22]
Migrations on both sides of the frontier are analyzed in parallel. The historian Paul Leuilliot points to "the inevitable effect of example that triggered a strong fever of emigration to the United States, gradually spreading from Switzerland to the right bank of the Rhine and then to the left bank."[23]

The immigrants, bachelors for the most part, were very young, between 15 and 18 years old, when they left their country. It is generally thought that they had no profession or training, but in reality this was not always the case.

A Majority of Merchants and Craftsmen

If you consider the professional distribution of all passport applicants from the Bas-Rhin, Alsace, between 1827 and 1837, 42.67 % are farmers and day laborers, 19.11 % work in textile and 8 % in leather.[24] The socio-professional categories of the Jewish population emigrating from the Bas-Rhin, Alsace in the same period are more homogenous than the categories of Alsace as a whole. We find a very small number of day laborers and plowmen, a small number of textile workers, and a majority of merchants and craftsmen. The professions listed for the Jewish immigrants from the Haut-Rhin, Alsace are as follows: four farmers including one wine grower, a day laborer, twelve craftsmen, a worker, and forty-seven merchants in various areas, including livestock merchant, leather merchant, butcher, and the traditional job of peddler.[25] Added to this are the professions of office clerk and domestic servant. This immigrant group also includes professions requiring technical training — a printer, a bookbinder, a lithographer-and artists — a painter, a photographer. Lastly, there are nineteen single women included in the group of one hundred and thirty four immigrants. Nine among them list a profession: there are three seamstresses, two milliners, one ironer, one schoolteacher, and two maids.

The emerging middle classes of the small towns and villages are also part of the German immigrant group. Between 1845 and 1849, for example, among those leaving Württemberg, are twenty craftsmen, six small merchants and peddlers, and seven livestock merchants. Individuals and their families are helped by community institution, as well as by the administration.

It should be noted that, added to the political and economic conditions, is the role of the Jewish institutions, eager to get rid of an overly large population. During a short period of time-the 1850s-the institutions are influential in speeding up departures by giving subsidies to the families wishing to migrate.[26]

The Role of the Jewish Consistorial Institutions in the Departures

In order to deal with the poverty of Jews in Alsace — some of who were reduced to the status of beggars — and encourage their moral progress, on March 14, 1853, the Jewish Consistory of the Bas-Rhin created a committee for the material and intellectual improvement of its co-religionists. The object of this committee, presided over by Louis Ratisbonne, was to try to do away with the traditional, undignified practices of a number of Jews in the countryside, such as usury or begging, and to steer them toward useful professions.

The minutes of their deliberations, that same year, record the offenses of the Jews of the Haut-Rhin, Alsace, the legal indictments against them, and their appearance for usury before the Jewish Committee. Besides providing assistance from 1853 to 1858, the committee also dealt with the issue of emigration. It asked all the consistories of France to send subsidies to help families who wished to settle in the United States but were too poor to cover the costs of the trip. In the years 1853-1854, thirty-seven requests for financial contributions were submitted to the committee, including ten from families with children. Between 1855 and 1858, 29 requests for financial contributions met with positive responses. On May 6, 1857, the Jewish Consistory decided not to help immigrants leave without cause. Emigration became a subject of discussion within the committee. One of the members suggested organizing the departure of idlers and indigents so as not to attract the attention of Christians. Emigration networks are contemplated by one of the members of the consistory but are not accepted:

To put it into effect, we must obtain sufficient funds by appealing to the government and request it organize an information bureau used both in the countries to which we would direct the immigrants and by the persons whom we will have to send preferably in order to come to an arrangement with the travel agents to obtain the transportation of immigrants at the lowest possible price.

The suggestion of getting rid of the burdensome rural Jews was rejected in favor of improving their condition by leaving them in their present homes, the objection being that forced expatriation would expose them to extreme poverty. It was better to create schools to help train and educate young Jews.[27] Thus the immigrants did not arrive uneducated and ignorant. They were often better educated in Germany or France than in America. A small number of them attended the *lycée* or *Gymnasium* or, like Léon Cahn, who emigrated in 1863, the Professional Trade School of Arts and Crafts in Strasbourg founded in 1820. However, establishing a Jewish school was a significant expense, especially in small rural towns. Hence in Germersheim (Palatinate) Jewish children, in the 1840s, were initially educated in Protestant or Catholic schools. A Jewish school, in an insalubrious room adjoining the synagogue, was founded in 1839. Philip Sartorius writes in his Memoirs that later, when the Jewish community received larger subsidies with the arrival of more affluent members, a building was rented, on condition that the State pay the rental and the salary of the schoolteacher.[28]

The young Jewish elite, eager to retain its specific religious rites while acquiring a more universal knowledge, asserted its concerns clearly. This commitment to the handing down of knowledge and its acquisition can be seen in the story Rabbi Stanley Dreyfus tells about his father who was a student in the Wissembourg Gymnasium at the time of the German annexation:

> *He used to tell a story, when he was in the gymnasium, he had a mathematics master in Berlin, a Prussian. The Jewish community had arranged that the Jewish boys would not have to write on Shabbat. So they arranged a special minyan at daybreak-a complete orthodox Shabbath service. And the kids went there and went through the entire ritual — went home for a bite of breakfast, and then went off to school where they did not write. The Prussian said one day: "Why don't you Jews ask the rabbi for a dispensation, so that you can write?" And my father somehow found courage enough to stand up and say, very politely-he didn't want to argue with him or insult a German master. He said, "In Judaism, the rabbi has no authority to grant dispensations, we really cannot write. And they didn't; that was the end of it.*
>
> *In their new home country, Jews had the same rights as other citizens; they were fully-fledged members of society without having to convert or conceal their origins as they had so often been forced to do in Germany.*
> *— Stanley Dreyfus, New York, October 20, 2000.*

In order to let their nationals leave, each State asked its administration to organize the migratory flows, but only after having deplored them. The organizing took place very progressively as of 1803; starting in the mid-nineteenth century the French administration favored immigration while controlling it. This was not the case for the other European countries.

The Role of the Administration in Regulating and Controlling the Flow of Immigration

To be more specific, in 1855 French legislation was implemented to legalize emigration: fixing the price of passports, railroad travel, and other forms of transportation. Migratory flows started to be monitored under the Second Empire; an Emigration Service was created within the Ministry of the Interior and put in charge of checking the visas of immigrants and compiling statistics. At the same time, emigration companies and agencies, some of which were found guilty of abuses, were put under supervision. Starting in the 1850s, the emigration requirements involving the delivery of passports for foreign travel became much more stringent, particularly for young men wishing to emigrate in order to escape military service. Hence, in September 1858, the young Émile Baumann from Forbach, supported his request for a passport with a certificate guaranteeing his ability to pay the price of his military exemption, the sum of 2,450 francs, should he be chosen by the drawing of lots.[29]

The aim of this policy was to monitor population movements, but also to contribute to the economic development of transportation and tourism. According to the Napoleonic Code, French citizens lost their nationality if they settled abroad with no intention of returning. Under the Restoration, new restrictions were imposed and, under the Second Empire, frontier checks were reinforced and the activities of foreign agencies were scaled down.[30] Moreover, departing individuals had to show proof of their financial capacities by means of a receipt and certificate from the tax collector. The mayor had to make sure:

That persons soliciting passports have settled their personal and real estate contributions in full; name, first name, age must be shown on the passport and they must show proof of having the financial resources to meet the costs of the trip. I will not deliver a passport to immigrants if their request is not accompanied by a receipt stating that they have already paid their contributions for the current year.[31]

The same circular required sub-prefects to write down the names of young people who belong to recruitment categories because of their age, and to record their exact position, the number they obtained in the drawing of lots, and whether or not they were to be drafted. Under the Second Empire, Jews who drew an unlucky number were allowed to find a replacement if they could afford it. But the view on emigration changed: "It was noticed that far from decreasing, the population tended to increase in the centers from which there was a regular and large wave of emigration." By 1850, according to the historian Gustave Chandèze, "the Germans had recognized that the amount of capital withdrawn each year by immigrants was far from as large as they had initially assumed. They also understood that the emigrants, who had been mediocre consumers in their home country, became substantial consumers thanks to their business prosperity in countries overseas and opened up new prospects for commerce and industry in their native country. Emigration could therefore bring genuine advantages."[32]

Commerce: a Proliferation of Cross-Border Emigration Agencies

The growing number of emigration agencies between 1855 and 1870, with America and Algeria as destinations, was a factor in the regulation of emigration as well as in its attraction and development. These agencies signed agreements with transportation companies in Le Havre for the journey to America. Their representatives were sent to all the small towns in Alsace, the Baden region, the Palatinate and Switzerland.

Offices were created in Pirmasens, Saverne, Wissembourg, Brumath, Landau, Kaiserslautern, Saint Louis, Pfaffenbronn, to organize departures to Le Havre. Many Jewish émigrés departing from Wissembourg, chose the firms of Boell Henry and Krauf Philippe, "two wealthy, highly regarded merchants offering all possible guarantees to justify public trust." The networks set up are very impressive. Hence, among the six large agencies in the region operating as local representatives of Le Havre shipping companies, the Wissembourg agency of Dreyfus Frères, which started booking the transportation of immigrants in 1865, had seventy-two emigration agents whom they sent out into the smallest and largest towns in Switzerland, Germany, and Alsace. Nor is it surprising that, parallel to emigration from France, foreign emigration, departing from the port of Kehl or the Wissembourg train station and crossing though Alsace, was also considerable. It played a part in influencing the Alsatian populations and contributed in improving the travel conditions of emigrants.

According to the report of the Ministry of the Interior to the prefect of the Bas-Rhin, in 1853, 16 to 17,000 foreigners crossed Strasbourg on their way to Le Havre. In 1854, 20,000 were expected. Prior to 1830 only a few thousand crossed into France. This ascending curve demanded improved welcoming facilities in Alsace and well-coordinated departures for Le Havre. The cost of transportation from Strasbourg to Le Havre was 33 francs whereas from Mannheim to Le Havre it was 32. The possibility was raised of attracting the German population from the center of Germany and transporting it to Le Havre. Three quarters of German immigrants chose to travel from Bremen to Hamburg, Rotterdam, or Antwerp. Mannheim-Mainz, Rotterdam-Antwerp cost half the price of the trip Strasbourg-Paris-Le Havre.[33] But up until the 1860s, the majority of Alsatian and German immigrants converged on Le Havre.

In Alsace, foreign emigration caused a problem: it was sometimes clandestine and the foreign emigrants leaving for America often had insufficient financial resources. The facilities for hosting immigrants needed improvement. Up until 1854, immigrants leaving from Le Havre were transported almost entirely by returning American cotton vessels empty of their cargo. It was necessary "to organize permanent regular transportation by steamship independent of the varying frequency of American cotton vessels." Reception in the Strasbourg inns had to be better organized; innkeepers' registers had to be dropped off at police headquarters, and a number of good quality, clean beds had to be provided. Good relations were to be established between Paris and Le Havre with information and plans. The wellbeing of the ship passengers had to be ensured during the crossing.[34]

The departure of German Jewish emigrants and Jews from eastern France surely caused disruptions in families and villages, in periods when the departures were most frequent. "The villages are emptying out, the children, a living force, are going away." But on the whole it provided relief for the remaining populations. They suffered from over-population, food shortages, rebellions and successive wars. Families hoped to be helped financially, their debts repaid by the young pioneer. They also considered leaving in turn. Emigration became "serial immigration," a new concept elaborated by historians. Though separation was difficult, with time the hope of a better life healed the wounds.[35]

Emigrants in Search of Documents

Emigrants had to submit to a waiting period before leaving and minors had to obtain parental permission. There were institutional requirements: a certificate of good conduct from the schoolteacher or certification from the law court that the person had committed no offence. The emigrant had to testify that a family member or connection in the host country would give him a job. In the Alsatian archives I consulted, I found the remarks of Léon Geismar dating from July 28, 1909, when he left with his uncle for New York and then on to New Orleans: "The way things are here at present, there is no future. I intend to stay in America and be naturalized American." He wished "to work in my uncle's business and earn my living on my own." "I request that you give me permission to leave."[36]

The town hall or schoolteacher delivered the moral certificate. Hence, in support of Léo Cahn, Monsieur Lévi, schoolteacher in Saverne, certified, on July 22, 1871, that he had "behaved in an irreproachable manner."[37] Theodore Dennery, originally from Vésoul (Haute-Saône) and a manufacturer in Wissembourg, left for New Orleans at age 36. He obtained permission to leave from the mayor on the following terms: Dennery, Theodore declared at the town hall that he "wanted to transfer his home to America," along with his wife Fanny Salomon and his two children, Charles and Marguerite. On July 17, 1871, the mayor certified "that Mr. Dennery, Theodore leads an honorable life and has good morals."[38] This meant he was departing without leaving any debts.

The passport was valid for one year. It requests that "the civil and military authorities of the French Empire and of countries friendly to France allow Monsieur Léo Cahn, tapestry-maker and upholsterer, living in Strasbourg and leaving for America, to pass through freely and to give him aid and protection." A complete description of the head of household is given at the bottom of the page: age, eyes, hair, chin, face, skin color and distinguishing marks.[39]

At the same time as the conditions of emigration improved, the report of the sub-prefecture of Wissembourg (7/12/1853) details the clandestine emigrations of inhabitants from the Palatinate, in Rhenish Bavaria, organized by a mayor in Uhrwiller (near Niederbronn, Bas-Rhin, Alsace) who provided the necessary documents for crossing France in exchange for a small fortune. In order to be admitted to France, foreign emigrants were required to pay 200 francs in cash or assets per adult and 80 francs for children between 5 and 15, unless they had a contract that ensured their transportation through France delivered along the requisite forms.[40]

Choice of Destination: Researching the Requests for Passports

After they had disembarked in the large ports of New York, New Orleans, Galveston, Savannah, Charleston, the immigrants chose very different destinations. The choice was first determined by the families or friends who had provided the affidavit required for transatlantic passage. It also depended on which languages they spoke, on their economic prospects, or the associations that could help them find lodgings and work. The Lazard and Weill families left New Orleans for California after the great fire of 1848. Others, like those from Phalsbourg, embarked directly for California in 1855.[41] Indeed gold was a strong attraction in the 1850s for certain families who would become the "French colony of San Francisco."

In compiling the choice of different destinations, requests for passports and personal narratives provide valuable information. According to the numbering of the passports for foreign travel from the Bas-Rhin, Alsace, between 1846 and 1865, the choice of North America by Alsatian immigrants increased considerably starting in 1853, with one third of the total requests being for America. The demand decreased as of 1856.[42]

The destinations of Jewish émigrés from the Haut-Rhin, Alsace, between 1840 and 1870 are as follows: out of 134 Jewish immigrants, 12 list New Orleans, 2 San Francisco, 1 Pennsylvania, 1 Minnesota, 1 St. Louis, 2 Washington, 1 Buffalo, 1 Canada, 89 New York, 5 South America; the remaining simply list America. Sometimes, the ports of New York and New Orleans were their first stops before traveling deeper in the new continent. In the Bas-Rhin, Alsace, in the lists of immigrants departing from the Wissembourg train station from 1865 to 1869-a transit station for Germans-we find 103 Jews among the 764 French and 16,686 Germans. Looking at the destinations listed, we can tally 66 immigrants destined for New York, 10 for New Orleans, 1 for

Pittsburgh, 2 for Cincinnati, 2 for Rio de Janeiro.

Taken together, the lists of the two regions show that close to two-thirds of the immigrants chose New York, whereas 8% to 12% chose New Orleans. Only a tiny number of small towns in the Northern United States were chosen as a first stop.

But it is important to see the immigrant as a person who makes his unique voice heard. His personality first appears in the way he takes leave of his family and country, a sensitive preliminary stage. Memoirs and letters offer emotional accounts conveying the joy of the person leaving and the despondency of those remaining. The young immigrant engrossed in his impending adventure was often unaware that this was a definitive separation.

Rupture and Separation Rites

For the departure and integration into the new society to be successful, each stage of the individual's undertaking had to be prepared well in advance. At the time, people did not talk about immigrating but rather about "a better opportunity in America," and "seeking one's fortune." But the journey was not rushed into but planned for several years. For it to be accepted by the family and the community, each candidate's departure was ritualized in various ways. Considered a rupture, families reconciled themselves to it provided a certain number of cultural norms were respected. Without such rituals, the departure could be perceived as a betrayal towards the family, the laws of the nation, and the social customs. The separation had to be carefully considered for one or several years prior to departure.

Isaac Levy kept a diary between 1886 and 1895. He left for New York on December 13, 1892, at age 22, from Lembach (Bas-Rhin, Alsace) after waiting for one year. His brother had left five years earlier and he was afraid of seeing his mother take to her bed a second time. After having filled out all the necessary papers, obtained a passport and the contract for the transatlantic passage, he waited for his friends and family to accept his departure. A few weeks before leaving, on November 27, 1892, he wrote in his diary that he could be satisfied. He had not been excluded from his circle of friends and ties would be maintained in spite of his departure: "All day long I had the visit of people coming to say goodbye to me. They say that when a person goes on a trip, he can see whether he is liked. Well, I can put my mind at rest; I don't think I'm leaving a great many enemies behind."

But he was aware of his mother's suffering and grief.[43] Another example is Julius Weis, who, in his autobiography written in 1908, reminisces about the preparations for his journey in 1845. His objective was to join his cousin in Natchez. His parents refused. His brother, who had left in 1837, at 19, had died of yellow fever in Baton Rouge a few years earlier. He was now their only child and he was called upon to remain. Realizing he had no future in the Palatinate, he was prepared to leave without their permission. His father finally obtained a travel contract for New Orleans via Paris-Le Havre, costing of 125 guineas ($50). He bought the contract on the other side of the border, in Wissembourg, ten miles away from his village. The sum was partly covered by Julius's savings; the remainder was borrowed.[44] On August 22, 1845, Philip Sartorius, another immigrant from the Palatinate, left his village of Germersheim, near Spire, at age 14. He embarked at Le Havre for New Orleans, on September 25, 1845, with 600 other passengers, and arrived on November 1, 1845.

Two things motivated the young immigrant: money and independence. Sartorius had the advantage of knowing both German and French. His position in the family counted; he was the youngest child. By leaving his elderly parents by themselves, in a certain way he was violating his filial duty. Though his mother was very distressed on the day of his departure, he didn't feel any regret at the prospect of never seeing her again. Nearly 60 years later, in writing his memoirs, he realized it had been traumatic for his family. "Just like a young boy, I thought of it as going for a picnic. I had no idea how great a step I was taking, nor the great pain it would cause my family. I was the youngest."

But, by and large, many of the young people who were swept up into the immigration, were not completely alone. Edmond Uhry, the son of a grocer in Ingwiller (Bas-Rhin, Alsace) who immigrated to New York in 1891 during the second migratory wave, writes in his Memoirs that almost all the families in his hometown had sent sons far away.[45] When one person settled, he was joined by others from the same region. And he observes that New Orleans is the primary destination of émigrés from Ingwiller, an inaccurate impression, as we pointed out earlier. When his first brother leaves for New York in 1886, the whole family is very worried during the ten days of the transatlantic crossing: "My mother prayed throughout days and nights. When a cable announced his safe arrival in New York, I galloped through the streets to broadcast the good tidings."

Though leaving could be considered as disloyal to the country of origin, the immigrants often saw themselves as being in the avant-garde, the pioneers preparing the ground for the whole family, the clan, or the village. Concerning the Bavarian emigration from the Palatine border region, the historian Avraham Barkaï does not speak of rupture but emphasizes that contacts were maintained by letter and financial support. "In many aspects these young immigrants considered themselves to be-as they often actually were-the pioneer vanguard that was clearing the way for the transplantation of whole families, clans and even communities."[46]

Indeed, thanks to the immigrants and their networks along the Mississippi, brothers, sisters and relatives would have the possibility of emigrating in turn, but not without difficulties.

The Crossing and Its Dangers

The journey itself, once the papers were obtained, was no simple affair. The danger of storms, the problems of discomfort and food supplies-the passengers had to bring their own food-the risks of disease-these were the new hardships. In the mid-nineteenth century the crossing could take to two months.[47]

Hence Julius Weis, born in Klingen, near Landau, in 1826, left for Paris in a stagecoach at the end of August, 1844. He stayed in Paris for two days. The trip by land took twelve days. He did not make the trip by himself; his group included twelve young people, six young girls and a family. They embarked on a sailboat on September 21, 1844. The vessel carried 400 passengers and there were only three cabins. The crossing lasted 42 days. During that period of time, the author records seven deaths and two births. What did the passengers do for food? They had to think of bringing supplies. The women cooked their food, mostly rice. The group arrived in New Orleans, on November 2, 1844. The entire trip had lasted three months. In his reminiscences, Philip Sartorius recounts how he left Germersheim one year later, on August 22, 1845. His itinerary, via Germany, Holland, and France, was less direct. He took an omnibus to Spire, a steamship to Mainz and Rotterdam. After staying for a week in Le Havre, he embarked on the sailboat Taglioni, on September 25, 1845. His transatlantic crossing lasted two months; his entire trip, three months. « We had five deaths on the trip. The bodies were put in a canvas bag with a heavy stone in the bottom, »writes Philip Sartorius in his Memoirs.[48]

And here are the recollections of Rosine Cahn written in 1908, describing her 1850 journey from Le Havre to New Orleans:

We were sixty-one days at sea and were in trouble several times, the large mast broke and it was necessary to fix it as best as we could; once a wave lifted off a part of the side of the boat and it was necessary to repair it with planks from the bunks since there was no other lumber in reserve for that : those poor people who had prepared for a voyage of forty-five to fifty days began to run short of provisions but mother had brought an abundance and as she always did helped out the others.[49]

Ten years later the journey was still hazardous because of epidemics and the lack of regular lines leaving Le Havre for America. According to the family archives he deposited at the Jacob Rader Marcus Center of the American Jewish Archives in Cincinnati, the tapestry-maker and upholster Léo Cahn, born in Saverne, left Strasbourg, his place of residence, in 1865, at age 36. Two of his children died of cholera in Le Havre, on October 18, 1865. He stayed there for one month and three days, helped by Catholic nuns. Having very little money left and unable to find work in Le Havre, he finally decided to leave for New York by sailboat. He embarked on November 21, 1865, with his wife and last-born child, and sailed into New York harbor on January 24, 1866. The crossing had lasted five weeks and the entire trip, over four months.[50]

So the journey undertaken by the immigrants was long and perilous. They faced hunger, epidemics, lack of money, and the suspicion of the natives in the regions through which they traveled. As they met in the ports and on the ships, the French and German populations forged ties and intermingled, as the historian Louis Chevalier points out: "The Alsatian and German emigrants end up intermixing. They share the same social and professional characteristics. They are crammed together on the same quays of Le Havre, waiting for endless months for a ship, and prompting the same hostile reactions among the port populations who blame them for bringing cholera."[51]

The Surprises of the Promised Land

Here is the account made by Benjamin Louis Geismar, originally from Grussenheim (Haut-Rhin, Alsace), of his arrival in 1879, an account published in The Jew of America.

It was a dark night in 1879 when Louis Geismar got off a steamboat at New River Landing in Ascension Parish (present site of Geismar. It was the New River Landing because the head of the river meets the Mississippi River here following an ocean voyage from Paris, France). He was dressed in a tuxedo, for one of his distant relatives had painted a glowing picture of the social life of the area and the fortune to be made in the new world. Imagine his dismay when he found that the bustling metropolis he expected to find was a riverboat landing from which a dirt road led back in the interior. Unable to find work-even for his room and board-Louis took the 55 dollars his parents gave him when he left home and opened a small store on the levee. The business grew and prospered and soon became the center of commerce for East Ascension Parish. The customers were the rice and cotton farmers in the area. In about 1884, Louis Geismar married Seraphine Heymann. They had two sons-Simon (1886-1953) and Minel (1889-1962).[52]

Flo Geismar, born in 1923 on the Geismar plantation, emphasized the myth of the pioneer, as both visionary and pragmatist: "Louis immediately recognized the potential and it was one of the few waterways that emptied directly into the Mississippi river and all the farmers from the inland came there to trade as well as people from upriver as down river. It was a natural landing."

Twenty years later, on September, 1992, in New Orleans, during my conversation with Flo, she related another, even more realistic, version of the story. Louis was not alone, he was with Jo Picard, and the two men took over a bankrupt business. She picked up the founding family narrative as if the latter, to be credible, had to include a fantastic element:

> *Louis Geismar born in 1857 arrived in the United States in 1879 with his cousin Jo Picard who had settled in a community up river about five miles of what became the village of Geismar, Louisiana. When they arrived there was also a Mr. Dreyfus also from Alsace*

whom Jo Picard had left in charge of a business and this business had gone bankrupt and he was now the owner of the store[...] Louis put up a small trading post near the coast and began to trade with the ladies and get his supplies by river from New Orleans and Memphis. Coming up the river, a young man by the name of Abraham Heymann. His father was a cotton producer and distributor in New Orleans as a shipping cotton exporter to Europe. He invited Louis Geismar home as he had three daughters home: Seraphine, Carolyn and Lena...
— Flo Geismar, New Orleans, September 8, 1992.

In spite of obstacles and a great many hardships, the narratives emphasize the capacity of the pioneers who, like the heroes of mythical tales, set off to conquer the wilderness and make it civilized. The pioneer stops at the pier or landing, propitious for doing business with people. The American adventure can then begin.

The Choice of Mississippi and New Orleans

A whole range of reasons led to a specific location being chosen: acquaintances, family connections, economic possibilities, languages spoken (German or French), previously settled groups, associations of supporting *landmannshaften*[53].Immigrants, the low price of land and businesses, the peddling and trade possibilities, or as the writer Eli N. Evans points out, the spot where "the mule dies."

Why the choices of Mississippi and Louisiana in such large numbers, after New York, Alabama and Texas?

Families and their relatives of the same generation settled in many small towns in Louisiana; as well as in Natchez, Vicksburg and Port Gibson, Mississippi; in Montgomery and Mobile, Alabama; and in Dallas, Texas. In 1850, New Orleans was a flourishing port with 116,375 inhabitants and an industrial production amounting to over one million dollars. It represented one fifth of the nation's population, after New York, Philadelphia, and Baltimore. Carl A. Brasseaux, a specialist of French emigration to Louisiana, puts the figure at 136,448 immigrants between 1840 and 1848, which is 12 % of the total number of immigrants in the United States. New Orleans is the second port of entry for immigrants, after New York City, with 77, 1401, in other words, 66 % of immigrants. Among these immigrants, there 11, 531 who are French.[54] These figures are to be viewed with caution. According to the statistician James Dunwoody Bronson, about half the immigrants entering through New Orleans were undeclared. Others were listed under the more comprehensive designation of immigrants from the North West, which included the Netherlands, Belgium, Switzerland and France.[55] Among them, were 11,425 Germans in 1850, with 126,000 German immigrants pouring in during the five subsequent years. Close to 2,000 Jews lived there in 1860.[56]

In 1850, 19,000 persons of mixed race were living in Louisiana. This population included soldiers, craftsmen, and very active businessmen. Mixed race creoles were free to sign contracts and accept donations of goods and property from other people of color or from whites. They engaged in business freely and lived in the same neighborhoods as whites, rubbing shoulders with them until the Civil War. The interdependence of the two groups, free men and women of color and whites, weakened the class differences in spite of the barriers established by the Spanish and French during the colonial period. In 1860, on the eve of the Civil War, free people of color owned 2.5 million dollars in property in New Orleans.[57] Women were present in the food trade, in markets, and they exercised the professions of milliner, hairdresser, seamstress. They owned boarding houses and ran taverns. A small number, free women of color, were placed under the protection of white men. The *plaçage* or left-handed marriage constituted an informal social institution specific to the French and Spanish slave territories. Creole concubines acquired real estate as per their status as "placed" women.[58] Their "natural" children, educated in special schools reserved for them, became businessmen, in the apparel, footwear or cigar industries, owners of plantations and slaves. Gradually a heterogeneous Creole group emerged whose interests and culture were different from the white group, an elite who became the spokespersons of a community of men and women of color.[59]

There were also whites in New Orleans who were members of the liberal professions, rich planters, and wealthy businessmen. In 1870, the city counted over 170,000 inhabitants including 15,239 Germans, 8,845 French, 960 Spanish, 936 Cubans, 668 Swiss, 254 Austrians. By 1890, the population of the city reached

242,000, but the German population kept decreasing. There were only 13,944 in 1890 and 8,733 by 1900.[60]

Growing Economic Activity Despite Epidemics and War

The historian Ronald Creagh offers a description New Orleans in 1850: "Steamships, barges, schooners, brigs are docked in the port. Rows of cotton, sacks of salt and all sorts of merchandise are piled up. [...] Raw material comes from the Mississippi valley and manufactured products come from Philadelphia." Business is transacted with Mexico and the West Indies. This was the period of import-export, and of industrial and commercial development. Cotton mills were set up. Sugarcane plantations prospered along the banks of the Mississippi and the sugar production became industrialized.

Abel Dreyfous, a young immigrant originally from Belfort, started out in a New Orleans soap factory in 1838, then trained as a notary public clerk and by the 1850s, became a well-established notary public.

According to Ronald Creagh, after 1830, the profitable sales of cotton and sugar led to the State's economic development and population growth. In 1860, with close to 5,000 workers, New Orleans was seventeenth in the nation it terms of manufacturing revenue. It was the warehouse for the entire Mississippi, and the great port for screening immigrants and sorting out agricultural goods. In 1854, Anglo-Americans were predominant in the Garden District. Prior to 1852, there was no central government uniting the French and American quarters.[61] Real boundaries existed in the city. In the first phase, the minority of immigrants that settled in New Orleans lived in the heart of the Vieux Carré and along Canal Street, the main shopping avenue bordering the Anglo-American section. When families became more prosperous, in the next generation, the 1870s to 1890s, they built beautiful houses in the Garden District and on St. Charles Avenue, Audubon Park or Carondelet Street.[62] The more impecunious immigrants settled a few miles away, in the villages of Lafayette and Carrollton, already populated with Irish, Germans and Alsatians, a place of intense port activity, where the congregation Gates of Prayer was born in 1850.

Still others, like Rosine Cahn's family, rented small shops near the sea wall to store merchandise peddled along the river. Her family's shop was next to stalls kept by immigrants who had arrived before them. Rosine Cahn remembers the area as having a mix of peddlers and stallholders, selling clothes and other non-perishable products.[63]

But the majority of Jewish immigrants settled initially along the fertile bends of the Mississippi river and its tributaries, the bayous. Between water and earth, the immigrants confronted the two great scourges of Louisiana: water and epidemic fevers.

The Importance of Hygiene and Water

The foremost question in New Orleans was hygiene. The streets were muddy, unpaved, often flooded, and livestock roamed freely. The drainage system of New Orleans, a city built below sea level, was still a major problem. Cathy Kahn, archivist at the Touro Infirmary, explained, "In 1890 a system of pumps allowed the water to be poured back into the river. But the drainage ditches served as sewers. The private companies polluted the water supply. At the time the city had 242,039 inhabitants. This is when the committee on water and sewers set up a purification factory."[64] It is hardly surprising that epidemics, yellow fever, cholera, malaria ravaged the city endemically between 1786 and 1847, then in 1853, 1858, and 1867. The year 1878 was particularly tragic. In a population of 216,000, 27,000 deaths were caused by epidemics.

The Civil War (1861-64) affected the cotton business. It slowed the city's growth and business activity. But the city was reduced to a state of immobility during the post-war epidemics: yellow fever in 1873 and 1878 resulted in 3,977 deaths. According to the historian Howard N. Rabinowitz, it only regained its competitiveness in 1888.[65] Patients were cared for by interfaith aid associations, such as the Howard Association, or community associations such as the Ladies Hebrew Benevolent Association. A home for orphans and widows was founded in 1854. The city was studded with hospitals. The Hebrew Hospital of New Orleans, also founded in 1854, became the Touro Infirmary after the Civil War, in 1874.

These epidemics impelled the inhabitants of New Orleans and much of its immigrant population to flow into the small towns along the river and inland. Whenever they could, newcomers quickly took refuge in the small towns; however, for reasons of trade, they stayed close to the Mississippi. Accordingly, Rosine Cahn's family took up residence in Pascagoula; Philip Sartorius's settled near Vicksburg; the Benjamins, Lowenburgs and Ullmanns in Natchez.

Nevertheless the appeal of New Orleans remained strong.

The development of the port of New Orleans played an essential role in the economic integration of immigrants.[66] The products coming into the port included food, but also non-perishable products or dry goods, hardware, clothes, footwear, china, building material. This merchandise required retailers for the companies in New Orleans and for the general stores in the small towns along the Mississippi. They were conveyed by riverboat.

The majority immigrated, initially, to small rural communities. Of the hundred or so families I studied, only about a dozen or so settled in a large city. Because of family connections and work opportunities, the first choices of immigrants were the small towns along the Mississippi river, and the bayous, the drained marshlands that had become fertile areas: Bayou Sara, Bayou Sainte-Marie... Perhaps this was because they found a world that was on their own scale, where they were close to their neighbors and future customers, and integration and exchange was easier? Very often they were the only merchants in these areas, or at any rate, they were so few in number that competition was less fierce than in the large ports.

They stopped in the small towns near New Orleans-Lafayette, Raceland, Lutcher, Thibodaux, the ports of Donaldsonville and, further North, the cities of Opelousas, Alexandria, and Shreveport in the Texas border. They also settled in Clinton, Woodville, Plaquemine, St. Gabriel, east of New Orleans, near Baton Rouge. Then they went to live further North, traveling upstream on riverboats, to St. Francisville, Vicksburg, Natchez, Port Gibson, Greenville, in the vicinity of Jackson, Mississippi. They could also be found in the North, in Brookhaven, Indianola, Lexington, Greenwood, Osyka. The immigrants' choice of small landing stages along the Mississippi was an economic choice. Indeed, up until the 1880s, the river remained the easiest mode of the transportation for merchandise. Therefore doing business required being on the riverfront. It was not until 1889 that the railroad linked New Orleans to Memphis, Tennessee.

Fully invested participant in America, a citizen adopting the models and practices of his new country, the new immigrant adapted to his environment.

What Were the Different Phases of the Settling Process?

In the course of my conversations, I often heard the terms adaptation and assimilation. The South was a land that had to be tamed and domesticated, a land from which the Jewish immigrant sometimes saw himself excluded...

CHAPTER II
The Paths to Success

"Americanization" in the South of the United States

The migration process raises the issues of reproduction, innovation, and change. It poses the problem of adjustments by immigrants, both collectively and individually. The lifestyles adopted by immigrants in their new country are elaborated slowly. Initially they try to reproduce their long-standing habits faithfully, but when circumstances forbid it, they adapt to the new professions offered by the local resources: farming the land, conducting trade from port to port, working in import-export. Their behavior fits the economic constraints of the environment and reflects the acquisition of a new expertise. It also reflects the specific history of the South, which was organized in religious associations and communities and structured by the ideas of class, race, and a ruling aristocracy.

The settlement of the immigrant raises the more general question of "Americanization." What does the term mean? For this group of immigrants from Western Europe, Americanization proved to be a necessity and an obligation in order for them to fit in with their neighbors.

Is Americanization feasible, is it attainable?

In the *Encyclopedia of the Social Sciences*, first published in 1930 by the adherents of the Chicago School of Sociology, the sociologist Read Lewis introduces the definition of "Americanization" in this way: "Americanization involves the social adjustment of social assimilation by which immigrants in the United States come to participate in the common life of the nation and to identify themselves with it with thoughtful feeling [...] Fundamentally the problem of Americanization is the problem involved in any migration from one social group to another..."[67]

In the same publication, Robert Ezra Park, one of the founding members of the Chicago School of Sociology, emphasizes the slowness of the assimilation phenomenon: "In the United States, an immigrant is ordinarily considered as assimilated as soon as he has acquired the language and the social ritual of the native community and can participate, without encountering prejudice, in the common life, economic and political. [...] "Assimilation may in some senses and to a certain degree be described as a function of visibility."[68]

In the course of the survey I conducted, essentially in the States of Mississippi, Louisiana, and Alabama, the term "assimilation" had no pejorative overtone; quite the contrary, it was used by my interlocutors to mean "integration," namely the different political, social, religious, and economic ways of being included in the new home country; the choices made and values adopted in order to adapt to it. The term "Americanization" was also often used by the descendants of immigrants who, looking back, narrated their itinerary, their paths to integration, and the ways in which they adopted predominant models.

However, the Americanization process raises the question of whether it is possible to maintain former customs in a new country. What is the meaning of the word "loyalty" in this context? Wouldn't it be preferable to use the expression "acculturation," which emphasizes the notions of contact, mixing, imitation, change, resistance, interaction and predominance, but, when all is said and done, the preservation of two cultures? Acculturation is the exchange of cultural traits among groups that are in continuous contact. Either or both of the groups might change slightly yet, overall, the groups remain distinct.

For the immigrant, the paths to acculturation must first involve opportunity and economic success. The immigrant's respect for the country's laws and his acceptance by others go hand in hand with his putting down roots and his financial success. In any case, migration does not presuppose a complete uprooting, or, conversely, the newcomers' complete assimilation into the society hosting them. It does require, in order to be as close as possible to reality, a non-monolithic view of the identities of immigrant families for they have very varied origins and personal journeys.

Every small town had its Jewish store but the Jews remained very dispersed along the Mississippi. It was not always easy to become affiliated to a religious community. It often had to be created and, in order to do so, sufficient numbers were required. The pressure in the South with regard to religious adherence was strong. Americanization meant commitment to the community in the narrow sense of the term, the organizing of religious life and charitable works. This involvement took place with a time lag of a few years. Religious life was not the priority of the pioneers and their families when they first settled.

The experience of the immigrant was defined by his aptitude for change and his mobility. His way of life and living space changed according to the vagaries of his experience. From temporary living quarters in a boarding house, the immigrant's family life was organized according to his economic activity. The family lived in the back of the store and later had a separate family home. In the photographs of well-to-do families of the period, you see a black governess among the masters. Objects, photos, and utensils brought over from the old country are exhibited in the houses, as a way of seemingly preserving the memory of a part of themselves. There is nothing distinctive about the architecture of the French, German, or bi-national family houses; they look like Southern colonial houses: wooden houses with an outside gallery and, in some cases, an inside patio.

Americanization did not just imply a professional activity and putting down roots, but also knowledge of the local customs. This knowledge was often made possible by integrating into a religious community and learning the language of the new country, English. How the language of the new country was acquired is an interesting question: on the job, in evening courses, in school. And in all these cases, what ties did they maintain between French, German, Yiddish and the English language?

The process of adjustment also entailed an adaptation to new styles of life and new tastes. By examining the objects, the décor of houses, the kitchen and cuisine of immigrants-the latter being at the heart of Jewish culture-you see that they gradually moved away from the traditional rituals in their ways of doing things. Finally, the feeling of belonging to a nation is demonstrated by an aspiration to civic commitment on different levels, that of the city, that of the State. The immigrant participates in the political life of his country. He bears arms, sees himself as a patriot and shows his attachment to his new land.

The interesting question is whether, when all is said and done, the Jewish immigrants originally from the Rhine valley who came four or five generations ago, feel like full-fledged participants in American society. It is surprising to hear Jane Godchaux Emke, the great-great granddaughter of the well-known planter Léon Godchaux, who made a fortune in sugar in the nineteenth century in Louisiana, express the following reservations: "Today I'm also keenly aware," she said, "that I've been ostracized from some clubs and organizations only because I'm a Jew. I'm aware of prejudice."[69] Does this comment hold true for the entire group concerned or is it just one person's opinion?

From Small Town to Small Town: The Insecurity of Birds of Passage

The reasons for emigrating were economic: such is the leitmotif. The promised land was the land where you could make a fortune, a land where prospects were wide-open. Where foreigners were free to travel in search of opportunities, and equally free to leave after a given time, a year or more, if business did not prosper. The pattern of upward mobility could take one or two generations, sometimes three. Very often success involved moving from small rural towns or bayous to the big city. The phases were usually identical, for many families. Indeed, they profited from the development of capitalism in the nineteenth century, whose scale was still family size. A distinction should be made between the city and the rural world. Capitalization methods were not the same for planters and owners of rural stores, as for city wholesalers, department stores, and stockbrokers.[70]

Though some families settled in the city, over a third settled in the bayous. Two thousand Jews lived in New Orleans in 1860, six thousand were scattered throughout Louisiana, in Shreveport, Donaldsonville, Alexandria, Opelousas, Monroe, Clinton, Bayou Sara. They were peddlers, or storeowners selling various products, among them products derived from cotton.

Using various census sources, the historian Jacob Rader Marcus, estimates that there were 1,200 Jews in Mississippi in 1859.[71] He notes an appreciable increase in thirty years, due to the second wave of emigration from Germany and from Central Europe in the years 1870 to 1880. In 1878, he comes up with a total population of 2,262 Jews: 220 in Natchez, 109 in Port Gibson, and only 88 in Jackson. In 1859, Alabama has 2,000 Jews. In 1849, there were only 30 Jews in its capital city, Montgomery. By 1878, the number had gone up considerably, to 600, with 200 in the city of Selma and 20 in Demopolis.[72] In 1860, according to Elliott Ashkenazi, the Jewish population in the South totaled 33,200. Louisiana had the greatest number of Jews, ahead of South Carolina. The residents of small towns in Louisiana are more mobile than the immigrants living in New Orleans:

They generally began as peddlers, an occupation that made them itinerant by necessity. Even Jews managed to open stores, they did so with little capital investment and hence with little or no risk. The overwhelming majority of Jewish storekeepers in rural Louisiana owned dry goods stores, or general stores. Their customers include slaves, large and small landowners, and other village residents. They bought their inventory from larger stores in Shreveport, Baton Rouge or Donaldsonville but most often in New Orleans. Some went directly in the North East of the United States or Europe for merchandise. They depended for their sales and terms of payments from their customers and to their suppliers on the prevailing agricultural economy based on the growth and marketing of cotton and sugar. Many of the rural storekeepers became active traders in these staples. [...] In a sparsely populated is State, Jewish merchants were visible even if their numbers were small.

In the small towns of Louisiana and Mississippi, Jewish businesses played a pivotal role on Main Street. Jewish stores competed with the stores that preceded them. The stores were open to all the categories of the population, without color prejudice; the prices were often lower and the products more innovative. The new immigrants' respect for the standards and values of the South led them to obtain, with time, the trust of the local population-in spite of the prevailing suspicion of traveling strangers and foreigners.

A good case is that of young Philip Sartorius. He arrived in New Orleans in 1845 and set out, with his brother, to explore the possibilities in the small towns along the river. He is an outstanding example of that rural and urban mobility, with his capacity to adapt to the opportunities offered by the river, to open a business and then set off again to another location. His Memoirs, written in 1910, a half-century after his arrival, are invaluable for understanding the risks, the insecurity, and the uncertainty that the immigrant had to confront.

In 1845, Philip's brother Isaac purchased merchandise for him in an auction sale in New Orleans. This first business venture was unsuccessful. He then tried to sell supplies to tailors and office employees, with no success either. After that Philip Sartorius was hired by Goldsmith and Haber, a large wholesale firm of non-perishable goods in New Orleans. But he stayed with the firm only a year. Thanks to a cousin who offered him a higher salary, he moved to Princeton, Mississippi in 1849. There too he stayed only for a short time. After a third job, he partnered with his brother Jacob; they bought a boat together and started a peddling business along the river. First they opened a stall in Richmond, Madison Parish, Louisiana. Because of the bad roads and the high cost of transportation, in the spring of 1850, they moved again, further north, on the other bank of the river, to Milliken's Bend, Madison Parish. The city of Vicksburg is just across the river. They opened a store selling furniture and household equipment. Business improved. So much so that in 1852 he bought a house. The store was on the lower floors and the living quarters upstairs. Within two years, in 1854, nine years after arriving in the United States, he was very respected and no longer treated like a pariah. He had acquired a house and his business was prosperous. He settled down for good. His brother settled in Memphis, Tennessee in 1858, still near the river. Philip Sartorius traveled to New Orleans by boat three or four times a year to buy merchandise. The trade in cotton bales completed the store's activity. Many shopkeepers were also cotton merchants. Darker times loomed ahead for Philip. He was drafted into the confederate army in 1863. He fought, was wounded, and returned home. After an epidemic, in which one of his children died, he felt he should move to St. Louis to protect his family, which he did in August, 1863. One of his nieces lived there. The armies were close, in Vicksburg. He obtained a permit to cross, exchanged his confederate money into dollars and three days later, arrived in the Union zone, in St. Louis. He needed money and sold all his valuable possessions, his furniture, his piano, his merchandise. He dispatched everything by boat and sold the cotton he still owned to the Union.

In St. Louis he entered into a partnership with an acquaintance and opened a cigar factory, hiring twelve workers. He stayed in the city for two years. Cigars were taxed too high. In 1865 he accepted another job, in partnership again, selling alcohol beverages in Vicksburg.

Philip Sartorius's life story is emblematic of the vagaries of an immigrant's life when he first settles. At first, the immigrant adopts the logic of economic survival. He moves from the big city to the small towns on the edge of the Mississippi and finally settles in

Milliken's Bend until the Civil War. The Civil War constituted a rupture because of the destruction, the bankruptcy of the plantation owners, and the reorganization of property. The former slaves, now free, became sharecroppers or a labor force that had to be paid.

In order to survive, Sartorius began by relying on his family, his acquaintances from his former village, and partners he met in his travels. Under pressure, he sailed up and down the river and exercised pragmatism, switching from one profession to another, diversifying his activities. He adapted to circumstances in order find accommodations, buy a house, find a job, start a business. Above all he was inventive and showed business acumen, providing his customers with previously unknown products, as he explains in his *Memoirs*: "We kept many articles not kept by other stores and in this way we soon established a nice business."[73]

The new resident, if respectful of social norms, can be integrated into the country, fully recognized and honored, after only a few years. From being a social pariah he becomes a responsible member of society, involved in civic and political matters. This sets him apart from the foreigners who transgress the rules and are perceived as unreliable businessmen.

> *We were strangers and foreigners. Those who were there before us, also foreigners, did not observe the laws, for instance they would sell goods to negroes at night without a permit from their masters and do other irregularities. We were distrusted and envied by the other merchants, but in time when the people learned to know us that we were law abiding, they trusted us and became friendly. [...] The people before the war immediately back of the river were friendly and sociable, and anyone that appeared respectable was welcomed and gladly entertained and treated, not like a stranger, but like an old friend.*[74]

There are other models of success.

The Peddler

Starting out in a small town, traveling from small town to small

town, and ending up in the big city. Once the first generation is established in a rural area, the second or third generation moves to the big city. The length of time needed to establish oneself and make oneself known varies. A small number of immigrants —
such as Julius Weis, originally from Klingen (Palatinate), who settled in Natchez, Mississippi, or David Wolbrette, who came from Alsace in 1870 and went to live in Plaquemine, Louisiana —
moved to the city after about fifteen years, once they had become prosperous.[75] In these examples, the success factors are a well-managed mobility, a flare for opportunity, a knack for innovation, and austerity. At a time when French was widely spoken, the fact that all the Jewish merchants spoke German-as a common, shared language-facilitated relationships and business partnerships. This was the case for both the German immigrants-Julius Weis, Philip Sartorius-and the Alsatians-Abraham Levy, David Wolbrette, Félix Fraenkel. In the 1850s and 1860s, in New Orleans, Shreveport and Alexandria, success was tenuous. The immigrants often started out with more modest positions, such as peddler or employee.

Let us focus on the job of the peddler, or more accurately riverboat peddler.

The peddler is an emblematic and traditional figure of Judaism in literature, an object of nostalgia, criticism, and often caricature. Peddling, in Europe and the United States, is a profession that requires very little capital but a great deal of persistence, stamina, and a willingness to hit the roads and sail the rivers. Lucile Aron, the daughter of a peddler, painted a lucid portrait of her father in one of her letters. With pride and amazement, she described her father's immigrant know-how, his ability to adapt to the most difficult situations, his qualities as a salesman, his persistence, his thirst for knowledge, and his love of books. Here is an excerpt:

> *He came to America in third class, in steerage, a seventeen-year-old Jewish Alsatian boy. He had only his strong sturdy young body, and an eager alert inquiring mind as his stock in trade with which to conquer the new world in which he found himself...*
>
> *He started as many young men did in those days, a Peddler! He peddled, he bought and sold, he planted crops on lands he acquired, he dealt in skins and pelts, he made sugar and milled lumber, he raised truck and there passed through his ownership many Louisiana*

plantations, for he was ever the born trader.
— Mrs. Lucile Lazare Aron, November 15, 1935.[76]

The peddler is a man whose main asset is his ability to work hard. Though he arrives with nothing, the newcomer contributes to the development of domestic trade. The peddler brought merchandise to the Southern plantations along the Mississippi. In New Orleans, the merchants in their boats circled around the big ships that arrived in port; they loaded their boats with merchandise, which they unloaded in the smaller ports along the Mississippi, Donaldsonville, Port Gibson, Natchez, and Vicksburg.

The peddler follows the pioneers inland. When the roads were laid out, the peddlers set off, either on foot carrying their bags or in mule-drawn carts, establishing a liaison between the waterways and the facilities located inland. Their philosophy is to be on the move: "Here today, gone tomorrow." These traveling salesmen sold a variety of useful everyday objects: notions, fabric, hides, pelts, shirts, boots, household objects, trinkets. They could not travel with heavy loads and had to limit themselves to small specialized objects. After about ten years, if they had have made a profit, they would open a small retail store, most often in a market town or port.

A good example is Léon Godchaux, who came from Herbeviller (Lorraine) in 1840. He started out, like many, by borrowing money to buy merchandise from Leopold Jonas, a well-known New Orleans wholesaler who trusted him. He was probably recommended by his companion Tassin, a free man of color from New Orleans and a cook, whom he had met on the boat. According to his biographer and great-great granddaughter, Jane Godchaux Emke, his main assets were a good knowledge of French, an ability to appraise people, and obvious maturity.[77] He sold notions, pins, thread, needles, ribbons, combs, mirrors, the usual things peddlers sold. He covered the area of Destrehan, a plantation about thirty miles from New Orleans, in St. Charles Parish. The women in the countryside did not go into the city often and needed merchandise. After about a week, he would return to his wholesaler, Jonas, to get new supplies. He understood that he could also sell his trinkets to slaves. Later, when his business began to prosper, he went into partnership with Tassin, who had become his friend. The two men sold silk and lace collars. Then they bought a cart and a mule and, thanks to this new equipment, their business grew. After that, the two friends bought a building in

Covent, Louisiana, not far from their customary route, which they used as a warehouse for their merchandise, thereby shortening their travel time. Four years later, at 20, Léon Godchaux opened his first clothing store on a shopping street in New Orleans, Levee Street: "Léon Godchaux French and American Clothes." Tassin became his salesman. Beginning in the 1840s, clothes were imported from France and New York. You could find ball gowns, hats, and even ready-to-wear clothes, in small towns like Franklin, according to the historian Edwin Adams Davis.[78] In 1858, Léon moved to New York and opened an apparel workshop where he employed two hundred people. Between 1862 and 1880, the brothers Léon and Mayer Godchaux manufactured and sold clothing wholesale, and sold retail in two other stores. In the next phase, they acquired a six-story store on Canal Street, "The Léon Godchaux Clothing Store"; on the top floor they manufactured men's suits.[79]

After the Civil War, Léon Godchaux helped develop the sugar cane industry by centralizing and industrializing the refinement process in several plantations. His first purchase, from the Boudousquié family of free African Americans, was in 1868. This marked the beginning of his second sphere of activity.

Other peddlers did not attain success as rapidly, according to the autobiography of Julius Weis; they attained it in stages.[80] Weis traveled around Mississippi, near Natchez, and only began to earn a bit of money after his second trip in 1845. He had a poor command of English, but started out, at 19, with a horse, a saddle, and a bridle. At first he was helped by a cousin, but they parted ways very soon. Julius left for a month, from November 20 to mid-December. He learned how to visit farmers who were likely to purchase his merchandise. He encountered slaves pursued by dogs, others who had been flogged, and expressed his indignation at the treatment they endured. He suffered hardships for a much longer period than Léon Godchaux.

Competition among peddlers became less fierce starting in 1850. The price of a peddler's license in the state of Mississippi rose from $20 to $100. Many people left the profession for lack of capital, explains Julius Weis. In 1850, after five years of peddling, he gave up on going to California and bought a mule and a cart. He started earning a good living in 1853 and says he saved $6,000. It took him eight years to prosper. He gave up peddling and bought a building in Fayette, Mississippi, a small town he had got to know as a peddler, about ten miles north of Natchez, and converted his newly acquired building it into a store.

The connections he had established during his peddling years allowed him to make a name for himself when he opened his various stores, in Fayette, Natchez, and later New Orleans.

As the historian Hasia Diner points out, the profession of peddler was a temporary one in America. It was the job of the first years, until the time when the immigrant could buy a riverside business.[81] Yet in the eyes of the local population, the image of the Jew was intimately connected to peddling. When the Plotchnikoff family came to Tennessee from New York to open a store in Concordia in 1920, the first question the father was asked was: "Are you the new Jewish peddler?" To which he replied: "Jewish, yes, peddler, no."[82]

Though he could sleep overnight on farms and plantations, the peddler could not share the farmers' meals because they were not kosher. He traveled with a can of tuna fish: this was the only acceptable food for him, just as potatoes and coffee were for the peddlers in eastern France during the same period."[83] In Natchez, the Millstein house was the place where "many peddlers who came home [...] after a week's work would gather [...] for the Sabbath."[84] In his contemporary memoir, the writer Edward Cohen relates that his grandfather used to spend his Saturday evenings in New Orleans, after a week peddling in Hinds County, Mississippi, carrying a twenty-five-pound load on his back, selling everything from coffee to boot laces. He used to rest, drink whisky with Alsatian peddlers, and play poker all night.

Peddling in the City is Different

In the city peddlers went to the homes of a select group of people. Their status was different. They were not traveling salespersons as they lived in the city. They traveled much shorter distances and visited people who were recommended to them. In her Memoir, Rosine Cahn recalls that her mother and aunt, helped by their connections, made money selling trinkets to the wealthy Creoles of New Orleans. Her father worked in rural areas, exchanging merchandise for animal skins, which he succeeded in selling very quickly in the city. Women peddlers in New Orleans were accepted thanks to the tolerance of the Creoles, the old French and Spanish families living in Louisiana since the colonial period.

Rosine Cahn, notes in her *Memoirs* that her aunt "had a good business among the Creole women who had all good hearts and who did not mind doing some business with people a little cultivated who were trying to earn their living honorably."[85] She emphasizes the importance of respecting the social codes in order to be accepted but adds another factor, that of being educated and knowing the code of good manners. As we have already pointed out, the society of New Orleans was tolerant but was also very stratified.

There were over 10,000 peddlers in the United States in 1850 and 16,594 in 1860.[86] The peddling profession endured until the end of the nineteenth century. It should be noted that they were physically more vulnerable than other immigrants. The lists of patients in the Touro Infirmary show that in 1869, 7 of the 17 Jewish patients were peddlers; in 1884, 4 of the 13 Jewish patients were peddlers."[87] The profession gradually disappeared, supplanted by that of street vendor in the city, salesman of non-perishable dry goods, or general store manager in the rural areas, such as the Lorman Store owned by the Cahns near Port Gibson, Mississippi, and the Dreyfus Store in Livonia, near Baton Rouge, in the Tête Coupée bayou. The two stores run by these families of Alsatian descent, who settled respectively after 1850 and after 1870, were once rural general stores, but today they have become a secondhand store and a restaurant-inn. Both these places preserve family memories thanks to the objects collected at the end of the nineteenth century, which makes them into genuine little museums of the rural world.

The image of the peddler associated with the immigrant is a familiar one. However, in the lists of people emigrating, peddlers are in the minority. The majority found positions as employees, traders, and craftsmen. Accordingly, the 1850 and 1860 censuses consulted in Louisiana show a wide range of professions. There are indeed peddlers and junk dealers-about one tenth of the Jewish population-but also butchers, cobblers, barmen, grocers, bakers, a large number of tradesmen, accountants, tailors, jewelers, cigar salesmen, schoolteachers, dentists.

Usually at the very bottom of the business hierarchy, peddlers played an essential role as informers, linking villages and various communities. They served as intermediaries, offering an opening on the world and the latest city fashions and novelties. Peddlers also "forged relationships with customers, helped stimulate desire for new goods, and served as the fixtures of many local economies." Moreover their comings and goings gave them the opportunity to explore the inland areas, the plantations and the way they were managed.

The peddler, in the South, crossed boundaries, as the historian Hasia Diner points out. He had direct relationships with African-American families, ate with them, helped families in difficulty. Morris Wittcowsky, the author of a peddler's life asserts that peddlers were probably the first white people to show African Americans respect and address them as Mr. and Mrs.[88]

A new identity of the Jewish Diaspora was created in this manner; it was no longer based on the origins of people, but on the places where they had traveled. This peddling experience was an important, founding phase in the new history of immigrants and their children, an experience they shared with many other families.[89]

The next stage was putting down roots.

The Figure of the Established Businessman: The Necessary Diversification of Activities

Metz Kahn, whose family has been living in Louisiana and Mississippi for five generations, describes the main steps to putting down roots. The tradesman sells farm supplies and equipment on credit; the farmers mortgage their lands in order to pay; the tradesman acquires the land after their death.

> *I think it was Wolff who used to sell the supplies for plantations on credit and who owned part of the land after the deaths of these people. That's how it started. There was a Lehmann family in Donaldsonville, I think their plantation was called Bon Séjour[90].*
>
> *The plantation was still there. Somewhere in my two boxes, I have photos. But none of the members of that family is Jewish nowadays. Some of the Lehmanns married into the Godchaux family.*
> — *A. Metz Kahn, New York, September 9, 1992.*

The store opens. With profits from sales, it expands and becomes a general store, with a range of different departments. The change in scale involves a move to a slightly larger town, still close to the small town, where a partner, usually a compatriot or relative, is found to share costs and help finance the business. The cities that develop for retail at the time are Donaldsonville, Montgomery, Mobile, Shreveport, New Orleans.

Suppliers are able to wait for their bills to be paid. Suppliers and traders become organized in rural Louisiana and Alabama, the majority coming from Jewish backgrounds, though not exclusively. There were 2,455 businessmen between 1840 and the Civil War, according to the historian Elliott Ashkenazi "...more than 50% traded in the clothing business or dry goods. Jews sold jewelry, tobacco, and fancy imported goods."[91] The most daring became cotton merchants and brokers supplying wholesale merchandise to customers both in the city and the countryside. The businessmen depended, for payment and supplies, on an agricultural economy based on the cotton and sugar markets. They acted as the intermediaries for the large importers and dealers, the New Orleans cotton and sugar markets, and the small rural towns with their property owners, large and small. Up until 1880, steamships remained the main means of transportation. However many businesses were short on capital and therefore very precarious. Between 1840 and 1866, there were one hundred and twenty Jewish stores in New Orleans, but 30 to 38 % went bankrupt.

Once a store was acquired, merchants added plots of land bought with the mortgages from the estates of the local customers. Plantations varied in size. Before the Great Depression of the 1930s, the Geismar family owned three stores, a sugar factory, and three plantations-sugar cane, corn and cotton. Three families, the Hymans, the Picards and the Geismars, lived on the plantations, whereas the plantation employees and the inhabitants of Geismar village lived in the surrounding area. It was a 10,000-acre property. Initially cotton was grown, but after the cotton disease of 1907, they switched to sugar and combined it with the dry goods business (groceries, hardware) and the selling of bales of cotton. They were also able to develop a wholesale business and sit as members of the board directors of banks, or become General Postmasters.

The descriptions of plantations tend to evoke an old aristocracy and are sometimes tinged with nostalgia. Flo Geismar's account of the family plantation, purchased by the Geismar-Heymann families in the 1860s, seems closer to reality. She was born in 1923 and lived on the plantation until her marriage. What was daily life like on the plantation?

In the 1930s, there were about two hundred African American men and women on our plantation and about seventy-five whites. The whites lived in the surrounding area in large houses, and owned stores. My parents owned a house for the guardian, the carpenter, the employees, and the bachelors who worked in the store. They had a cook who prepared their meals, which they ate in the kitchen, not in the dining room.

The African Americans had their own living quarters that gave out on to the sugar cane fields. Previously it had been cotton, but it had been destroyed by the epidemic. In the plantation there was an overseer who managed everything, a groom (a horseman) who looked after the plantation's horses, a locksmith for the farm equipment.

> *My father used to start his day very early, at daybreak; his horse was ready to go into the neighborhoods, and when he returned, he had breakfast with us, at about 7 o'clock. Rosa, the black servant, was already there. He opened the store. He managed the plantation and the store. The store worked on a credit system. People made purchases throughout the year and once a year, at harvest time, they came and settled their debts. Some of the plantations were very large. There were at least six accountants who worked on this all day long.*
> *— Flo Geismar, New Orleans, October 6, 1992 and October 23, 1997.*

A wide range of activities was a necessity in order to survive but it lets us foresee the many obstacles and uncertainties of the business enterprise. According to Flo Geismar's account in the 1990s, and the survey conducted by Brenda S. Babin, completed in 1970, the recession of the 1890s, the natural disasters and floods, were very onerous for the Picards and the Geismars. In 1893, they lost their entire crop and the crops of their neighbors in which they had invested large sums. Their company ran a $75,000 deficit. They declared bankruptcy. By some miracle their business survived nevertheless. After the flood in 1893, the levees were moved back and Louis Geismar built a new store in 1898, facing the river. In 1889, a railroad linking Memphis with New Orleans was put into service. The river traffic declined and railroad traffic increased rapidly. In 1900, Louis Benjamin Geismar built a new store facing the railroad. This was when the village took the name Geismar. It had a post office and a railroad station. But there were still obstacles. During the Great Depression, in 1930, Geismar and Picard had to cope with new difficulties. Most of their land, i.e. 10,000 acres, was sold at auction at the low rate of $14 an acre instead of the real price of $2,500:

> *The Geismars owned 10,000 acres of land, three plantations, a sugar mill, three stores in Ascension Parish, and we lost it all. The sugar market fell, we were able to survive. But then we had a great frost two years in a row. We lost our sugar cane crops. Not only did we lose ours, but also the others that we had financed all around.*
>
> *We were so wealthy that we had coined our own money because when merchandise came up the river the boats, when the money didn't come on time, there were no more coins. So we had our own coins. They were all stamped Picard-Geismar. We had a set of them.*
> — Flo Geismar, New Orleans, September 18, 1992.

The remaining properties were administered by Léon Benjamin Geismar's son, Minel Geismar. Louis Geismar died in 1934. Léon Geismar, his nephew, worked with the Geismars and Picards, who became the administrators of the plantations in 1930. Then he started his own business. He reorganized the store and made it into the Progressive Stores. In 1932, he opened a branch in nearby Gonzales, which he gave to his son Léon Sol. In 1955, the Geismar Waterloo plantation burned down. It was the end of an era. The landscape changed and new residents arrived-engineers, chemists, and workers attracted by the exploitation of the region's energy resources in gas and oil. In 1958, the Wyandotte Company opened a chemical processing plant.[92] In the city, some of the traders became auctioneers. They sold supplies at auction, a very popular but unpredictable profession in New Orleans.

When, unlike the Geismars, or the Marxes in Port Gibson, the owners of general stores were not plantation owners, "a parallel activity occurred," says Elliott Ashkenazi, "between small cotton growers and the country storekeeper who acted as a factor [moneylender] for them." This traditional diversity of activities could also lead to variations. After having opened a store with a range of products including cotton, the owner sometimes chose a single activity, such as finance, and became a cotton broker. Such was the case of Julius Weis.[93] Along with his son and an associate, he opened an exchange office and became a financier, establishing relations with the big banks in Paris and London. Other families I met, such as the Geismar-Toledano family, chose the import-export business in the 1920s. Alfred Geismar was the son of the founder of a family company dealing in cotton linters with headquarters in France. He emigrated in 1926 and opened a branch in New Orleans, working on both continents.[94] These firms remained family firms, but were able to make use of the networks in the large metropolitan areas in America and Europe. It was possible, as in the case of the Godchaux family, to go from being a small peddler to being Louisiana's Sugar King within one generation. The plantations Léon Godchaux purchased in Louisiana each had their own sugar mills; he went on to consolidate processing and refining in a single facility at Reserve Plantation. By the 1890s, the harvests were conveyed by railway, then processed at Reserve Refinery and Mill, a big mill on his plantation located about thirty-seven miles from New Orleans. The mill would process 200,000 pounds of raw sugar in twenty-four hours. In 1895, Godchaux Sugar Inc. started using steam locomotives. To increase output, the company also imported sugar from the West Indies. Sugar was made into white sugar, using new processes invented by the manufacturer himself. In 1892, Godchaux owned 60,000 acres of woods and eight plantations growing 10,000 acres of sugar cane. The centralization of the business was necessary because Godchaux had to deal with competition from the West Indies, where sugar cane was a year-round crop with a higher yield and the cane's sugar content was higher. Sugar cane was not native to Louisiana and grew only from spring to fall. Godchaux Sugar Inc. remained one the largest refineries in the United States until it was sold in 1958. In 1975, it was acquired by Sugar Cane Refiner, which restricted itself to refining and which shut down in 1985. The Godchaux had kept the firm in the family for over a hundred years.[95] Economic development at the end of the nineteenth century was not just due to the diversification of activities, but also to the importance of networks-family networks, country wide economic networks, and intercontinental networks. These networks played an essential role in the integration of immigrants. There were strong business relationships between the big cities of

New Orleans and New York and the countryside, for non-perishable commodities, apparel, and fragile merchandise, as we already noted. There were also exchanges between the big cities on the banking and financial levels-Paris, New York, San Francisco, New Orleans-with the Lazare bankers for example. Business and family relationships were established between Hamilton (Ohio), New Orleans, and New York by the families of Lazard Kahns-industrialists and manufacturers of cast iron stoves in Hamilton-and the Lemanns, sugar cane growers and owners of a department store in Donaldsonville, Louisiana. Indeed the Lazard Kahns owned shares in the Lemann plantations and supplied them with cast iron stoves.[96] The Lemanns' cotton broker in New York was Abraham Sons. But the business was also transcontinental: Geismar and Company was established in Paris in 1925. Business was transacted mainly between Paris and New Orleans; a branch also existed in Brazil, as Geismar's daughter, Jackie Toledano, told us. Her father founded the subsidiary company of cotton scrap and an import-export business in New Orleans in 1925-1926.[97]

Another factor contributed to the development of the region: the rural and urban interconnections due to the traders. It allowed for the economic growth of these different areas and brought prosperity to the intermediaries. Jewish immigrants played a pivotal role as moneylenders in the cotton market and in a wide range of merchandise. These professions were linked to the specific characteristics of the region and were not easily transferable.

Professions Adapted to the New Country: Cotton Factors and Brokers

The new immigrants forged professions as intermediaries in the cotton economy and became traders. They were "factors": they bought crops of cotton bales and resold them to the textile plants. They adapted the traditional profession of banker to their new environment, lending money to cotton growers in anticipation of the next crop and being reimbursed after the harvest. These professions were exercised over several generations among the families I met who sometimes also owned a general store.[98]

The profession of intermediary in the cotton business illustrates the interaction that existed between the city and the countryside. Cotton and sugar in the South-in Alabama, Louisiana and Mississippi grew in importance because of the agricultural and commercial chains that ensued from them. The biggest dealers were the Weils. The Loebs, known cotton dealers in Montgomery, sold their cotton through the Kohlmeyers in New Orleans, who were the cotton brokers for the dealers in the region. These families originally came from Vieux Brisach in the Baden region, Lembach and Reichshoffen, in the Bas-Rhin, Alsace. For generations, the Kohlmeyers handled transactions on the cotton exchange market, first in New Orleans, later in New York and Liverpool.[99]

The factor finances a transaction. This archaic word is still used to describe the houses that provide funds to apparel retailers so they can acquire supplies, appliances, beauty products. Initially, the cotton factor lent funds to farmers to help them at the beginning of their season. He was paid back with interest and was entitled by tradition to buy the cotton when it was harvested. The dealer bought the cotton from the grower in order to subsequently sell it to the textile mills.

As Elliott Ashkenazi points out, the cotton grower and the factor, the person who lent him money, had many dealings. These dealings varied with time. Before the Civil War, the factor was the grower's most important intermediary; he financed his crop, transported it to the trading center, and sold it. He provided the grower with supplies. As the growers spent more and more time on their plantations, which were located further and further away from the cities where the cotton was sold, the growers began counting exclusively on their factors in the port cities. The most important port was New Orleans where factors were numerous.[100]

The profession of factor was not a simple one; it required talent and knowledge. The factor took responsibility for the crop and paid for the freight expenses to New Orleans. He lent money to the growers until the crop was sold. He bought supplies for the growers and their slaves, expenses that were not paid back until after the sale of the crops. "And for this service," the historian Elliott Ashkenazi explains, "he charged 2.5 %."

But it is already apparent that the big cities attracted businessmen who wanted to see their businesses flourish, the expansion of their clientele, the creation of wider networks, and a greater proximity to the markets. In the majority of cases, the families moved to a big city in the second or third generation. The urbanization phase took place mostly between 1860 and 1880. Today there are very few Jews or Christian families of Jewish descent still living in towns such as Donaldsonville, Opelousas, Alexandria, Louisiana, or Vicksburg and Natchez, Mississippi.

The small museums, like the one in Utica-Jackson, Mississippi, served as reminders of that earlier period and showed a wish to preserve the traces of the rural past of these families.[101] The desire to preserve the memory of that period and make it live again was evident in the exhibit "From Alsace to America" held in Jackson from May to August 1998, which drew close to 70,000 visitors from different parts of the United States.

During our conversation, Flo Geismar, who collects antiques, china, dolls, and toys and has kept the account books of the former family firm, explained the reasons for her attachment to the history of the small rural towns: she had spent her childhood in one. This was expressed by her taking part in the exhibit and helping to collect objects from the rural past of the Jewish pioneers:

> *The Jewish museum was set up in camp Henry S. Jacob (Utica, Mississippi) eight or ten years ago and we have been collecting things from all over Louisiana, Mississippi, and Arkansas, especially from the small towns. With the change in the economy from an agrarian society to an industrial society, the small towns are gradually disappearing. There is a second and third generation of Jewish people. They left the farms and plantations and came to the city as doctors and lawyers. They were stockbrokers. They're businessmen, teachers, and college professors. You name it and you have it.*
> — *Flo Geismar, New Orleans, September 6, 1992.*

Michel Bandry, a French specialist of United States, provides more background detail.

> *The South underwent a radical transformation starting in the 1950s: agriculture changed with the development of large-scale agriculture, the introduction of new crops like peanut, and the quasi-disappearance of cotton. Sharecropping disappeared as a farming method and was replaced by a genuine agribusiness*

> requiring a smaller workforce, the hiring of seasonal workers, the planning of various crops, and a greater use of machines. As a result the population became increasingly urbanized, with an influx of the black population into the big cities [...] and interstate migrations.
>
> In 1940, the South had nine urban areas of over 250,000 people, among them Atlanta, New Orleans, Birmingham. By 1960, there were 16; and by 1980 there were 45 cities of that size.[102]

Upward mobility and the acquisition of wealth often meant leaving for the big city. Yet these departures were not necessarily permanent exile. It often implied a return. Some of my interlocutors told me that their parents, though they received a university education, returned to the plantation and the family business instead of exercising their professions. This was the case of the Haas family in central Louisiana. Was this a losing proposition? Not in the opinion of Dr. Posner and the local historian Rebecca Manouvrier with whom I spoke in 1995 in the small town of Opelousas, in northern Louisiana. As we talked, we gathered pecans that had fallen in front of the little brick synagogue, built in 1892 and which looked like a chapel. In the lovely house of Dr. Posner and his wife Isabelle, we discussed their experiences as Southern Jews at length, for they had lived in the South for three generations. Getting an education, being open to the world, were their priorities. Their remarks revealed the primacy of the book, which did not preclude the gift of being a good businessman, quite the contrary:

> Samuel Haas's son, John, who was a physician, did not practice medicine because he became a businessman. He bought a property and managed it. [...] It was an advantage to have received an education. This was years ago, particularly in this region, which was isolated. The communication route in Louisiana was the river and the people who lived along the river were exposed to the outside world. They were interested in what was going on, but the people who lived in this part of the State, Acadiana, were isolated. This was the case up until the arrival of the railroad... When they settled, Jews wanted to send

their children to the schools in New Orleans or on the East Coast. When the children returned, they worked in the family businesses. But at least they were educated. That way they were interested in what was going on elsewhere and very open to the world.
— Dr. Gerald Posner, Opelousas, October 25, 1995.

The family businesses prospered thanks to economic growth and the movement of goods and merchandise. This raises the question of the specifically Jewish contribution to the development of capitalism. The contribution of Jews to modern capitalism-with efficient methods and planning, an adaptation to the market, and investments based on financial loans-began in the mid-nineteenth century. It was due to efficient financing, well-coordinated family businesses, partnerships, and a frugal moral code, as Julius Weis points out in the concluding words of his autobiography: "I emigrated, in my early teens, to the American Eldorado, and here, by my own efforts, have succeeded in establishing not only a comfortable fortune, but also a reputation beyond reproach for fair dealing and a name scarcely second to any for worthy charity."[103]

Families from France and Germany developed their family businesses, traveling from the heart of the city to the outskirts in order to expand their companies, boost production, diversify, and open branches in other Southern cities. Moreover, they also developed industrial activities, using scrap as raw material to manufacture consumer goods, finding markets for selling them, and buying trucks for distributing them. We should add that this industrial development was possible because of the gradual opening up of the South politically, thanks to the civil rights movement. This development was also due to the South's economic modernization, which attracted an entirely new population from the northeast of the United States. They saw opportunities for acquiring wealth in the region's new resources in gas and oil and the development of tourism. As the historian Isabelle Richet points out, these new alliances between religion and politics could only have occurred as a result of the deep changes in the South after the Second World War.

Up until the Second World War, the South remained a poor agrarian region, secluded from all the changes affecting the rest of the country. Its small rural communities, where the churches are the place where social ties are forged, had preserved a homogeneity that protected them from the culturally corrosive effects of the pluralism characterized by the big urban centers. The move of the centers of production into the region during the war, then the relocation of many industries seeking a cheap and non-unionized work force in the following decades sped up the transition from an agrarian economy to an industrial economy, along with the rapid urbanization of the population, and a greater number having access to higher education. The process became more pronounced in the last decades of the century with the arrival of high-tech industries and services, the exploitation of oil resources, the activities connected with tourism. These changes led to a process of social differentiation and shattered the solidarity of the white caste that had been a major cohesive factor in the region.[104]

As an illustration of this analysis, let us examine how three families from France and Germany thrived before and after the Civil War.

The Lazarus Family and the Cotton Route

The fate of the Lazarus family is unique though not really exceptional. The family was originally from Romanswiller in Alsace and settled in New Orleans after 1870. The pioneer started out as a cotton factor. His son worked as an accountant in a company that made stuffing out of cotton scrap and eventually became the manager of the company. His son, the third generation, became a professional, a dentist.

The business activity of the Lazarus family illustrates how the cotton industry developed over several generations. The grandfather, in the late nineteenth century, first worked as a moneylender. He worked for a company, as a kind of rural banker:

> *Grandfather Lazarus worked in the cotton business prior to [my father]. He was what was called a cotton moneylender, a cotton factor. He went to the farms and lent the farmers money to buy seedlings and then, at harvest time, he sold the cotton. He was the accountant. He was more or less a banker in the cotton business. He wasn't the owner of this business. He worked for someone. Thanks to his cotton connections, Daddy worked in the cotton trade. Instead of working for someone else, he found a way of setting*

up his own business in that field. My father's business was in cotton padding. The workers changed it in their factories and made it into stuffing for mattresses. He did this work for thirty or forty years. During the Second World War, he manufactured mattresses for the army and for hospitals, because initially he had made mattresses for the private sector, for stores that sold furniture. During the war, he was asked to supply the army. Many of his employees were drafted and served as soldiers.
— *Will Lazarus, New Orleans, September 12, 1992.*

The second generation, in the 1910s, wanted to be autonomous. They wanted to set up their own companies. With this in mind, Will Lazarus's father attended the Soulé business school at the turn of the century, following the example of future businessmen. He professionalized his knowledge, enhancing his family experience with an accountant's knowledge. He used cotton as his business focus, but turned away from the pre-production stage to concentrate on the post-production stage-the point at which cotton had already undergone changes. He worked as an accountant in the Southern Mattress Company, which used scrap, inexpensive products, stuffing, to manufacture the mattress felt. Later he was promoted to a management position. About twenty workers worked under him. Jules Jacob Lazarus used automatic felt manufacturing machines; the workers were in charge of operating the machines and, in the final phase, of sewing the mattresses. Two generations worked in the same industry, but the second generation became prosperous thanks to the mechanization of labor and the expanding furnishing market. The company worked for private firms, as well as for the public sector, including hospitals and the army during the Second World War. The third generation changed course. Thanks to Jules Jacob's business success, his son studied dentistry at Northwestern University in Chicago from 1933 to 1938.

Another example of success, in this case in the bakery and restaurant business, illustrates the same economic know-how. Fred Kahn worked in the Dennery Company until it was bought by a large industrial group. In his interview, he describes an enterprising bourgeoisie, attached to both New Orleans and the French lifestyle. Fred Kahn remained proud of his heritage and the French language, which he used in his family.

The Dennery Family: From Craft to Industry

Some French families are well-known in New Orleans. The Dennery family, whose origins can be traced back to Vésoul, shaped its immigration narrative: the first Dennery arrived in New Orleans by train from St. Louis; hearing French as he stepped off the train, he felt comfortable. He chose to work in the wholesale bakery trade and then in the supply business: the Baker's and Confectionery Supply Business was created thanks to the genius of Charles Dennery, who had left Wissembourg as a child with his parents in the 1870s. Charles employed his three brothers and his brothers-in-law, Alfred Schwartz and Fred Kahn. Fred Kahn was hired in the family business after the war and worked in the firm until the eighties. He agreed to describe his experience:

Charles Dennery started his bakery business in 1894. Twenty years later, he opened a bread and supply factory, Charles Dennery Inc. that sold equipment and restaurant products to restaurants, bakeries and hotels throughout the entire South and South West. The business flourished and became a company. It had offices in Houston, Dallas, and Atlanta. It was bought by DCA Food Industries in 1964 and shut down in 2001.[105]

The successive moves of the company's headquarters are a sign of its expansion. The business was first based on Canal Street, the shopping center where all the department stores are located, like the one owned by the Godchaux family. Then it moved further west, to Magazine Street, which runs parallel to the Garden District's wide avenue, St. Charles Avenue; then it left New Orleans and moved to Jefferson Street in Jefferson Parish.

The plant was also linked to a large house where the Dennery family lived and where Fred Kahn Jr. resided as a child. The fact of working together and living together strengthened the family ties. Four or five generations worked in the company.

The company grew from a small-scale cottage business to an industry in the second half of the twentieth century. Industrial capitalism developed: an investment in equipment; an efficient, well planned infrastructure; the diversification of products; a large commercial network.

The third generation turned its back on business. Charles Dennery II became a lawyer. This third generation maintained contact with their relatives in France, spoke French and travelled to France regularly.[106]

Capitalism spread to the cities. In the small towns, too, there were forms of expansion that required capital investments and fine-tuned economic ties between business income and agricultural income. The fortunes of the Lemann family exemplify this fact. The Lemanns handed down their expertise over several generations, and enlarged their properties thanks to the profits they earned from their plantations and their knowledge of business circles in the city.

Jacob Lemann and Bernard Lemann, Store Owners and Sugar Cane Planters [107]

In 1836, Jacob Lemann, 27, originally from the duchy of Hesse, settled in the small town of Donaldsonville, Louisiana. In 1850, Ascension Parish, which includes Donaldsonville, had a population of 10,752, 68 % of whom were slaves. It was a small, rapidly expanding port, the former capital of Louisiana in 1831. Donaldsonville was surrounded by large sugar plantations with its own molasses mills and houses, initially built by the Creole aristocracy, later by the English one. The town attracted many immigrants. Jewish immigrants from Germany and Alsace started settling there beginning in 1849. In 1856, twenty-five among them founded a benevolent association in order to bury the dead: the Bikur Cholim, Parish of Ascension.[108]

Bernard Lemann started out as a peddler for the surrounding plantations; then, in 1840, he opened a general store. According to Elliott Ashkenazi, the success of Lemann father and son was due to the personal and financial ties they developed with the local growers and the city merchants. The father lent money to the growers, using his profits from the store and with outside help. Very soon, by 1850, these loans put Lemann in the position of building up capital. He acquired land with mortgages.

The Lemanns owned both a general store and plantation stores that met the needs of the plantation workers and the resident population. Moreover, the Lemanns did regular business with the New Orleans merchants. From the beginning they established contact with the Jewish merchants in New York and

Cincinnati. They found funds in New York to reinvest after the Civil War and buy a new store in 1877. After the Civil War, the success of sugar production in Louisiana was dependent on their business contacts with storekeepers. They supervised the expenses of the harvest production and the finances of their stores. Production required salaries and cash for the workers. The Lemanns were clever at seeing that this money be spent by the workers in their stores, either on credit or in cash.

Jacob Lemann became a grower, even though he was a tradesman. He had a good knowledge of his territory and of all the branches of the business in New Orleans and New York. He also relied on the cohesion of the Jewish businessmen and the network of suppliers, including Léopold Léon, originally from France, who bought merchandise in New York and New Orleans for his dry goods store in Donaldsonville. The Lemanns succeeded as landowners but also thanks to capitalist business techniques. The fluctuations of the Lemann department store reflected the sugar crop cycles.

The harvest was collected in October, but the sugar was only ready to be sold two or three months later, in December. The harvest and refining of sugar required additional supplies. Therefore, sales at Lemann's went up every fall. Molasses and sugar went on sale only at the beginning of the year, in January. The sales went up during the first months of the year. The growers made half their purchases between January and April, also settling their debts from the preceding year. The Lemanns gave planters credit for one year and lent them money regularly.

Having left in 1858, parents and children returned from Europe and the north in 1863, to try to recover their rights to their lands. Far from discouraged, they acquired new plantations, Peytavin and Palo Alto in 1867. Their success was due their good knowledge of sugar production. They found partners, the Jacobs, who invested with them. Furthermore, their New York contacts lent them money. Their son, Bernard, was able to invest in a new store, also in Donaldsonville, in 1877. He went into partnership with the Loebs. The family worked in sugar production while also selling its merchandise in the new general store:

The most distinctive feature of the Lemann's plantations management is the integration of their general store with the needs of the plantations. This integration involved sales, of course, but also payment of wages and a system of accounts that permitted the plantations and the stores to be viewed as what they actually were, a single economic unit.[109]

Once they had fit in economically and won a place in the community where they lived, immigrants wished to remain a homogenous group. Though the French group of Jewish immigrants was smaller in the 1850s than the German one, the two groups united to organize a community structure.

CHAPTER III

The Emergence of Communities

Birth of the American Israelite

After arriving in New Orleans in 1845, Joel Sartorius noted in his *Memoirs* that the congregation of German rite Shangarai Chassed Synagogue in New Orleans, established in 1842, was only open on the high holy days and that the *shohet* (traditional slaughterer) was also the *hazan* (cantor). Sartorius was not indifferent to religion. He had brought his *Sefer Torah* (Torah scroll) as had his brother two years earlier.[110]

How religious practice was organized can best be understood by closely examining the modus operandi of the community, the local congregation, the place of worship, as studied by the sociologist Norbert Bellah. The community of worship was an adaptation of the Jewish synagogue. Jews and Christians "view their communities as existing in a covenant relationship with God". The practice of the Sabbath, around which religious life is focused, celebrates this Covenant.[111] The three functions of the synagogue correspond to the three main activities of Judaism: the synagogue is a place of prayer, a place of study, and a meeting place. The Jewish world is organized around these three obligations: service to God, study of the Torah, and charity, *tzedaka*, managed when the congregation meets.

The community of faithful (the congregation) is part of a larger group, the community itself, a human society with a historical, cultural, social, and religious specificity. The subjective belief in a common origin refers to a territory, following the typical ideal category of community as defined by Max Weber. But the territorial element does not have the same importance for Jews as for other groups, given their scattering and the successive relocations of the Jewish Diaspora.

In the United States, communities have a degree of autonomy in interfaith relations. Indeed, though Americans have by and large accepted the doctrine of the separation of Church and State, most of them believe that religions and their communities have an important role to play in the public sphere. For all that, the religious factor did not always have the same importance. Indeed, there has been a shift "from a 'communalism' valued order, of harmony, and obedience to authority, and these values centered on the figure of the settled minister, to a plurality and a privatization of the religious", as Norbert Bellah points out.[112] At the same time, there was the development of civil or public religion, which disposed of the concept of secularism, the founding principle of the French model. Norbert Bellah defines the American model in the following terms: "the civil religion at its best is a genuine apprehension of universal and transcendent religious reality as seen in or, one could almost say, as revealed through the experience of the American people."[113]

The question then arises of knowing how the immigrants adopt and set up the community model, and what they call themselves-communities, ethnic groups, Jews.

Up until the Civil War (1861-1865), the set of rituals followed by the immigrants from Alsace-Lorraine and Southern Germany were in the German tradition. The community archives were written in German. The rabbis, up until 1850, spoke German. The synagogues — buildings that were built about ten years after a congregation was formed-were initially architectural carbon copies of the synagogues in the home countries, according to the historian Arthur Hertzberg.[114] Gemiluth Chessed Synagogue, the synagogue in Port Gibson, Mississippi, built in 1891 in neo-Moorish style, with two onion-shaped domes, might be an imitation of the synagogue in Saverne, Alsace. Originally, in 1871, the congregation had a majority of Jews from the Rhine valley.[115] Liberal Judaism exists in the tension between tradition and modernity. How can the ancestral traditions be preserved while taking into account the changes in societies and customs, in brief, the passage of time? If religion fails to adapt, it becomes sclerotic and is bound to die; if its original message is not preserved, it is emptied of all content and legitimacy. The mission of Reform Judaism, a religion of progress, is to adapt to the surrounding environment.

The experience of liberal Judaism in Germany, as early as the 1840s, showed that Jews could adapt to a modern society and that their emigration could justify "their future Americanization" in the United States.[116] Large cities such as Hamburg or Berlin and small towns had instituted reforms focusing on the propriety and respectability of synagogues in the mid-nineteenth century. They had adapted the rites and made them conform to the standards of decency of German society of the period. The power of adjusting to modernity was exported to the United States. Arthur Hertzberg explains, "In roughly twenty years the vast majority had been transformed into 'Reformed congregations'. Almost everywhere the sexes were no longer separated; there were organs and prayers in German, and soon in English. As was to be expected, these changes were deplored by the Orthodox, who were ever weaker and more on the defensive, but the dominant tide in midcentury favored 'moderate reformers' who were creating respectable American Judaism."

If, in Europe, there is a model of the "Israelite" that can be contrasted to that of the contemporary Jew, if we change contexts can we speak of the birth of an American "Israelite"?[117] Reform Judaism could be seen as the shift from a "German Orthodox" tradition to the liberal movement initiated by Isaac Mayer Wise. This movement led to the building of new temples and the introduction of new customs.

What Is Its Origin?[118]

As this process is well-known, let us briefly recall that liberal Judaism took a structured form in the declaration of principles adopted by a group of Reform rabbis in Pittsburgh, in 1885, subsequent to lengthy deliberations between radical rabbis led by

David Einhorn, a German *émigré* with an austere and rigorous German yeshiva education and more moderate rabbis such as their flamboyant leader Isaac Mayer Wise of Bohemia. The Reform rabbis established Classical Reform Judaism. Jewish immigrants could thereby adapt to a modern society. Their great principles included the idea of progress, a single God, religion used for moral and spiritual elevation, and the recognition of a changed interpretation of the texts. The texts belonged to a given period; hence adapting the ancient rites to the present period was not a violation of the texts. It is worth remembering that under the influence of the Enlightenment era these thoughts made their appearance in 1828, in Charleston, under the influence of a young generation of Sephardim who created an independent society "The Reformed Society of Israelites." The Jews were not, as in Europe, a tolerated sect, but "a portion of the people." The great innovators, Isaac Harby, Abraham Moise, David Nunes Carvalho, rejected the idea of the chosen people. They wanted to introduce English in sermons and prayers and requested a simplified service.

This resulted in an acculturation phenomenon, the reformulation of Judaism as a religion cleared of the political and national concepts of the Jewish people and the Jewish nation, a reformulation that matches the one made by the French Israelites subsequent to their emancipation in 1791. As our readers are familiar with the Reform movement, let us evoke it very briefly.

Reform Judaism rests on some of the great founding principles of the American nation: institutions must be based on the principles of reason and equality for the public good, and must have beneficial effects on society. Reform Jews appeal to social pragmatism; the laws must be useful and applicable to the period we live in. They have a conception of Judaism as a factor of progress, evolving historically. The first Reform temple in New York (Temple Emanu-El) was founded in 1845 under the aegis of Rabbi David Adler, who integrated the principles of human rights into the religion.

The Foundations of the Reform Movement?

The religious must play a forward-moving role. Each person's freedom must be respected. Given this view, each person's faith, which is not imposed but chosen, must be respected. Faith is the product of experience given as a heritage. There are two major ideas in this reform: patriotism and Americanization (much like the idea of citizenship and the French language for French Israelites). The stake for Reform Jews is to prove their capacity for integration and their loyalty to the American nation. For Isaac Mayer Wise, going beyond the principles of integration, Judaism could fully participate in the American national destiny and find a delicate equilibrium between national unity and individuality. The point was to give Judaism a new and unique fate and to assert that Jews form a religious community, not a national one. "The United States was the modern Jews' promised land." In 1854, Isaac Mayer Wise founded the weekly *The Israelite*, which competed with the Orthodox-leaning newspaper *Occident*, published by Isaac Lesser, and with Robert Lyons' *Asmonean* in New York. The term "Israelite" is used often, as of the 1850s, in the archives of the New Orleans congregations and in the reference book of the New Orleans elite, *The Book of Israelites of Louisiana*, published in 1904.[119] We find the same foundations as those attributed to the Israelites of the French Third Republic: devotion to the civic and philanthropic cause, with religious practice confined to the private sphere. Interestingly orthodox immigrants from France and Germany kept to their old faith first and only gradually adopted the new movement.

The Adoption of Reform Judaism by the Immigrants

Liberal Judaism, being unostentatious and having no apparent features to distinguish its followers from the rest of the population, seems more easily accepted by the Christian population. It is also better adapted to the professional elite and individuals. It is less visible than Orthodox Judaism and expresses an "assimilation" of

Jews to the dominant culture. It seems closer to a code of ethics than a religion.

The most progressive urban elites became members. Provisional rules were set up in traditional temples. The ostentatious signs of Judaism were eliminated. The service took place mostly in English; Hebrew was no longer taught; young girls and boys became confirmed in white clothes at thirteen and then sixteen. Keeping kosher was no longer a requirement. Odd forms of acculturation were instituted in which the dominant Protestant and Catholic models were influential. The vocabulary that was adopted is revealing: temple, confirmation, sanctuary, chapel, minister, congregation.

Liberal Judaism spread to different cities: Cincinnati, an important seat of Judaism became the training center for Reform Judaism in 1875, with the creation of the Hebrew Union College, the educational center for Reform rabbis.

But the first immigrants were slow to join these societies. Most of them, married to young Jewish women, considered themselves Jewish but were not religious. In large cities like New Orleans this first generation participated in the life of charitable associations that were the starting point for the existing religious congregations-thus the founding of the Hebrew Benevolent Societies that would give rise to religious congregations in the mid-nineteenth century. Initially they were founded in order to find a location for burying the dead, the first stage in the organizing of a congregation. One of the functions of the philanthropic societies was to preserve and administer these sacred locations.

The first newcomers joined the Gates of Mercy Congregation (Shangarai Chassed Synagogue), founded in 1827 at the initiative of Jacob Solis, whose background was Sephardic, and they participated in this little congregation that began by observing a traditional Sephardic ritual. The community was very tolerant of the Catholic wives of Jewish immigrants, as a way of protecting themselves from the threat of exclusion from this first congregation established in New Orleans.[120] Then, starting in 1842, with the growing number of new members, the Ashkenazi rite was adopted. Other immigrants from the banks of the Rhine, arriving later, went to live in what was then a suburb of New Orleans, Lafayette, and founded Gates of Prayer in 1850.[121] On May 3, 1901, the local Jewish paper, *The Jewish Ledger*, founded on January 4, 1895 by Aaron Steeg, whose parents were Alsatian and German, described this now established congregation emphasizing the diversity of the members as well as their proclaimed tie to Judaism: "Within this busy town, Israelites lived and labored in joy and sorrow, the cheery Alsatians, the excitable nervous Lorrainese, the steady Badinser, the methodical Rhinepfalzer, a heterogeneous aggregation of Israelites from many nationalities but all Yehudim in the full acceptance of the term." The more traditional Jewish congregations, in the cities and large towns, were founded when the Jews from Central Europe arrived in New Orleans in 1858 and a little later in Alexandria, Shreveport, and Montgomery.

Indeed, by 1870, a new modern and Americanized figure was born: the American Israelite, representing the majority of the Jewish population in the South. A number of Orthodox congregations gradually changed while Reform temples such as Temple Sinai were born in New Orleans. Congregations in rural areas were instituted between the 1850s and 1870s and gradually became liberal, except for the ones in Shreveport and Alexandria.

The first generation of immigrants subscribed to a non-traditional Judaism according to the testimonies of their grandchildren, but actually did so more than twenty years after their arrival to Louisiana. The grandparents or great-grandparents of my interlocutors were founding members of the liberal Temple Sinai in 1870 in New Orleans. Salomon Marx, born in Mainz in 1831, the great-grandfather of Abraham Metz Kahn, first joined the traditional community at Rampart Synagogue but in 1871 he became a member of the liberal Temple Sinai. He was joined by the notary public Abel Dreyfous who belonged to the Orthodox community Tememe Derech. The Alsatian-born banker and chinaware merchant Michael Frank became the first president of Temple Sinai in 1872.[122] As Abraham Metz Kahn puts it, "By his choice, my grandfather Salomon Marx was clearly giving up tradition for new rules". For Ruth Dreyfous (Abel Dreyfous's granddaughter), this new affiliation was seen as a "form of ethics."

In central Louisiana, in towns like Opelousas and Gonzales, the children gathered in Baton Rouge, the meeting place and educational center for rural Jews in the 1930s. Few liberal Jews in their seventies or eighties at the time could read Hebrew and conduct prayers. Once religion was seen as a form of ethics, it became acceptable for American Israelites to become secularized. Religious practice was not the chief point, as my interlocutors explain: it was important to be involved in the various activities of the synagogue and participate in the social and civic life. The word "involvement" resonates very strongly in the American context. It is in itself a line of conduct:

> Marx was the founder of Temple Sinai in New Orleans. At first he was a member of an older synagogue but the rabbi didn't want to ease some of the Orthodox rules of procedure — this in 1869. Touro Synagogue was more conservative. The founder himself, Touro, was Sephardi, the family originally came from Rhode Island. He had come from Spain and had first settled in the West Indies. I think that Judah's father was Isaiah Touro and was part of a congregation whose religious service George Washington had attended and Washington allowed the style of the monument to be preserved.[123]
> — Metz Kahn, September 2, 1992.

Liberal Judaism seems an obvious choice for my interlocutors: "We didn't want a Jewish State, we wanted to be integrated, assimilated. We're Southern religious, which means not very religious, but I'm very involved with my synagogue." The commitment of families is both moral and social. For the majority of my interlocutors, liberal Judaism is an obvious choice: "They were not ready to be traditional Jews," Joel Myers says, speaking of his grandparents in the 1880s.

My interlocutors try to dispose of Orthodoxy as though it had never existed. It is true that in liberal circles Orthodox practice is incomprehensible. It seems like a stigma for families that have been living in the South for three or four generations. The Jews of Eastern Europe were seen as representing a return to the customs and rituals of an ancient world from which the liberal families rapidly wanted to free themselves. Parallel to the Reform movement, a number of Orthodox synagogues founded by Jews from Central Europe in the 1880s became Conservative in the mid-twentieth century as a way of keeping their members and adapting to new times. Indeed Orthodox synagogues are in the minority in the different regions I visited. The historian Lee Shai Weissbach, who has studied the history of small towns and the image of Eastern European immigrants notes that "a survey of the 81 towns in the South that have total populations of under 50,000 and a Jewish population of at least 100 but less than 1, 000 around 1907 reveals that in 44 of these towns there was a synagogue affiliated with the Union of American Hebrew Congregations (since 1873 the umbrella of Reform Judaism) and that in another 15 towns there was an unaffiliated synagogue that can be identified with Reform on the basis of its practices or its name (the Greensboro Hebrew Reformed Congregation in North Carolina for example.)"[124]

The behavior required to become Americanized went beyond religious behavior. It was a daily lifestyle that included manners, clothes, names, and adopting a new mentality in order to be considered American and no longer appearing like a foreigner. Indeed, recommendations were written up after the massive immigration movements from Central Europe in the 1880s gave rise to the 1897 rulings restricting immigration and a strong nativistic backlash.[125]

Different newspapers, *The Reveille* of Port Gibson and the *Jewish Ledger*, both distributed throughout the South, ran articles on immigration issues. In 1906, there appeared a text titled "Immigration Problem" encouraging immigrants to leave the ports and seek work in the rural areas.[126] Advice on assimilation and the behavior to adopt in order to avoid being stigmatized as a foreigner appeared in the *Jewish Ledger*, on August 26, 1898:[127]

> *What the Jews want... The Jew in his synagog can be a Jew without being more un-American than a*

Christian in his church or agnostic in his lecture hall. But if outside of the synagogue is clannish or exclusive he is to be blamed for the odium which results. If he retains a foreign atmosphere that is no proof of his piety, but of his want of patriotism. If in manners, dress, name, he is still the foreigner, he needs not wonder if he is stigmatized as un-American, when he cannot overcome his own prejudices against the American environments. On American soil, the Jew must cease to be German, Russian, Polish and the rest. He must be American in a sense of illustrating the same ideals of honor, culture and good breeding as are embodied in the lives and careers of representative Americans in general.

The local newspaper of Port Gibson, Mississippi, *The Reveille*, pursued the debate between assimilation and the need to preserve a Jewish identity in its December 23, 1892 issue. The fear of nativistic reactions and anti-Semitic acts persisted. The Jews from Germany and Eastern France who had arrived earlier had achieved an acceptable economic and social status. They had been adopted by the local population and did not want their Americanization to be called into question by these newcomers. Their hostility to the immigrants from Eastern Europe, whom they stigmatized and distanced themselves from, endured until the Second World War: "In the minds of many non-Jews and even certain Jews, it is courteous to call us Hebrews. You might infer that there is a stigma attached to the term Jew. The newspaper is constantly trying to make this impression disappear. We are Jews, not Hebrews, not Israelites."

What are the ways of asserting a Jewish identity?

The Traditional Practice of Joining a Temple

Specific to American society is the fact that the temple or synagogue is primarily a place of sociability, a meeting place people enjoy going to regularly. This gives it great importance. It is also a place devoted to study and education as much as to religious practice. The synagogue is the central spiritual, cultural, and social venue.[128] It is the seat of women's associations, Sisterhoods, in charge of collecting funds, often for charitable activities, to help the needy and the sick. The seat of the philanthropic associations that manage orphanages, hospitals, old age homes, and the place where the B'nai B'rith chapters meet in support of human rights and the protection of Jews throughout the world. Beyond the many educational associations focusing on the life of men, women, and children, my interlocutors are affiliated with a specific temple.

The life narratives I collected emphasize the importance of the immigrants' commitment to charitable organizations and their social vitality. The families attach much less importance to the respect of religious practices, often confined to the basics, confirmation and temple attendance on Jewish holidays.

Membership in a specific congregation is a sign of loyalty to previous generations. The great-grandparents were founding members and their descendants are proud to keep their commitment alive. Hence I rarely met families that had changed temples; they maintained the same tie for several generations.

Families might identify with Classical Reform Judaism, or a more liberal Judaism, or a more conservative brand; these nuances depended on the history of each temple and its development. Changes are introduced by the rabbi and discussed by the board of administration. The temples are like small indoor cities, with a prayer room for big and small holidays, a meeting room, classrooms, a library, an administrative office, an office for the incumbent rabbi, and even a gift shop. All along the corridors, there are photos and names honoring different presidents, women and men, as reminders of the role played by each one. Donors are very highly regarded because they respect the duty of *tzedaka* (donation and charity). Their names are often inscribed in remembrance in gold letters inside the buildings, because they gave the synagogues decorations or sanctuary drapes. It is important to see the photographs of one's ancestors in the building. It is a sign of belonging, recognition, gratitude, and prominence.

The temple is a space of remembrance for older people, but above all a center where a life of study is structured and group identity is created. When the temples are confronted with contemporary issues they generally do not look to the past, except when it comes to commemorations celebrating jubilees of the community. These events are used as an opportunity for a historical overview or an exhibit on the history of the dignitaries and the associations. They underscore the longevity of the community and give it credibility in the eyes of its members and the city. The archives are rarely filed there.

What are its ritual events? Confirmation used to take place in white clothes at age 14 or 15 following an exam. Nowadays, for the last fifteen years or so, it has been replaced by the rite of the Alliance with God ceremony, the *bar mitzvah* (for boys) and the *bat mitzvah* (for girls). This ceremony is the mainspring of the rite of passage for boys and girls. Many parents regard it as one of the ways for their children to remain Jewish and, according to my interlocutors, it protects against inter-religious marriages:

> *It's good for them to have a bar mitzvah, that way, they'll remain Jewish. But it doesn't make you more Jewish. There are so many boys who are pushed into it by their parents but don't want to do it.*
> — Julia Marcus, New Orleans, March 9, 1997.

The choirs included both men and women. Different clothes are worn, depending on the individual attitude of the members. Indeed, personal choice prevails. Some men wear a *tallit* (prayer shawl), but it is not an obligation. Men and women sometimes wear a *kippah*. For the high holy days there are two or three rabbis, including women rabbis, as in Dallas and New Orleans. Families sit together, men and women are not separated as in the Orthodox ritual. The service unfolds as a dialogue between the congregation and the rabbi. Everything is organized so that the congregation can follow the service. Particular attention is paid to the singing and the talent of the *hazanim* (cantors) who are sometimes former opera singers, as in San Francisco. On the whole, there is a great tolerance regarding people's origins and their social circle. Reform synagogues can be seen as expressing a balance of vitality, propriety, and decorum. Great care is put into observing decorum and giving each person his proper place. The president of the congregation concludes each service with an inventory.

Article 14 of the American Constitution guarantees religious freedom; it is a constitutional right, intrinsic to the functioning of democracy in America.

> *Moreover, these congregations are grouped into federations that offer a whole range of social services, from child assistance to drug addiction treatment. The Jewish community center has its services there; there is an agency that is called the Jewish Service for Children and there is a group that takes care of orphans. The committee remained in the city. It became a Jewish family service for all the cities in the seven Southern States that don't have a Jewish federation. If you need advice, there is a health center, a boarding school, and if you don't have a local Jewish service, the federation's Jewish center handles it.*
> *— Julie Grant Meyer, New Orleans, October 24, 1997.*

Handing down knowledge is a duty. It guarantees the protection, continuity, and identification of the group. But in the beginning, it was more a matter of ritual than study.

The Handing Down of Judaism from the Late Nineteenth Century to the Present

In the rural areas, several towns were grouped together. There were few rabbis and they travelled to the small towns from the big city. For confirmations-the rite of passage that consists in an exam often transcribed in cursive script-the *paracha* (the section of the Torah that is read every week) was learned by heart. There are no Jewish Sunday Schools in the small cities.[129]

It may seem surprising that Jewish schools are called Sunday Schools, which shows how the Jewish cycle has adapted the Christian cycle of celebration. Yet, in spite of the attempts of some Reform rabbis, such as David Marx, to adopt Sunday as the day of the Sabbath service, Saturday was kept. Study and training for children are generally held on Sunday, even if some synagogues maintain Saturday schools (Sabbath Schools).

Nowadays the head rabbis chosen by the congregation are politicians and scholars. They may comment on current affairs and take positions. If they have the required diplomas, they teach Judaism at the university. They combine knowledge, religion, and politics. They are also friends, confidants, and educators. Liberal Judaism differs in this way from other forms of Judaism.

This branch of Judaism does not define Judaism by blood ties (the fact of having a Jewish mother) but by the children's education: children are Jewish when they are brought up in a Jewish home. When a liberal Jew marries a Christian, it has no influence on the following generations; the emphasis is on the children's education, in accordance with the platform of Reform Judaism adopted in 1961: "Reform Judaism, however, accepts such a child (from a non-Jewish mother) as Jewish without a formal conversion, if he attends a Jewish school and follows a course of studies leading to Confirmation. Such a procedure is regarded as sufficient evidence that the parents and the child himself intend that he shall live as a Jew. This paragraph was amended in 1988 because of the number of interfaith marriages. The Central Conference of American Rabbis (CCAR) stated, "the status of a child of a Jewish parent is under the presumption of Jewish descent." The presumed Jewish progeny of interfaith marriages must be established by appropriate and regular certifications of identification "with the Jewish faith and people. The performance of these *mitzvot* (obligations) serves to commit those who participate in them, both the parent and children to Jewish life."[130] As can be seen, the rules require the commitment not just of the child but of the parents as well. In any case, not all children from interfaith marriages are Jewish. We are dealing with a presumption. The parents and child must declare themselves as

Jewish, they must accept to follow a Jewish education, identify themselves as Jewish, and give up any other faith, in order to be part of the Alliance.

In cases when they affiliate themselves with Judaism, the newcomers are more devout and dynamic than the other members of the family; they teach the group Jewish values and reinforce them.

But in their trajectories, immigrants were confronted with a great diversity of situations in the South, given the vividness of the Christian environment, Catholic, Evangelical, Baptist and Methodist

CHAPTER IV
The New Configurations of Judaism

One fact dominates the South: the omnipresence of the Christian world. Its influences are not always experienced on a conscious level. Retrospectively, Joel Bert Myers, whose ancestors came from Alsace in the mid-nineteenth century, points to the impact the Christian world had on the Jews who had settled in the small towns: "They belonged to the Christian society even if they were Jewish," she says during our conversation. She mentions her grandparents who lived in Raceland, Louisiana, in the 1920s and 1930s: "We're assimilated to a Christian world, I think we protected ourselves," she adds.[131]

"Marrano effect," Christianization, the effect of vivid omnipresence and immersion. These remarks do not so much emphasize the Marrano effect on the population as its ability, as a minority, to fit into the rural environment. Indeed, most often arriving in small towns with no synagogues and in inadequate numbers, the immigrant could not observe the Jewish rites and holidays. When these families moved to New Orleans, they found a specific place to pray and meet for the first time. Some Christian customs were absorbed into the Jewish way of life but lost their original meaning. Will Lazarus, whose father was an accountant and later company manager in the cotton business, as described above, was in daily contact with the Christian world in New Orleans:

> We also had Christmas. My father received gifts from his clients and for Thanksgiving they gave him turkeys. We had a Christmas tree. This did not mean anything; it was just a pretty object. One of my neighbors with whom I had grown up used to call me to decorate his

Christmas tree. I was so happy. There was no religious content, the celebration of Christ. We didn't know these were religious vacations.

I wasn't aware of these problems, his wife Carolyn adds. When I was in the lower grades, most of my friends were Christian. There were quite a few Jews in Shreveport. But in a small town, you play with your friends and neighbors, whether Jewish or Christian.
— Will and Carolyn Lazarus, New Orleans, August 25, 1995.

Other interlocutors try to define liberal Judaism and describe their religious practice: "We were Reform Jews. We went to temple on the holidays." They mention the family traditions. The appropriate words are compromise, Americanization, and "cultural assimilation." For all that, assimilation in different circumstances is not total. The families we met are conscious of the separation between Christian society and the Jewish world: "We live together but we're also separated. There is a fine separation, there is always a fine, paper thin screen separating us," notes Joel Bert Myers, with lucidity. However, there are interfaith marriages within families. They follow particular rules.

In spite of its modernity, Reform Judaism was not initially very favorable to inter-religious marriages. "For a religion that looked forward to the unity of mankind, on the basis of prophetic justice there would be no possible objection to Jews marrying non-Jews many of whom already have accepted this outlook." says the sociologist Nathan Glazer. It was very rare for a Reform rabbi to adopt that position. Even the radical liberal rabbi David Einhorn was opposed to inter-religious marriage. The Central Conference of American Rabbis (CCAR), in 1909, declared that it was "contrary to the tradition of the Jewish religion and should therefore be discouraged by the American rabbinate."

The president of Hebrew Union College argued as follows: "Because of this universalistic Messianic hope...it is imperative...that the Jewish people continue its separateness...and... avoid intermarrying with members of other sects."[132] The initial orientations of Reform Judaism on this issue changed due to the large demand of interfaith marriages. But the change was slow.

At first, Reform Judaism preferred conversion and later, failing conversion, allowed the spouses to marry but stressed the requirement of a Jewish education for the children issued from interfaith marriages. Now it is characterized by openness and abides by the principles of Judaism defined by the platform of liberal Judaism adopted in 1999: "We are an inclusive community, opening doors to Jewish life to people of all ages, to varied kinds of families, to all regardless of their sexual orientation, to *gerim*, those who have converted to Judaism, and to all individuals and families, including the intermarried, who strive to create a Jewish home." In rare cases, interfaith marriages are celebrated by both a rabbi and a Christian minister. The priority of these rabbis is that the bride or groom not turn away from Judaism. Some liberal rabbis accept the idea of a joint service celebrated by a rabbi and a reverend. The marriage ceremony takes place in a non-denominational location. The rabbi who accepted this procedure in Temple Sinai, notes that in New Orleans there are many Jews who join other religions. Interfaith marriages are better than turning away from Judaism.[133] Cathy Kahn, whose daughter married an Episcopalian, explains how the marriage was celebrated:

> *There was a joint service performed by the rabbi from Temple Sinai and the reverend from Trinity Church. The ceremony was held in the non-denominational chapel in Newcomb. Some rabbis don't want to officiate with a reverend, but Rabbi Cohn accepted to. There are many Jews who practice other religions in New Orleans.*
> — Cathy Kahn, correspondence, August 12, 2004.

I found two examples of marriages contracted with Christian families. In the first, the Jewish family ended up assimilating "the foreign element"; they do not discuss it much and the Jewish lineage survived.[134] In the second instance, the marriage vows allowed for a dual affiliation, Jewish and Christian, which is accepted in families that belong to a tolerant elite.

At the beginning of the twentieth century, there were already Jewish families with a non-Jewish member and whose children were brought up in the Jewish tradition. "Nothing was said and it hardly changed anything, we were simply Jews, that's all," Carolyn Lazarus recalls in 1995. This example shows that Judaism is able to absorb a person from an interfaith marriage. The family, it seemed, was hardly affected by this fact. In cities like New Orleans, interfaith marriages took place earlier: "There were mixed marriages very early on, at the beginning of the twentieth century. We all have that in our genealogical trees in New Orleans," says the archivist Cathy Kahn.[135] But for Carolyn Lazarus's sister, Ruth First, who lived in New York, when one of the members of the family married a Christian, this is not always a welcome event. The family went into mourning and sits *shiva* for a week, as did her grandfather. Rhoda Abraham Dreyfus said the same thing happened in Montgomery, alluding to her grandparents: "Robert Dreyfus and Emma Jonas Dreyfus were very upset when their son married a Christian; today that would seem ridiculous."[136]

Dual affiliation can lead to a real religious cohabitation:

> *The father was half-Jewish, half-Episcopalian, but we didn't think about it. We were Jewish, half-Jewish, half-Episcopalian. Respect for the Christian and Jewish traditions then creates a real cohabitation of religions, with no apparent clashes.*
>
> *Our family is married with Presbyterians, Episcopalians, the children observe the Jewish Easter, sing the songs. The important thing is respect for others. The children will choose later.*
>
> *In the present generation, many children marry non-Jews. Conversion takes place either on the Christian side or the Jewish side. The important thing is for the family to belong to a religion: Jewish, Episcopalian, or Catholic...*
>
> — *Ruth Dreyfous, New Orleans, May 3, 1994.*

Cases of Conversion

Conversions take place both ways, most often because of marriages. When one of the spouses converts to Judaism, he or she often draws the family into new forms of practice. He is very "devoted," says the Jewish wife, about her converted husband. "He takes up religion and nudges the whole family into being Jewish... They do their best because they want to be part of this way of life."[137] In order to convert, study is required, but conversion seemed less difficult twenty years ago than it does now, according to Vicki Lazarus, who comes from a Los Angeles Methodist family.[138]

For the Jew converted to another religion, the doors are not shut. Sometimes the granddaughter keeps the name of her grandparents. She adds it to the names of her parents and husband. When she marries in 1998, the granddaughter becomes Leslie Geismar DeBardeleben McLaughlin: Geismar (her grandmother's name), DeBardeleben (her father's name), McLaughlin (her husband's name). Her three affiliations are strung together: Jewish through her grandmother, Episcopalian through her father, Irish Catholic through her husband.

Marriages into non-Jewish families can give access into New Orleans high society and this is sometimes the objective. Jews were long excluded (except for a few very wealthy families) from the very select Boston Club and Country Club.[139] Every chance of assimilation is given to the young woman who converts and makes her entrée into high society at the "debutante's ball." Conversely, if a Christian chooses to marry a young Jewish woman, he is no longer admitted into New Orleans high society. Because of him, his family will lose its rank.

> *He (the father of the bride) did not know anything about Jewish people. We were the first Jews he had ever met. And my daughter knew a lot about Christianity. She had attended an Episcopalian private school and because her grandmother, her uncle, her cousins on the other side of the family (her father's side) were Christian.*

— *Flo Geismar, New Orleans, October 23, 1997.*

The use of marriage by affinity or as a way of acceding to a new status, which dates back to the late nineteenth century, recalls the German Jewish bourgeoisie's conversion in the nineteenth century in order to gain access to higher administrative, political, and educational positions. One of the emblematic figures in Germany is Rahel Varnhaghen, a converted Jew who held a salon at the beginning of the nineteenth century.[140]

Another situation can arise: the converted person never completely gives up the religion of his or her father or mother. He or she seeks consistency and tries to make the two religions compatible. The person has chosen another religion but finds it is intimately related to his or her history. This option could be called "the postmodern individualist option."

Postmodern Individualism or Versatility

I found myself looking into disconcertingly diverse situations created by the choices made by individuals.

To account for this complexity, Danièle Hervieu-Léger points out that "religious identities are less and less inherited, either beliefs spread, or new practices are invented, it is therefore necessary to adopt new tools of thought."[141] She sets up two figures, the "converted" and the "pilgrim." The wide spectrum of choices reflects the multiplicity of religious offers in the United States. You can "travel" harmlessly from one church to another, the different Protestant churches being very close to one another. This cobbling together makes for a unique individual who organizes and rationalizes his affiliation. Danièle Hervieu-Léger notes in this regard: "What is postmodern is not so much the dissemination of beliefs as such. It lies in the explicit claim by individuals to have the right to personally combine the small systems of significance that give meaning to their life and to freely choose, if they wish (which is hardly automatic), reference to a tradition that allows them to enlist as believers, in a particular religious lineage."[142] In this case there is no claim to lineage;

religion is constructed according to the vagaries of life, family bonds, proximity, unpredictable factors. Some of my interlocutors with responsibilities in the Jewish milieu, present their family as homogenous. At the end of the interview, after trust has been established, they reveal a more nuanced picture. That is when it becomes possible to see how fragmented situations are. Indeed it is hard to preserve a Jewish identity given the religious dispersal of families. Is it possible to become assimilated without losing one's original identity?

> *There are some people who wanted to preserve the Jewish tradition and others who wanted to be assimilated. My brother, for example, never belonged to a congregation. His wife is the daughter of a Methodist pastor; their children have not been brought up as Jewish. His daughter was married in the Baptist church, his son in the Lutheran church. I have a sister. Her daughter joined the Mormon Church (laughter). My brother's family does not belong to any church.*
> — Metz Kahn, New York, September 3, 1992.

Within a single faith and a single family, the situation proves to be very diverse, matching the wide spectrum of Judaism-from ultra-Reform to ultra-Orthodox. Fidelity to a heritage and the idea of lineage are obsolete. No model is stable anymore. My interlocutor, the former president of the congregation in Baton Rouge, whose grandfather created the Reform congregation of New Orleans, Temple Sinai, interprets the situation as follows:

> *My son-in-law, with whom I live, is not Jewish, but comes from a very old Protestant family; the children were educated as Jews and had their bar mitzvahs. My other daughter belongs to a conservative congregation in Washington D.C. Her son was brought up as Jewish. The two parents are very active in their congregation. My youngest daughter, Kathy, lives in Bersheva in Israel, she has a diploma of service from the Jewish community in Brandeis. She works for*

> Jewish agencies, Jewish centers, federations, Jewish schools in Israel. She is married to a young man whose mother was Catholic, but who converted to Judaism. He works at Jerusalem University and comes from a very conservative, extremely conservative family, and they married in Jerusalem.
> — Metz Kahn, New York, September 3, 1992.

There is a wide range of possibilities: elimination of the heritage or inclusion of Jewish history along with a mixed Christian and Jewish practice, or a very distant affiliation following conversion and a sense of belonging to a remote history. In San Francisco, one of my interlocutors, originally from Lexington, Mississippi, insists on the fact that it is not necessary to practice Judaism in order identify oneself as Jewish. He demands the right to belong to the "Jewish tribe" while subscribing to another faith. For him, one is not Jewish by birth or religious practice, but by heritage and memory:

To write off people who do not adhere to a religion (for whatever reason) or those who have been separated from Judaism and adhere to another faith is to diminish "our tribe" in my opinion.

> The future of American Judaism is in that sanctuary: in the future, there will be converts in and converts out, and there will be congregations of people who had one Jewish great grandparent or great-great grandparent and who have belonged to an unbroken chain of Jewish ancestry.
> — Jay L. Wiener, San Francisco, September 28, 1999.

Liberal Judaism results from a choice that is not established by filiations. The heritage does not just derive from patrimony; it is also a handing down of knowledge; it is a choice based on work, on knowledge, and does not just reduce itself to filiations. Jay L. Wiener mentions a chain of legendary filiations. Jewish history has often known ruptures. Moreover, what do the following comments mean? I would not challenge whether a Jewish identity exists (i.e. non-Jews) for those attending the service with an open, prayerful heart." Reciting prayers or attending a service are simple identity markers. Judaism assumes another complexity. Jay Wiener's position is that of a small minority. There are two people in my survey who are converted to another religion but want to preserve Jewish history and its heritage, and feel Jewish, but in a loose and contradictory way. They demand the right to ambivalence. The interviewee is proud of belonging to a Jewish heritage even if he has chosen not to be Jewish anymore. These adjustments result from a need for internal coherence. The boundaries must be flexible in order to surmount affiliations that appear hard to reconcile and in order to recognize oneself in both, without cleavage. But wasn't this the position of the new Christians in sixteenth and seventeenth century Spain?

Leroy H. Paris, a lawyer in Jackson, Mississippi, whose mother was Lutheran and whose father was an officiating Jew in Lexington, Mississippi, is in the same position. He is Christian but holds on to his Jewish heritage as well. Every once in a while he attends the Jewish services in his father's family temple in the Lexington. It is the individual's choice that is most important:

> *I'm very proud and interested in my history, because that is where I come from on my father's side. As a Christian, it is very meaningful because I am like Christ, who came from a Jewish background, but now I am Christian. To me, that's very meaningful. When my first child was born I named her Rachel Marie and we call her both names. Rachel came from the Jewish side of the family and Marie from my mother's Protestant family. And, you know, I look at myself as a blend. I think that two different cultures came together inside me. I am proud and I like to say that I maintain my Jewishness... I am proud of my Jewish heritage; I take my children to the service here in Jackson. I am very interested in the Museum of the Southern Jewish Experience and all the different aspects of Jewish history.*

— *Leroy H. Paris, Jackson, September 17, 1992.*

He refers to the different cultures in America-Spanish, Irish, Baptist, Catholic-and America's ability to integrate this diversity better than any other country. At home, he shows me the Bible and the New Testament.[143] This attitude causes embarrassment in both the Jewish and Protestant milieus for each rejects the idea of belonging to two very different groups at the same time.

My interlocutors were interested in their family history and genealogy, and reconstructed their different family branches. Their choice is part of a "dual choice" with which they fully identify. In the South, added to the complexity and plurality of religious affiliations, there is also the issue of "inter-racial" marriages with mulattos, genealogical branches that have long remained hidden and/or were rediscovered thanks to genealogical research.

Judaism by Genealogy

By this term I mean an affiliation or filiations to Judaism in a remote way. One of the family members, an ancestor or a close relative, is Jewish. This association with Judaism is the fruit of personal research; it does not change the status of the person though it does give him a new opening. This affiliation can be more or less well accepted and people live with it in ways that are not always obvious. We observed gradations in Judaism by genealogical filiation. Indeed, different attitudes are possible: genealogical research can lead to renewing ties with different members of the family either with satisfaction, or with feelings of deep perplexity and a difficulty in integrating oneself in the maze of the rediscovered family. The Siess family, originally from Lembach in Alsace, now lives in small towns in Louisiana: Marksville, Mansura, Alexandria. Carol Mills, a member of the family, researched the Jewish branches, long concealed by her relatives. She discovered marriages with Jews and mulattos:

> *My great grandfather became Catholic. He had six children. His six children were baptized. However*

> Leopold Siess died and was buried in the Jewish cemetery in Pineville, Louisiana. His wife, Josephine Chatelain, is buried in Saint Paul's, the Catholic cemetery of Mansura, Louisiana. Among the six children, the first child, Auger Siess settled in Alexandria and married a young girl from a leading Jewish family in Alexandria... The inhabitants of that parish [Avoyelles, his mother's parish] had only one church and a single priest went from one church to the other. Natchez, one hundred and fifty years later, was in the same situation with its Jewish temple. A student from the rabbinical school goes there once a month. This is their rabbi. But in central Louisiana, where transportation was difficult and the weather was not always clement-there were often floods-it was not always possible to have a priest. My Catholic mulatto relatives, the Voorhies, when they had their civil marriage, went to Natchez. That way they could get married and be registered as "White" and avoid the stigma of being listed in the register reserved for "Blacks."
> — Carol Mills, New Orleans, June 24, 2004.

She discovered two religious practices, Jewish and Catholic, in three of her family branches. Sometimes, in the later years of life, there was a return to Judaism. Carol Mills notices the separation between the mulatto family and the other branch. Rural Catholicism is less controlled than in the city. The frontiers between Judaism and Catholicism are not always watertight. The discovery of a concealed Judaism causes a profound change in her:

> When I started to look, I thought of the family as a whole, not just the Siesses and the German family-the one that died in the Holocaust. This deeply affected me, as I never thought I belonged to that group. It's like something from the outside and suddenly you're part of it, and people to whom you're related have perished.

- Carol Mills, New Orleans, June 21, 2004.[144]

My second interlocutor, Philip Luchinger, lived in Mississippi and worked on the railroad. His wife is a college business teacher. He has explored his Alsatian Jewish origins. His great grandmother, Julia Abraham, came from the village of Reichshoffen (Bas-Rhin, Alsace), and married Abraham Klotz. She was buried in the small town of Donaldsonville, Louisiana, in 1871. We went together to visit the liberal Gates of Prayer congregation, where the Christian organist sings on Friday nights; in Metairie, the suburb of New Orleans, he showed me the different congregations, the Gates of Prayer temple, the new conservative temple, and the Creole kosher delicatessen where he sometimes dines with his wife. His youth was defined by religious changes. His religious affiliations are many, depending on his entourage-his stepmother is Catholic, his wife Baptist. Finally, he and his wife chose to become Presbyterian.

As Isabelle Richet points out, in the United States, religion is both individualist and pragmatic. Religion must be satisfying and useful.[145] Philip Luchinger is somewhat disoriented by all these successive choices. He has not renewed ties with his Jewish family. His criteria in choosing a particular religion hinge less on relatives or entourage than on the flexibility of the liturgy, the possibility of being an elder, and the tolerance of the church. The reasons seem vague and completely incidental: music, openness, autonomy, coincidence of discovery.

Freedom prevails in the United States given the vast number of churches. My interlocutor combines individualism, modernity, and fluctuations. His many choices are also characteristic of the American religious system, the multiplicity of Christian churches, and the minimal differences among them. The "religious marketplace" is the term commonly used to evoke this great diversity:[146]

> *I didn't hear my parents talk about religion. But all their friends were Jewish and many cousins were Jewish and many people in their address books were Jewish. I think I was eighteen when my father and his former*

girlfriend married in Starkville (Mississippi) in a Catholic church because she was Catholic, and I was the best man at the wedding. I had joined an Evangelical church in New Orleans because my neighbor had asked me to. He was my age. He knew its customs.

First Evangelical and then Reformed

I joined that church when I was seventeen and when I returned to New Orleans, I was in the habit of attending that church but when I was away in College I would sometimes go to the Catholic church with my father, and sometimes I went nowhere on Sunday. And when I got married, one Sunday we would go to the Baptist church, the next Sunday we would go to my "Church of the First Reformed Days"... Then one day, we were walking down the street and there was a trailer and a sign about this new Jean Calvin Presbyterian church, so we both started going. It was close to the house, there was good music and the message that was delivered was of high quality so we both changed and became Presbyterians. This was in 1967, about thirty-seven years ago.

You had no problem switching from the Evangelical church to the Baptist Church to the Catholic Church and then to the Presbyterian Church...

Everyone likes to change. These churches have the same idea of religion. The Jews don't believe in Christ, the Presbyterians think he'll return, the Catholics, I don't know. The Presbyterians think Christ will return...

Do you sing at the Presbyterian Church?

We sing. It's been the same pastor for twenty years. In the Catholic Church, there are the deacons. In the Jewish church, I don't know what they're called. In the Presbyterian Church, they have "elders" and members elect the elders who take care of daily life, pray, and

> *have different activities. I've been a member for thirty-seven years and an elder for ten years. I spent a year and a half looking for our pastor... My wife is going to be Chairman of the Presbyterian women.*
> *— Philip Luchinger, New Orleans, June 18, 2004.*

A scattered population, multiple affiliations, instability characterize postmodern American society. A spectrum of religious possibilities exists within the same faith. The Jewish religion covers a wide range of practices: from an absence of ritual practice to traditional practice, from liberal practice to ultra-Orthodox practice. Nowadays, new forms of Jewish tradition are being adopted. This attitude seems like another aspect of Postmodern Judaism.

The Contemporaneousness of Tradition

Flo Lehmann, whose two sons are rabbis in the South, emphasizes tradition and stresses the need for greater spirituality. This movement is one of the foundations of Reform Judaism. Her comments are echoed by the members of another congregation, Touro Synagogue in New Orleans. Reviewing the change in their temple over a period of about forty years, both Flo Geismar and Sylvia Marcus have similar observations about the request for a stricter observance.

> *We have an organ, in the synagogue and in the chapel. We have a large sanctuary. Touro Synagogue is a classic Reform community. I was there. I noticed that the young people wanted more tradition. They want to return to many of Judaism's ceremonials. Many members want kosher food when we they have a meeting. Before, they didn't.*
> *— Flo Geismar, New Orleans, October 23, 1997.*

> *I was confirmed in Touro Synagogue. We didn't know what a bar mitzvah was. But when the couple is mixed, liberal and Orthodox, it is not uncommon for the*

> *child to have a bar mitzvah usually to please the grandparents.*
> — Sylvia Marcus, New Orleans, September 23, 1994.

Actually children have been having *bar mitzvah* and *bat mitzvah* for only about twenty years. And a respect for the rules of traditional Judaism excludes women from the choirs. "We went from an all-female choir to a male choir. All of this means changes in relation to former times. They say we can't have music in the synagogue. That's going too far, "Sylvia Marcus explains.

As for the rites and behavior, they are edging closer to Conservative Judaism. Nowadays, many faithful wear a *kippah* and *tallit* (prayer shawl), which were long banned from Reform synagogues. Weddings are celebrated under the traditional canopy. Hebrew is making a comeback in the services at the request of men and women from the Eastern and Northern states, or from people who are taking Hebrew courses. One of the women I spoke to even felt the need for a *bat mitzvah* at age forty-five because she felt this rite of passage would be a way of being completely included in the community. The rabbi of this Reform synagogue pointed out to me that he was merely following the wishes of his congregation; nonetheless he seemed happy with this return to a more traditional Judaism. The change affects the new generation of twenty to thirty year olds too. It arouses the irritation of the older members who feel ill at ease with this excessive return to traditional Judaism. For others, it points to a new affirmation of identity that includes the religious: Hebrew, the observance of rites, study, and a respect for the heritage.

The term "heritage" becomes composite, covering a history, the experience of a culture, and a Diaspora, all of which renders the most diverse positions legitimate. The return can be explained by a need to identify with a form of Judaism that can be distinguished from other affiliations and avoids uniformity. The young generation insists on present-day differences. There is a clear-cut disparity between the generation of sixty and eighty year olds, who were attached to a cultural and charitable form of Judaism, the Judaism of the Israelites, and the younger generation who longs for greater rigor and observance. Judaism, according to them, has been too open to outside influences.

In Dallas, Myra Fischel, whose family comes from Central Europe, is married to a Jew of French-German origin. She completely agrees with the preceding remarks.

> In our Reform temple, Temple Emanu-El, many people wear the kippah and tallit. When we first arrived, in the 1970s, you didn't see anyone wearing a kippah. In my generation it wasn't accepted, ever. And you never wore a tallit. Today, it's accepted, it's our heritage. They are still Jews which means that people's minds have opened up to all sorts of Jews, but there are still some differences.
> — Bert and Myra Fischel, Dallas, October 8, 1997.

As an extension of this need for identification, for the last twenty years there have been summer camps that bring together young people from the Southern states. Minority families living in small towns send their children to these summer camps where they are taught the history of Judaism and of Israel. These places allow young people to meet other Jewish children, acquire a better knowledge of Judaism, and sometimes eventually lead to marriages between co-religionists. These camps offer a veritable reconstruction of Judaism's world view, founded on the Jewish experience and heritage whose values the active members are responsible for handing down in the future.

These days, instead of being based on universal values, identity is reconstructed by distinguishing and separating oneself from others. Given this movement of identity reassignment, it is not surprising that the relations between liberal Judaism and Israel have changed considerably over the years. Initially the liberals were fiercely opposed to the idea of a second home. But their position has evolved. It has changed since 1917. After the Holocaust and the creation of the State of Israel, their attitude mellowed. The Six-Day War in 1967 and Reform Judaism's last platform in 1999 contributed in establishing a clear attachment to Israel on the part of Reform Jews.

Changing Relations With Israel

Though liberal Judaism originated in Germany, the lively debates they sparked were exported to the United States.[147] The controversies, at the time of the creation of the American Hebrew Union Congregation in 1874, led to the resignation of some its members who supported the idea of a return to Zion.[148] Liberal Judaism, contrary to Orthodox Judaism, has as its foundation an exclusively American filiation. "America is our Zion." For Michael Meyer, specialist of Reform Judaism, "To Reform Jews, Zionism was a counsel of defeat, a surrender to the forces of anti-Semitism rather than the valiant fight to defeat them."[149]

Let us briefly recall how Reform Judaism evolved with regard to Zion in the course of the nineteenth and twentieth centuries. Institutionally, Reform Judaism was fundamentally opposed to political Zionism. At their first convention in 1897, just a few weeks before the Congress of Basel, the Central Conference of American Rabbis (CCAR) declared unanimously: "We totally disapprove of any attempt for the establishment of a Jewish State. Such attempts show a misunderstanding of Israel's mission." A year later, in 1898, the Union of American Hebrew Congregations (UAHC) reissued its condemnation: "We are inalterably opposed to political Zionism. The Jews are not a nation but a religious community [...] America is our Zion. Here, in the home of religious liberty, we have aided in founding this new Zion." But following the Balfour Declaration of 1917 allowing the creation of a Jewish home in Palestine, their position mellowed: the document was seen as "an evidence of goodwill toward the Jews" and the Union of American Hebrew Congregations supported the immigration of persecuted Jews to Palestine. Yet it could not subscribe to the idea of Palestine as a national homeland for the Jewish people and reasserted its view that "Israel is at home in every free country and should be at home in all lands."

Having briefly recalled the position of classical Reform Judaism in the early twentieth century, I do not propose to delve further into the changing relations of Zionism and the Reform movement, but more modestly, to show how Zionism was perceived by my interlocutors. With a few exceptions, the relation to Zion was never specially mentioned at the beginning of my survey, save incidentally. Flo Geismar, for example, pointed out that she had felt close to Israel very early in life and that she contributed to charitable causes, against the advice of her father and other members of her family.[150] The question of the relations between Reform Judaism and Israel was raised explicitly only later. It came up, first in the context of the commitment of philanthropic women who were less worried about the State of Israel than in assisting children who were in danger of becoming blind. Their effort was above all charitable; it was not political. Only one of my interlocutors, Rosalie Cohen, who is Orthodox, committed herself to the Zionist cause very early, in the 1930s, and made regular trips to Palestine. According to another of my interlocutors, Rabbi Stanley Dreyfus, Zionism was rare in Youngstown, Ohio, or Shreveport, Louisiana, during the first half of the twentieth century. He spoke of his Zionist convictions with pride, and of Zionism with admiration. Originally from an Orthodox Alsatian milieu, he was very isolated in his support of Zionism: "My father was one of the Zionists. But when I was an adolescent in Youngstown, in a Classical Reform congregation, perhaps only two or three of us students were proud of being Zionists."

At the beginning of the twentieth century, the Reform Rabbi Max Heller, who was very close to Orthodoxy and the Russian Jewish population, was a fervent propagandist for the Zionist cause. He was welcomed as a pro-Zionist lecturer in 1903 in the Orthodox congregation on Dryades and Decatur Streets, the Ohavei Zion center, where Zionist institutions were organized in New Orleans. He was the exception and his own community did not share his point of view, as confirmed by one of the descendants of his congregation.[151]

> *The Reform movement was not Zionist at all, except for Max Heller. Max Heller came from Czechoslovakia, and he brought his convictions with him; he wasn't a product of the Hebrew Union of Cincinnati.*
> — *Metz Kahn, Baton Rouge, October 11, 2000.*

Abraham Metz Kahn, who is from liberal family, points out that before the Second World War the distinctions between the Reform and the Orthodox groups were clear-cut, with a few exceptions, but later they became less so:

> *My great grandfather Salomon Marx was a very good friend of Max Heller's, the rabbi of Temple Sinai. Rabbi Max Heller was a precocious advocate of Zionism. My great grandfather wasn't a Zionist at all. The Reform communities in the South were never very enthusiastic about Zionism. When Rabbi Heller finished the service with the sentence, 'Next year in Jerusalem,' my great grandfather would stand up and raise his umbrella, "Speak for yourself, Max, I'm staying here.'*
> — *Metz Kahn, Baton Rouge, October 11, 2000.*

These words could be exchanged in the beginning of the twentieth century: "The repressive atmosphere in post-populist climate of Louisiana was as instrumental as his identification with the sufferings of European Jews in pushing Heller to Zionism."[152] Rabbi Max Heller came out for the equality of peoples and cultures in order to call attention to the sufferings of Jews and the racial prejudices against African Americans. He made a distinction between religious Zionism, a vital force of awakening, and political Zionism. Heller tried to reconcile his position with that of his congregation. His speech published in the *Daily Picayune*, on November 18, 1899, seems significant with regard to the birth of the Zionist movement and the dissensions it gave rise to, a combination of enthusiasm and recriminations. Max Heller tried to explain the elements and vitality of Zionism to his congregation in a speech which the press entitled "Rabbi Max Heller discusses Zionism: the difference between the political and the religious." The first is the result of despair, the second the birth of a wave of optimism. His speech begins thus:

The word Zionism is new and so are, essentially, the political projects, the national and commercial schemes which travel under that name; the sentiment which is its lifeblood hails back to the dim ages of Israel's antiquity. A movement such as this, drawing its strength from the oldest to the dearest association of a race, and yet eager to be ranked among the vital forces of the century, will naturally give rise to many misunderstandings.

At the end of his speech, he expresses the view that if "Zionism is an error but a necessary error. [...] it will fail from its inherent opposition to the core of Judaism but not until it shall have fulfilled its mission of sending life into the dead bones of lethargy and preparing the soil for a nobler movement of a grander scale." The organizations that were opposed to Zionism were united in the American Jewish Congress. They were opposed to the idea of a land for Jews. "They said it would have a negative influence on Americans," says Abraham Metz Kahn. After the Yom Kippur War in 1973, the state of mind changed completely:

> *Between these two periods (before the Second World War and the Yom Kippur War), they were against the creation of the State of Israel. In Baton Rouge, New Orleans, Atlanta, everywhere in the South they refused to participate in fundraising for Zionist movements. This was because there were two Reform congregations in Baton Rouge: one was made up of German refugees from the Second World War and they supported Zionism. This caused division between the two congregations. One had a pro-Zionist stance, the other, my community, had an anti-Zionist sentiment.*

There is a difference on this point between the families of Orthodox origin who adopted Reform Judaism and the others: Ellie Fraenkel is from a pro-Zionist, Orthodox family. Other families, of Romanian origin, were Zionist: the Cohens in Jackson, Mississippi, as the writer Edward Cohen points out, alluding to his grandparents.[153] Attitudes were not homogenous. Some liberal families supported charitable causes for a long time and used to send money to Palestine, The most popular organization is the Hadassah. Hence Joel Bert Meyers's grandmother, who came from an openly liberal French-German family, contributed money at a very early date to the Hadassah health organization, a women's association supporting Palestine that dates back to 1912. There was operation Blue Box. A number of boxes had to be filled with money in order to take care of a child who was in danger of losing his or her eyesight. Many children suffered from glaucoma due to the sand from the desert regions. Her granddaughter explains her motives as essentially philanthropic and charitable:

> *My grandmother was a very sensitive person. She wanted people to be happy and she tried to do things to help. Someone contacted her and told her that there were needy children in Israel who were in danger of becoming blind and that they could be helped. All they needed was help. My grandmother was asked if she could take a blue box. Very few acted like that, Thérèse Abraham Kahn, my grandmother, used to help children. I don't know if she was committed to Zionism, she had become involved only to help children. Her daughter Emilie continued. She was very committed to Zionism. I think she saw her do it, I think it was in the 1940s. But her mother started before then.*
> — Joel Bert Myers, New Orleans, October 18, 2000.

When my interlocutor refers to Zionism, I don't know if she means political Zionism, the recognition of a State, or only charitable Zionism. As we can see, her grandmother, Thérèse Abraham Kahn, had been a precursor in the 1930s. She did not erect frontiers; she was known for her generosity and involvement in all types of charitable causes. Nowadays, many people still participate financially in these causes. Joel Bert Myers makes a point of saying, "I give them money; I always do." It was not the same in those days. Today most people belong to the Hadassah and Jewish communities are now of one mind in their attachment to Israel, even if their involvement varies. The new platform of 1999 is evidence of this, for it divorces itself from the debates of 1885, when a dual affiliation was rejected in favor of a single homeland, America: "We have committed to the *mitzvah* of love for the Jewish people and *tok'lal* Israel, the entirety of the community of Israel..."

Subsequently, the platform is more precise and emphatic:

"We are committed to a vision of the State of Israel that promotes full civil, human and religious rights for all its inhabitants and that strives for a lasting peace between Israel and its neighbors. We affirm that both Israel and the Diaspora Jewry should remain vibrant and interdependent communities...."

It is true that today the support of the Diaspora is unshakeable. This new attitude does not prevent Reform rabbis from criticizing the Orthodox religious system. Still, they maintain their charitable support.

> *There's a difference between sending money and fighting for the creation of a nation. On an individual basis, people can send money for the poor, but they don't want to send money to help the army.*
> — *Metz Kahn, Baton Rouge, October 11, 2000.*

All the families are unanimous on one point: the danger Israel incurred during the 1967 Six-Day War turned them toward the Zionist State. In many families that I questioned, it is customary for young adolescents to make a trip to Israel, paid for by the grandparents, after their *bar mitzvah*. The relation to Israel is no longer a question of recognizing the State and supporting it as in earlier times. All the federations have become organized so that a portion of the funds raised is sent to Israel. The contributions are relayed by Zionist organizations such as WIZO, the Women's International Zionist Organization, and no longer pose a problem. This is confirmed by an official from the New Orleans Jewish Federation, who explains how the different funds are distributed:

> *You probably know what I'm talking about: we have a Greater New Orleans Federation; its function is to make the Jewish community go out and collect funds for this community. A portion of the funds raised is sent to all the local Jewish agencies. Another goes to Israel, to similar agencies, and another part is sent through the national route to social agencies in other foreign*

countries.
— Julie Grant Meyer, New Orleans, October 24, 1997.

As we reach the end of our analysis on the growth of congregations, we can note that the immigrants settling in their new country formed communities while they also assimilated socially and economically. Affiliation was a response to the pressures of the surrounding religious milieu and the need for cohesion in organizing newcomers: praying together, helping the most needy, finding land for burying the dead. The first wave of immigrants proceeded by imitating the old world. The model of Reform Judaism became preponderant at the end of the nineteenth century because it fits so well with the social decorum and liturgical demands required by the faithful and the environment. We could say it was an ethical Judaism rather than a religious one. It entailed the affirmation of the Americanization of its members and a complete loyalty to America. The service replaced Hebrew with English; the rites and garments were in no way dissimilar to the Protestant model, with its organs, the dialogue of the faithful, and the officiating minister. Assimilation, which was a very strong demand on the part of the immigrants, raises the question of the handing down of a Jewish identity in an environment that is not always favorable. In this context, we should also distinguish the larger cities from the small towns, in which the hundred or so Jewish families are identified and recognized. Tolerance sometimes means absorption by the majority, or conversely, a clear-cut cleavage between the Christian groups and the Jewish groups. A process of "de-assimilation" is taking place at present, a sign that expressions of identity are being asserted. The demand for greater spirituality comes from the younger generations and from newcomers from the Northern states. They give Judaism a new momentum but can also create new separations both inside and outside the group.

Observing a group also means seeing how it lives at close range, in its intimacy, at home, through its language and its ways of doing things. How do people organize their private space? What are the signs of prosperity? Does the group use the French language and what becomes of the language in the second and third generations? Finally, in a Creole environment, can it adopt Creole cuisine and make it kosher?

CHAPTER V
Dwellings, Languages and Cooking

It is very revealing to study the daily lifestyles of families through the narratives of the first immigrants and the descriptions of their descendants. How did they organize their living space, what languages did they speak, what kind of food did they eat?

A Makeshift Arrangement of Private Space

The separation between the professional and the private spaces occurred progressively. The ways in which families and unmarried immigrants settled reflect the unstable situations at their arrival. The ones who disembarked in New Orleans, or in New York with the intention of traveling on to the South, found accommodations with families. They also stayed in inexpensive boarding houses, waiting to find work. When they did find an apartment it was located above the store. Philip Sartorius' brothers, Isaac and Jacob, who emigrated two years before he did, welcomed their brother and sister into their home in 1848. Though Isaac got married, his brother continued to live with him, while his sister lived very close by. This is described in detail at the beginning of Philip Sartorius's *Memoirs*.

> *Bro Isaac had his store about [where] Cox and Henry's barbershop is now in 1910. Bro Isaac occupied the upper floor for residence. All the stores were thus inhabited [...]. "In 1846, Bro Isaac got married, we lived in the two story frame house next to Willie Lévy's house on Walnut street opposite to Phoenix Engine House. Sister Caroline lived there and [this is] where Emma Chan Kohlman's wife was born. Sister*

Caroline's first husband 's name was Michel Levy.[154]

Rented houses were divided into a private space and a professional space. Thus, Rosine Cahn's father found a home for his family in 1847 in Pascagoula, Mississippi, in order to escape from the yellow fever epidemic in New Orleans. He rented part of a house.[155]

> *The house was one story and had rooms on each side of a hall in the middle, this man (the landowner) used one side of the house, he rented the other side to my parents. My father had brought merchandise from New Orleans and beside our bedroom was a small room (which I supposed was used for the storage). There were shelves and a small window which looked out on the back of the house.*[156]

Unmarried immigrants who lived in boarding houses for several months paid on credit.[157] Private spaces existed but they were still makeshift and temporary. When the young immigrant Julius Weis landed in New Orleans in November 1845, he was put up for two days at the house of an acquaintance, Isaac Meyer, then he took the boat to Natchez, Mississippi, where he found a boarding house that his cousins had told him about. His relatives had paved the way for him. He relied on a network of family and friends.[158] More unusual were the immigrants who were put up in well-to-do houses in which the private space was already clearly defined. When he arrived in New York on March 21, 1865, Benoît Fromenthal, a Lauterbourg native, made the following description in French: "Spacious houses with water and gas on all the floors, a profusion of rugs, the wealthy are numerous and they display great luxury.[159] Rosine Cahn, whose family returned to New Orleans in 1848, when the yellow fever epidemic ended, described her new environment. The rented house was located in the French Quarter on Moreau Street. It was larger than the former one; the owner lived on the upper floors while the family lived partly on the ground floor. The house was split into two spaces, a professional space where products were sold and a space reserved for domestic activities. The rooms reserved for the black servants were separate from the main house and the kitchen was located outdoors in order to avoid the heat in summer. The professional space could encroach on the private space whenever needed. Indeed, the family's foremost consideration was earning a living. That is why the private rooms could be used to store merchandise. The two spaces were interchangeable and if the professional activity required it, the spaces had to be redefined. But in addition to this division between private and public space, the racial division should also be taken into account, the separation of African Americans and Whites. It was not acceptable for the African Americans to live in the same house as the masters, as Rosine Cahn recalls:

> *The first room in the corner was the shop, behind was a large room also, the living room, dining-room and bedrooms, that later became part of the store when the shop was no longer large enough to hold all the merchandise. Behind these large rooms, there was a courtyard which opened onto Moreau Street. There was the kitchen, the laundry room. Above were the bedrooms. It was there that I had my room when I was older. These rooms were for the servants. And since they were blacks they were not allowed in the main house itself. And then the kitchen was separate from the house to avoid the heat in the summer.*[160]

As for the plantations which the immigrants began to own after about twenty years, nothing is said about the changes between the private and public spaces. These seemed self-evident within the context of segregation. The spaces reserved for the black servants are the "quarters", clusters of rudimentary row houses, adjoining the main house. The slaves, and later the emancipated slaves, lived in cabins, separate from their employers. The overseer and master visited these quarters regularly and could intervene in the servants' space. The cast system implied a rigid separation between Whites and African Americans. African Americans were only admitted in the white man's house in order to work. The immigrants adopted the segregationist customs and values of the natives. On the plantations, the prosperous families who had arrived before the Civil War lived with a large staff of servants up until the mid-1920s and, above all, with a maid attached to the mistress of the house. Usually they regarded the staff of servants, slaves and, later, children of former slaves with kindness. Their lifestyle was very similar before and after the Civil War. Flo Geismar, with whom I had several conversations, felt nostalgic for this bygone way of life, and reminisced about certain aspects of this idealized vanished world. Yet she knows, from personal experience, that the ruptures were brutal:

> Louis Geismar's wife, Sera Heymann, told me that when she was a child, there was a hairdresser who went from house to house; the young woman came at least every other day, she took care of their hair. Aunt Sera had a personal chambermaid Blanche who took care of her bath, dried her, pinched her cheeks to make them pink. I used to sit in the bathroom while she was having all these little things lavished on her (beauty treatments). This was done every day when I was a child until Blanche got married and left the house. Her mother was the old woman who had been a slave on Minel's plantation. She had been the personal chambermaid of Minel's daughter. They were the owners of the Waterloo plantation before the Civil War. I would say that sixty-five years ago, aunt Sera would never have thought that the plantations had to undergo change. The thought never occurred to her. After all, she was born during the Civil War. Things did not change very much after the Civil War until much later. They paid the slaves. They all lived in the slave quarters that you saw.
> — Flo Geismar Margolis, New Orleans, September 27, 1997.

Flo Geismar was born on the plantation in Geismar in 1922. Her cousin Sera Heymann, of the previous generation, lived in the same place.[161] Flo describes the life of a little girl very pampered by wealthy plantation owners. Her father arrived in 1907. He was preceded by an uncle. This is prior to the Great Depression, which will bring about the family's bankruptcy, as mentioned earlier. Young girls and young women lived inside the house and were not involved in caring for the crops on the plantation. Women managed plantations only in exceptional circumstances. In 1879, a young Creole woman, Laura Locoul Gore, became responsible for the family plantation in Saint James parish, on the right bank of the Mississippi. The plantation that bears her name, Laura Plantation, has been restored and is open to visitors.[162] In the second generation, or after about twenty years, affluent families lived in impressive Greek Revival residences.

Life in the Cottages, Neoclassical Houses

In the late nineteenth century, the wealthy bourgeois French and German families had a style of education that was similar to the one in Europe, with a staff of servants appointed to every household task. Young women had the same musical and manual activities, an upbringing that lasted until the 1930s:

> I was educated like a young woman on a plantation. It was Aunt Sera who educated me. She believed that in order to be a lady, you had to know how to crochet and knit. You also had the choice of playing the piano or the violin. But you had to play one or the other. It was the bourgeois life. I don't know how you call it.
> — Flo Geismar, New Orleans, September 27, 1997.

The phenomenon of upward mobility and the adoption of middle-class values, due to the ownership of neocolonial or attractive residences, occurred in Europe as in the United States. In New Orleans, from the 1890s to the 1920s, the second generation of prominent families chose to have houses built on the thoroughfares near the residential Garden District. It is interesting to note that some of the townhouses had backyards, small orchards, even henhouses, such as the home of notary public Félix Dreyfous. His daughter Ruth, ninety-one years of age, described it to us:

> *My father lived on Esplanade Avenue (near the French Quarter). And his father died when my parents were on their honeymoon. When they returned, they stayed in my grandfather's house while they were building a house on Jackson Avenue, which is still there, five blocks away. There was a large courtyard and the children would come in the afternoon because we had this large courtyard. In the back we had plum trees and a henhouse and we used to cook the chicken.*
>
> **And how many servants, cooks and household help did you have?**
>
> *We always had someone to mind the children who used to clean the upstairs and the ground floor. We had a person who served, cleaned and cooked for seven people, a person who did the washing and ironing, and a cook. The only man was our chauffeur when we acquired a car in 1909.*
>
> — Ruth Dreyfous, New Orleans, October 23, 1992.

The Dennery family, another well-established New Orleans family, adopted a French style of life that bore a similarity to the postcolonial savoir vivre of the South. Théodore Dennery arrived from Vésoul with two children after the Franco-Prussian War of 1870. He had married Sarah Salmon in 1860, and a year after her death in 1866, he married her sister, Fanny, with whom he had a son, Charles, born in Wissembourg in 1869. They obtained permission to leave Wissembourg for America on July 17, 1871. Initially Théodore Dennery and his family lived with a Mr. Théodore who ran a wholesale grocery on Magazine Street. In 1917, Charles Dennery, his son, and Charles's wife Jeannette Frank, built a two-story house for the thirteen members of their family. Their grand-nephew, Fred Kahn, who lived there, described it to me:

> It is located on the large residential St. Charles Avenue, where the residences of the large plantation owners were built, the latter having made their fortunes in cotton, sugar or rice. These are antebellum Greek Revival cottages, in other words neo-classical, some of them dating back to the 1860s.
> — Fred Kahn, New Orleans, September 24, 1998; grand-nephew on the maternal side of the Dennery family.

This house provides us with details on the lifestyle of middle-class families: "There are three maids, a majordomo, a cook and the car, a Buick with glass panes, driven by a chauffeur. The best rooms are downstairs." Fred Kahn's mother moved downstairs to the rear of the house when his father died. At thirteen, Fred lived downstairs with the men. All the generations lived together. This is not exceptional. Relatives lived side by side: we can cite the Burkenroad family, coffee importers, who owned a spacious family house. Middle-class families adopted a French style of life. They dressed up for the evening meal. Two or three maids were in charge of the upkeep. "The china set took up several shelves as did the silverware: a fancy service," Fred Khan recalled. The rituals were in keeping with the social class. This formality was not just characteristic of urban houses. In the Geismar's more modest *post-bellum* house, their granddaughter, Vicki Stamler, recalls having to dress up for the main midday meal at her grandfather's in the 1960s:

> My grandparents were very attached to proprieties. They used to have French lunches. It was the main meal of the day. No T-shirts. We were told to button our shirts, wear a tie, wear a dress that was suitable for the meal. He (my father) was also told to speak slowly. He would go out on the grounds to smoke a cigarette and come back. He had been brought up on Staten Island, in Lithuanian New York. He fell in love with the South, its gentle lifestyle.

Decorative Objects, Hidden Objects, Fragments of Memories [163]

This style of entertaining still applies. When I was invited for dinner by families of French descent, they welcomed me with a tablecloth, fine china, a three-course meal and coffee served in cups and saucers. My hostesses put as much care into the table decoration as in the refined dishes they had prepared themselves or instructed their cook to prepare. Each of these families decorates their home with particular care, too. The furniture dates from different periods and is in various styles: English Chippendale, or French-style armchairs. Sometimes they have antique furniture, sometimes Japanese-style furniture, as was the case for Ruth Dreyfous who was ninety-one when I met her. Some of the objects came from Europe — clocks, large Napoleonic vases. One of my hostesses had Alsatian chairs in her kitchen, which had been brought over from France. She had arranged to have her grandmother's early twentieth-century bedroom furniture sent from Toulouse out of attachment to her family. And she wanted me to sleep in that bedroom whenever I stayed with her. Display cabinets with collections of china teacups from Limoges, Holland and England were not unusual in the homes that welcomed me. The furniture was handed down over several generations and their loss or damage during the 2005 Katrina hurricane, for example, was painful to them, like the disappearance of a part of their history.

In New Orleans, the taste for beautiful furniture is linked to the history of the city. The antique stores on Royal Street in the French Quarter and the secondhand shops on Magazine Street display period furniture. Moise Waldhorn, who arrived in New Orleans from Alsace in the 1870s, was initially a jeweler and went on to open the city's first antique store after the Civil War, in 1881. After his death, in 1910, the store was managed by his children, grandchildren and great-grandchildren, until it was acquired by Coleman Jewelers in 1997.[164] As for Henry Stern (1896-1963), an antique dealer on Royal Street, he "taught entire generations how to recognize what he loved, France and the French style," the historian Cathy Kahn explains in her most recent book.[165]

On the other hand, we see very few traditional Jewish objects in the homes of these families, whose lifestyle is secular. Indeed, there is no apparent sign of religiosity. Georges Simonnot, a French-speaking Cajun friend of Metz Kahn's, born in Lafayette in 1903, and whom I met in Baton Rouge, knew Samuel Klotz, the former mayor of Napoleonville, very well and attests to this fact: "A few frames [Mizra, folk-art paintings hung facing Jerusalem in the homes of religious Jews] with Hebrew lettering in the house. There was *no mezuzah* as far as I could see. There was nothing else. Nothing else. But I didn't pay attention to all that."[166]

Furniture is a constant reminder, a keepsake and a sign of attachment to a history that pre-dates emigration. It is also a sign of distinction. Some families have carefully preserved family photographs that span several generations, and these are discreetly displayed on the second floor of their homes. Such is the case of the family members of Nancy Kohlmeyer, originally from Riga. During our first conversations she remained silent about her origins. The pictures led her to relate the family's stories about the atrocities of the Cossacks. Photos have an enormous importance. They preserve the trace of faces and are the only remaining portraits of the families who came from Europe. They form a tie reaching beyond dispersal, distance and time. These mementoes reunite partially destroyed or deceased families. In a recently built house outside the city, the pastis handed down over four generations, thanks to photographs of four children in four different frames wearing the same dress. This garment deliberately shows both unity and continuity: "Thanks to recollections, keepsakes, objects, photos, the past is excavated, lists are made, landmarks are traced. It is the archeology of an earlier civilization, a land of the dead that can be surveyed... It allows us to say that we are not alone, that we come from somewhere. Allows us to be proud or, on the contrary, complain of being weighed down by family memory."[167] There were also families who were very attached to their books and who showed me their personal libraries, which included the classic works of French, English, German and American authors. Whether in two-story neo-colonial wooden houses, architect's houses inspired by Frank Lloyd Wright, modern one-story houses, smaller more modest houses, luxury apartments located above the House of Blues in the French Quarter, apartments for pensioners-in each of these dwellings a fragment of history was preserved: an ancestor's slave contract, a genealogical tree, a naturalization certificate, prayer books with family birth dates, ancient Bibles or — perhaps more prosaic but equally cherished-the account books of their parents' store. Some families who no longer spoke French, Jewish-Alsatian or German, asked me to translate their documents. Prayer books are often similar to family record books; marriages and births were inscribed in them, in accordance with the Jewish tradition.[168] Other documents are more accessible. These include translations of French marriage and birth certificates or requests for French citizenship. Translating these documents enables the families to understand the itinerary of their ancestors in greater detail. The first two generations speak French, German and the dialect. The third or fourth generation rediscovers these first languages.

Does this mean that we are witnessing the obliteration of French, German and the dialect? This is the delicate question we will now broach.

What Remains of the Languages Spoken by the Immigrant

The language my interlocutors are attached to, first and foremost, is French. German, Alsatian and Yiddish-Daitsch were also spoken by the first-generation families of immigrants. However, my interlocutors hardly ever told me, on their own, about their ancestors' use of Jewish-Alsatian or Jewish-German. Jean Meyer in Strasbourg was an exception. His great grandmother, Pauline Weil Hirsch lived in Hazelhurst, Mississippi, at the time of the Civil War. Jean Meyer, her great grandson, recounts that she usually spoke in Alsatian in emotional instances: "She went looking for her Hirsch, who had been drafted, and in her anger she spoke to the officer directly in Alsatian."¹⁶⁹ The immigrants spoke Alsatian and Jewish-Alsatian or the Rhine valley dialect. However, aside from my interlocutor in Strasbourg, I heard no other oral confirmation of the fact.

The historian Elliott Ashkenazi notes that Jacob Lemann, merchant and plantation owner, did his bookkeeping in Yiddish: "His European heritage, however, never left him. He continued, for example, to keep his personal accounts in Yiddish, which, incidentally, may have provided a guarantee of secrecy."¹⁷⁰ There are only scattered traces of Yiddish. Benoît Fromenthal's correspondence with his parents includes a few comments about the holidays written in Jewish-Alsatian and German on March 3, 1865.¹⁷¹ When Benoît Fromenthal does not want to be read by others, he uses Jewish-Alsatian. This is also the case in the correspondence of Lazard Kahn with his family in Ingwiller.¹⁷² The Société Israélite Française de New York includes the first generation of immigrants from 1910 to 1930; the need to speak Alsatian explains why they lived clustered in the same neighborhood in Jamaica.¹⁷³ Some of its members point out that Alsatian was used often. Speaking of her mother, originally from Brumath (Bas-Rhin, Alsace), Janet Rothschild points out that "she spoke Alsatian a lot."

I found very little trace of Yiddish among the immigrants of the French-German families settled along the Mississippi. Louis Benjamin Geismar wrote in Yiddish to his family in Alsace but his descendants did not. In contrast, the immigrant families of Polish or Russian origin, who arrived in New Orleans at the beginning of the twentieth century, spoke Yiddish and passed it on to their children. Rosalie Palter Cohen began to learn Hebrew with the poet Ephraim E. Lisitzky in 1910 and speaks Yiddish fluently.¹⁷⁴ A good knowledge of Yiddish is apparent in the cookbooks written by Sylvia P. Gerson and Mildred Covert with the use of expressions such as Schnapsy Seder Chicken, Ma Nishtanah Stuffing, etc., mixing Yiddish and English.¹⁷⁵

Use and Handing Down of French

In Louisiana, among the Jewish families that were predominantly French, the French language was spoken until the 1930s. It was also used in school courses, when it is not prohibited, as usually happens. Knowledge of French is not always a sign of distinction or integration. It all depends on who the speaker is and the kind of French spoken. Some families chose Louisiana, such as the Dreyfous, Dennery, Geismar families, because French was spoken there. From the strictly legal standpoint, contrary to what some people believe, there is no present-day law making French the official language, nor is there one for English, actually. The State of Louisiana's linguistic policy has become a policy of non-intervention. Not only is there no law establishing an official language in the State (neither French nor English), but the State has delegated its powers to a state agency, the Codofil (Conseil du Développement du Français en Louisiane). According to their present homepage, since its inception in 1968, Codofil has worked very closely with the State Department of Education to promote the study of French in Louisiana's elementary and secondary schools. For many years, the speaking of French at schools was discouraged through means such as humiliation or corporal punishment. Great steps had to be taken to reverse the psychologically-ingrained belief that the French language was inferior and not worthy of study. The greatest of these steps came in 1983 when the state's Board of Elementary and Secondary Education voted to require five years of second language study at the Elementary school level". However, the Codofil has no legislative power and must restrict itself to measures that are strictly administrative and educational. Out of a total of sixty-six school councils, about forty require the teaching of French in school. The councils that do not require French are located in the poorer parishes in the north of the State, which does not have a Francophone heritage. In the southern part, designated as the francophone region of the State by the legislature in 1971 and given the name Acadiana, there are ten school councils that teach French by immersion. In 1997, there were 54,694 students who were learning French as a second language and 1,623 in immersion programs. 20 schools offered immersion courses and 460, courses in French as a second language. 269 French language specialists and 190 foreign teachers, including 28 from northern Acadia, were teaching these students.[176] In Louisiana, French was widely used up until the 1930s. Abel Dreyfous encountered no difficulties when he became a notary public in the mid-nineteenth century. The French Civil Code applies in Louisiana and still governs the relations between private individuals. Moïse Dennery, whose family was originally from Vésoul, (Lorraine), acknowledges that his good knowledge of French was an asset in his education. When I met him in September 1992, he was a lawyer connected with the French consulate. For him French was "more than just a language because he was of French descent."[177] Because it was spoken by the upper classes, French was a sign of distinction in Louisiana.

The French language is part and parcel of the history of the French immigrants, but it also reflected a patriotic attachment to the Confederacy, as evinced by the experience of Félix Dreyfous, Ruth Dreyfous's father. In 1862, after the Civil War, Félix, like all the children his age in public school, was required to pledge allegiance to the Union and sing the national anthem. He was seven years old and he refused. He was expelled from the public school and received the rest of his primary and secondary schooling in private French schools. When he later traveled to France his excellent French astonished his family.[178]

> *My father spoke perfect French. They would go to Paris and people couldn't believe that my father Félix wasn't born in France. The only mistake he made was tiny, the gender of moustique (mosquito); he used to say "la" moustique.*
> *— Ruth Dreyfous, New Orleans, September 23, 1992.*

You can see in the archives how, after the Civil War, with the arrival of the "Yankees" English is gradually substituted for French though there is a persistent attachment to French. Actually French was not the only language used. The regions where the immigrants settled were often bilingual or trilingual. French was spoken, but also German, by the German immigrants of the 1840s and 1850s.[179] In fact, rabbis usually conducted their services in German in congregations in New York, Cincinnati and San Francisco. It was the language for prayer, used as much as Hebrew. It was taught in Jewish schools. It was also the language used in the archives of the Jewish congregations until the mid-1870s. Afterward, the second generation of immigrants appeared, strongly influenced by the prevalence of the English language. Churches introduced English at the time. "Every church introduced services in which the English language was used exclusively, although the German language remains the official one of the pulpit, the classroom and the meeting room."[180]

> The reason they could conduct business along the Mississippi was because they were Alsatians and spoke German. My father spoke Alsatian, he spoke French and he learned English very quickly, I think, but he actually didn't need English very much because the first language spoken in Louisiana was French and the people who came inland from the bayou were mostly French. It was very easy to do business. My father learned English with the Blacks. He would go into the fields to speak to the Blacks in English. The children made fun of him in school because he spoke Paris French.
> — Flo Geismar, New Orleans, September 8, 1992.

French was taught in the public schools at first, then, after the Civil War, it was primarily taught in private schools. The convents, like the Ursuline Convent and the Catholic schools, Saint Martin School or the Sacred Heart School, are the best teachers of the French language today, along with Catholicism. Other private non-parish schools are sometimes run by Frenchmen, people of French descent, or people specialized in the French language like the École Classique. Other kinds of schools still exist. The Newman Manual Training School was created in 1904 by Herman

Kohlmeyer's great-grandfather, Isidore Newman, to train children of all denominations in a manual skill. This school now accepts children from primary school to high school and includes the teaching of French. Still considered above average, it has an excellent reputation; the school attracts some of the urban middle class and celebrated its hundredth anniversary in 2004.[181]

For the first two generations-according to many testimonies- French and German became languages of collusion between grandparents or parents. But some children learned French easily during the 1930s and 1940s. Fred Kahn pointed out that he used to speak French rather fluently. When he spoke it in primary school, no one could understand him except the professor, but his syntax was poor. He said, "he speaks a little, but it comes back to him when he returns to France."[182] Some families are trilingual, with French or German mothers or grandparents:

> *My great grandparents spoke French and German. They alternated between French and German. My grandparents spoke French, my parents spoke French. They always spoke it when they didn't want me to understand. I also chose French. And when I was at the stage where I could understand them, I didn't speak French because I didn't want them to know that I could understand them. The first time I went to Paris, I tried to speak French and my cousin said: "I want to use my English. Speak English with your Southern accent and I'll speak English." I never tried to speak French again. But I understand it very well and I can read it.*
> — Joel Bert Myers, New Orleans, October 18, 2000.

Though the first, and occasionally the second, generation knows French or German, a great many of my interlocutors from the third and fourth generation can only say a few words for having learned them in school or heard them. The children and grandchildren choose their grandparents' language to meet their foreign language requirement. Everything depends on their family environment and education.

After the 1940s, French was largely supplanted by English in Louisiana. Nowadays Spanish has become the second most widely spoken language. Dr. Posner in Opelousas, Louisiana, whose mother was German from Frankenbourg, nonetheless emphasizes the importance of French. It must be said that he lives in Acadiana, the southwestern part of Louisiana, where French is still spoken:

> *This region is a French area. French was spoken until 1937. The original registers in the court and in the town hall are in French. The language spoken in the streets was French.*
> — Dr. Gerald Posner (zal), Opelousas, October 25, 1995.

Georges Simonnot also emphasizes the importance of French. He was over eighty years old when I first met him. Originally from Cajun country, in southwestern Louisiana, he is a good observer of how the use of Cajun French evolved, as he himself speaks French fluently.[183] He has noticed important differences: for the last twenty years or so Cajun French has been favored again thanks to the tourism campaign in the Cajun region; French acquired a new prestige. But a clear distinction is made between the Cajun families in the bayous-farmers, small craftsmen, fishermen and often, in the Lafayette region, hunters-and the French Creole bourgeoisie in New Orleans who speak French French. "There was beautiful French and Cajun French." Since the beginning of the twentieth century this distinction has been fading. The Geismar grandchildren are very proud of having had a Cajun grandmother, Evelyn Vessier. In fact, one of the granddaughters uses the Acadian grandmother's name, Vessier, in her e-mail address.

Why is French losing ground?
Georges Simonnot: *In order to be socially integrated, you must speak English. It's good to have success in society.*
Is it possible to find work if you speak only

French?

GS: I don't think so. Baker. There are a lot of bakers in Lafayette. If you know how to cook in this region, Opelousas, New Iberville, Alexandria, Ville Platte, or Washington, Arnaudville, there are a lot of French people. Codofil promotes French. That's good, there's an exchange of schoolteachers. It's the promotion of French. My grandmother used to sing in French in Lafayette.

Metz Kahn: When I was a child in New Orleans in the 1930s, we used to speak French.

GS: In Ascension Parish in 1919, the rules were written in French until 1919. At that time, French was used in the court. You could have a trial in French. Now you have to request it. In 1933, it was over, but the Napoleonic Code is still applicable in Louisiana. Lawyers went to learn law in Paris. My parents spoke French, never English. My parents never spoke English. My mother had a little Negro woman who used to clean her house and she spoke to her... My aunts who are 100 years old don't speak English.

We learned English in school.

There was a huge argument between my mother and my grandmother. My mother wanted us to learn only English and my grandmother wanted us to learn English and French. French was first.

My mother won out.

At the time, I was 5, 6 years old (1921), children were punished in school, in kindergarten, when they spoke French. In primary school, they had to wear a yellow star. We were discouraged from speaking French. In my class, there were ten students who didn't speak English at all. The sisters came from New Orleans. They didn't speak English very well; they spoke with a French accent.

— Georges Simonnot, Baton Rouge, September 29, 1997.

But this region is an exception. Cajuns speak a type of French that is very similar to French Canadian and which has hardly changed since the eighteenth century when a population of 12,000 was expelled from their lands in New Brunswick and Nova Scotia. This event was called the *grand chambardement* (the great upheaval). Nowadays French is mainly spoken and sung in the Southwest Louisiana. However a number of archivists and librarians can read French, even if not all of them can speak it; the same is true of genealogy specialists

Names and the Host Country's Language are Factors in Americanization

In spite of the attachment of families to the language of their parents or grandparents, to France or Germany, the imperatives of integration and university access are paramount. For the first and second generation, English played a role of cohesion. This occurred as soon as they arrived in America. Some families deliberately changed their names, sometimes using a literal transcription, sometimes using a translation. The result can be surprising:

> *My grandfather went to Louisiana, to a city called Opelousas.*
> *There was a man there that his family knew and who owned a store. His name was Dreyfus. There were some Dreyfuses living in St. Gabriel which is very close by. Many people changed their names. My grandfather changed his name from Blum to Bloom. There are some Blums that went to Alabama and who took the names of flowers. Dreyfus became Three Foot.*
> — *Metz Kahn, Baton Rouge, September 3, 1992.*

Flo Geismar's story is emblematic: her family did not speak French at home, even though both parents knew French. French became the vernacular. It didn't allow you to get into college, the ambition of the new generations. English, the *lingua franca*, then became the first path to Americanization.

> *I got into the class, there was someone whose name was Major as department head, when he saw my name, he spoke to me in French. "Are you Léon Geismar's daughter?" I understood that much of course and I replied, "Yes. Excuse me I speak very little French. And he launched into a tirade: "How can your father, who speaks French so well, let his family grow up not speaking French?" And I explained to him that when I went to school, it was important to know how to read and write in English especially if you wanted to go to college. If you didn't, you couldn't get an education. My mother spoke Cajun French. They spoke French only when they didn't want to be understood. Otherwise the first language at home was English because they wanted us to have a university education. I have a sister, she has a Master's in education and I have a brother who studied management.*
> — *Flo Geismar, New Orleans, September 3, 1992.*

Later in our conversation she added that she had to take remedial classes in English grammar because hers was poor. For her, taking courses in public speaking was essential. Her brother too had difficulties because he translated English from French and he too was required to take additional courses in remedial English. However, in the State of Louisiana, French has a place of honor again. This was clear in 2005, on the occasion of the bicentennial celebrations of Louisiana's incorporation into the United States. All the organizers were required to take French courses. On the scholarly level, Louisiana State University in Baton Rouge is very active in publishing studies in the field of Acadian language and literature and is interested in French immigration. It has a prominent Department of French and Francophone Studies, and organizes seminars and summer sessions in France, as well as colloquia in French. The same emphasis on French and its diverse aspects is made at the University of Louisiana Lafayette.

We are seeing the renaissance and expansion of the Acadian language thanks to its being taught in the Louisiana primary schools, high schools and universities, and also thanks to the dissemination of Acadian music, the presence of its artists, and the annual meetings and festivals in Lafayette and Quebec. At the same time, French is being taught at the Alliance Française, a center for events, meetings, French courses and language practice for various groups in New Orleans-business people, museum employees and newcomers. The Alliance Française is a necessary step in successfully integrating into the city.

The social integration process also includes matters of lifestyle. How do the culinary customs of households change? What becomes of *kashrut* in the regions where the Jews are very much in the minority; what rules are followed, those of the host country or the home country? Cooking is a language that borrows from the rules of substitution so it can reinvent itself.

The Invention of Creole Kosher Cuisine

Traditional Jewish cuisine in eastern France, Germany, Central Europe and the Mediterranean borrows heavily from the different countries where the Jews happen to be living. The cuisine mixes local habits and respect for the Jewish dietary laws, *kashrut*. Introduced in New Orleans, Jewish cuisine is soon subject to new influences, partaking of the way of life of the historically multicultural population of the American South. It absorbs the habits and food products of other-voluntary and forced-immigrant and foreign groups, including African-Americans, Native Americans, Caribbean natives and Europeans. How did these cuisines become intermixed? Which dietary laws were respected and which were abandoned? What is meant by the terms Creole cuisine and Jewish cuisine?

Jewish cuisine conforms to rules that separate the sacred from the secular; it is punctuated by the holidays in the Jewish calendar, Jewish history, its commemorations and life on a daily basis. It has to respect the distinction between milk and meat and comply with many Biblical bans, food defined as kosher and food considered *treife* (non-kosher). The main ban is the eating of pork.[184] As for Creole cuisine, it arose out of a complex multicultural mix in which customs, a diversity of local and imported products, the contributions of African and European population groups, created crossbreeding and specific culinary knowledge. Both Jewish and Creole cuisines have a very coded language. In order to establish its pedigree, and combine the two cuisines, "Jewish Creole cuisine" has to implement substitutions and re-elaborations. It can only exist if it is named, or re-named. Cuisine is a language in which the Creole and Yiddish languages will mix; dishes will be given new names and be re-appropriated. The names confer a new life on traditional dishes, ensuring their dissemination and recognition.

Classical Jewish cuisine is made up of very rudimentary products, such as chopped chicken liver, split pea soup, *matzo* balls, inexpensive cuts of meat, like *pikelfleish*, tongue, *tcholent* (meat stew) or *borscht*, herring, and *gefilte* fish. Sweet and salty are mixed as in noodle and *raisinkugel*. It includes a great many deserts: *chaleth* (French toast) with apple, cheesecake, strudel, *kreplach*, cheese and fruit *blintzes*. The Sephardic Jewish tradition from the Mediterranean region is very distinctive as well, with its many vegetables and spices, carrots with saffron, chicken and rice, lemon and artichokes, fried fish, *tfinas*, *bourekas* (small pastry filled with tuna, cheese or mushrooms) and walnut biscuits… These cuisines were adapted to the local culinary customs, which themselves arose from the nomadic populations and their products.

Creole cuisine is an integral part of the Louisiana lifestyle. It is valued by all the inhabitants: whether German, Spanish, French, Italian, Black and métis, they all find something of themselves in it. Indeed the cuisine results from the contributions of the original Amerindian populations, brought over from Africa, escapees from Santo Domingo in the late eighteenth century, European colonizers and immigrants. They all adapted their habits to the local resources, inventing what was called "Creole cuisine" at the end of the nineteenth century.

The city of New Orleans welcomed population groups with heterogeneous cultures that came to seek their fortune in the New World. The (White) Creoles, the French and the Spanish of New Orleans, who settled prior to the Louisiana Purchase in 1803, formed a mixed group economically and socially, as we already pointed out. They were the first to arrive and they settled in the downtown area, the French Quarter.

Throughout the nineteenth century, the city adopted the French language and French lifestyles, with its immigrant cafés in the Vieux Carré, its boarding houses and hotels, its vegetable and spice markets. It was an import-export hub, one of the most important cotton exchanges in 1860, a cultural center with a theater and the oldest opera house in the United States, built in 1859. Businessmen came for trade but also "to let the good times roll." There were renowned chefs downtown at the Tremolet Hotel on the Place d'Armes, the main square of the French Quarter, as well as in the American section, in the Saint Louis Hotel on St. Charles Avenue.[185] In 1860, the city's white population numbered 144,601; there were 10,939 free people of color; and 14,484 slaves; in other words, a total population of 170,024. Whites made up 85 % of the population; free people of color, 6.4 %; slaves, 8.5 %.[186] From 1860 to 1900, the métis Creole population created a genuine culture with qualified craftsmen, architects, artists, musicians, associations, Freemasons and political personnel. Louisiana gave citizenship and voting rights to free African Americans in 1870.[187]

The Birth of Creole Cuisine

The cuisine, as we have said, reflects the presence of a multilingual population with contrasting culinary habits. In New Orleans new seasonings will be added to the traditions of French cuisine-the roux, grilling, boiling, sauces-seasonings introduced by the Spanish, Italians, American-Indians, African-Americans and free people of color living in the old section of the city. It is described as follows by the writer and journalist Lafcadio Hearn who lived in New Orleans between 1878 and 1888:

> La Cuisine Creole (creole cookery) partakes of the natures of its birthplace-New Orleans-which is cosmopolitan in its nature, blending the characteristics of the American, French, Spanish, Italian, West Indian and Mexican. In this compilation will be found many original recipes and other valuable ones heretofore unpublished, notably those of Gombo filé, Bouillabaisse, Court-bouillon, Jambalaya, Salade à la Russe, Bisque of Crayfish à la Créole, Pousse Café, Café Brulé, Brulot, together with many confections and delicacies for the sick, including a number of mixed drinks."[188]

The cuisine in hotels and small boarding houses is a combination of the French tradition and the Creole tradition, which includes both the Creole aristocrats, the Grandissimes of 1881, described by George Washington Cable (1844-1925), and the lower classes. Creole identity was created in 1884-1885, on the occasion of the great cotton exhibition. Lafcadio Hearn contributed to the book *Historical Sketch Book and Guide to New Orleans*, where he recorded local eating habits, listed different menus and set down criteria. At the same time, the *Christian Exchange Creole Cookery Book* contributed to the fashion for Creole cuisine, a native cuisine served in homes and restaurants around the French Market. In 1885, the restaurants on St. Charles Avenue offered copious menus: oysters, turtle soup, baked pompano, game with two vegetables, a second dish with duck and turkey, *soufflé*, desert and coffee. An ordinary dinner, therefore, included soup, fish, sweetbread, lamb chops, chicken, roast beef or mutton or veal, one of two vegetables, cheese, desert, fruit, jelly and coffee.[189]

Creole dishes are mixed preparations: *gumbo*, of African origin, *jambalaya*, Spanish influenced (a transposition of paella with ham and sausage), adapted traditional French dishes: *pannequets*; Norman soufflés with apples, pig's feet and calvados; *beignets* coated with walnuts and served with syrup. Creole cuisine innovates with knowledge. It adapts traditional dishes of French cuisine using local products and tastes. It uses familiar designations and names, combining them innovatively. The *mirliton* is in other words chayote squash or christophene (the Caribbean name), a vegetable originally from Mexico; *court-bouillon* is a way of cooking fish with a spicy sauce; *calas* are fried sugared rice cakes; *pain perdu* is toasted French bread served with sugar cane syrup.[190] Creole cuisine has a recognizable French vocabulary. The French terms have been retained: *étouffé*, *bisque* trout *meunière*, *soufflé*, *café brûlot* (coffee with Armagnac eaten with sugared pecans).

The New Orleans lifestyle is one of refinement, elegance and good taste; the local savoir-vivre includes eating well. This pleasure is facilitated by access to a wide range of different products: rice, corn, shellfish, vegetables from Africa and the Caribbean, okra, christophene, sugar cane; the cuisine uses an infinite variety of herbs and spices. Starting in the first half of the nineteenth century the wealth of products and flavors was interpreted by chefs such as Antoine, Galatoire, Brennan, who knew how to create new dishes. Black cooks ,more modestly but just as effectively, were also important in adapting soul food to Jewish cuisine and vice versa. At present, in the context of a syncretic culinary tradition, Jewish families from the large northern cities are ill at ease and losing their bearings. Kosher habits have become very discreet, the remaining Jewish delis, grocery stores and restaurants are completely unlike the ones they used to know.

The foods themselves are not in question, but some combinations are. The mixing of meat and butter fails to respect the separation of *milchig* (milk) and *fleischig* (meat). Therefore the dishes are no longer kosher but *treife*. An unusual, shocking new taste is created. The South leaves its stamp immediately after a mere visit to a delicatessen. When these newcomers become members of a Jewish temple, they meet black cooks or caterers who have long been employed for weddings, *bar mitzvah*s and receptions and who have brought their knowledge to bear on Creole cuisine.

Gumbo and matzo balls, mixed cuisines

As a result, strange combinations appear, such as barbecued

matzo balls and *gumbo* soup, a soup that is found in all the restaurants, from the most modest to the most sophisticated. This soup, the unequivocal introduction to Creole cuisine, is itself a combination of okra (a vegetable originally from the Congo), *filé* powder made from the dried and ground leaves of sassafras (planted by Native Americans), and herbs and spices from the Caribbean to which fish, rice and onions are added. The Cabildo Museum uses *gumbo* as a metaphor of the mixed populations of the region. The cultivation of okra is closely linked to the development of plantations. Initially it was the food of slaves. Nowadays, *gumbo* is a complex soup. Its elaboration uses the know-how of different immigrant groups. The Cajun population in southwestern Louisiana favors "oysters and sausage file gumbo." The Spanish population has added rice and spices; the French, the art of making *roux*. It is essential that the *filé* be served with sliced and diced fresh vegetables, long available at the New Orleans French Market at the heart of the French District. Today, *gumbo* is most often made with shrimp, crab, sausage, tomatoes, *filé* ("shrimp file gumbo") or with chicken and sausage, or game. Nourishment from the sea, nourishment from the earth.[191]

Around the city, crops of sugar and rice and significant supplies of fish come from the bayous. The Cajun population has made shrimping a specialty. Many fishermen had settled around the Mississippi delta and Lake Pontchartrain. Small houses were built there to make crabbing and oyster gathering easier. In an old fishing village, in Bucktown, there were a few houses and small restaurants that were supplied directly from the banks of Lake Pontchartrain. The Bruning family, originally from the Baden region, had been living there since 1859 and ran a casual seafood restaurant overlooking Lake Pontchartrain that was regularly visited by Jewish families.[192]

For many of these families, shellfish is not considered non-kosher: "Shrimp isn't pork, it's different," said one of my interlocutors.[193] Hence, in the course of a meal in Baton Rouge, our hostess served shrimp soufflé in the rabbi's presence. Indeed many families consider that shellfish are an ingredient of Creole cooking and allowed by Reform Judaism. These foods are completely acceptable among Jews in the South. There are other reasons for this acceptance. Not eating these ingredients would hinder contacts with the majority group, interrupt the conviviality rites characteristic of the city and make Southern Jews more marginalized. Tricky negotiations take place during official ceremonies in order to intertwine Southern ways of life and the Jewish heritage and the Jewish way of life. Attesting to this fact was the commemoration of the hundredth anniversary of the Jewish temple in Natchez, Mississippi, on April 29 and May 1, 1994, presided by Chief Rabbi Schindler. For this ceremony, Elaine Ullmann Lehmann, whose great grandfather, of German stock, had founded the B'nai Israel temple in 1872, was in charge of the seminar on cuisine, under the auspices of the Museum of the Southern Jewish Experience. She found a middle solution by offering ham biscuits, an inescapable dish of the region, at one end of the table and biscuits without ham at the other end. For lunch the participants had a choice between catfish (non-kosher) and fried chicken for the more observant, while the meal was served to the music of the Klezmer All Star Band of New Orleans.[194]

On perusing the menus of Jewish families established in the South, the Creolization of dishes is clearly apparent as well as their respect for Southern eating habits; they maintain a "pinch" of Sabbath practices. The major influences are French, Creole, Cajun, Black and American. This is apparent in my interview with Ruth Dreyfous whose family immigrated to New Orleans from Belfort in the 1840s:

> ***Do you remember any particular dishes?***
> *On Friday nights we didn't eat meat, of course. Jewish families like ours always ate the same thing: gumbo, a light soup, always soup no matter how hot it was, fish and deserts. On Sunday morning, we used to have a copious breakfast: grits, bacon, oysters. And then dinner at two o'clock, we used to have turkey or chicken, salad, artichoke, and for desert, ice cream.*
> *— Ruth Dreyfous, New Orleans, September 23, 1992.*

The Dreyfous family combines oysters and bacon. Oysters (non-kosher) are loved and cooked in all sorts of ways-in *gratins*, in cream, on skewers, with bacon, French fries and even in sandwiches. There are almost eight different oyster recipes in the books I consulted.[195] It is clear that cuisine is prized in New Orleans. In the warm regions, soup is served in the evening. It is also the first course of the Sabbath meal, often with *matzo* balls and chicken soup. On Passover it is customary to serve soup with *matzo* balls; on Friday evening, fish is eaten rather than meat. Meat is *treife* (non-kosher). This family has its own personal way of respecting the Sabbath. No one knows what kind of fish is served, trout or catfish. It is interesting to note that on Sunday, everything is allowed again: a copious breakfast and the combination of a very popular dish in the South, grits, and oysters. Grits are pan-fried coarsely ground hominy with ham, bacon or sausage; it is the ritual breakfast dish in the south. In some inns, in St. Francisville near Baton Rouge, the menus list French, American and Jewish dishes. *Blintzes*, pancakes stuffed with fruit, mushroom, cheese or potato, are prominent: "Breakfast is a complete buffet served in the main house. It includes scrambled eggs, muffins, bread, grits, sausages, blintzes, fruits and much more."

    I partook of meals that were quite unfamiliar in the bayous, as if I were returning to a world where lifestyles were most rudimentary and table manners unheard of: mounds of cooked shrimp, ten kilos worth, on a blue oilcloth shared among five or six people, without plates, sauce or forks. That was the entire meal. Sometimes the meal relies on Cajun hunting or fishing and the first course is turtle soup, a very sought-after dish that can be found in some of the restaurants in the city. The influence of black Creole cuisine or soul food is far from negligible. Rice and red beans or pecan pie are served in almost all the restaurants as well as the traditional *jambalaya*, prepared by black cooks on plantations and in Creole restaurants. There are a great variety of *jambalayas*; rice is the central ingredient of Creole cuisine and the basis of many recipes. Its low cost makes it a shared ingredient.

    Creole cuisine is a style of cooking that uses very local

specialties, which explains its many versions. Leah Chase, the most famous restaurant owner, opened her restaurant, the Dooky Chase, in 1939 and has written the *Dooky Chase Cookbook*. She has maintained very friendly relations with Jewish families for many years.[196] I attended exchanges of Jewish and black recipes; Leah Chase was given a Jewish mother's book of recipes. Jewish cuisine with a Creole influence is a symbolic language, a collection of ways of doing things. It conveys a particular relationship to the world. It is also a way in which immigrants became integrated into the American middle class.

American Eclecticism: The Influence of the Middle Classes

Famous Jewish cookbooks were published beginning in the late nineteenth century. In 1889, *Aunt Babette's Cook Book: Foreign and Domestic Receipts for the Household*, and in 1901, *Lizzie Kander's Settlement Cook Book*. These two books were handed down for several generations and provide essential information on running a household and organizing a kitchen. For the author of *Aunt Babette's Cook Book*, Bertha F. Kramer, "Nothing is *treifa* [sic] that is healthy and clean." *Aunt Babette's Cook Book* was first published by the Jewish publishing house, Bloch Publishing in Cincinnati. Marci Cohen, who, in the late 1990s, conducted a survey of 107 Southern families on Jewish cooking, points out that "Aunt Babette's (the pseudonym of Bertha F. Kramer) was passed down through generations of American Jewish women, southerners included," but as Marcie Cohen adds, they "turned to this quietly Jewish cookbook more for its *charlotte russe* and escalloped oysters, than for its *matzo* balls."[197] Kramer's book highlights German "Kaffee klatch" habits as well as simple traditional American Sunday dinners, "Portable luncheons" and "Thanksgiving Dinners.[198]" For Barbara Kirshenblatt-Gimblett, non-kosher cookbooks like Aunt Babette's "reveal how Jewish identity was constructed in the kitchen and at the table through the conspicuous rejection of the dietary laws and enthusiastic acceptance of culinary eclecticism." Anne Bower suggests that women authors like Lizzie Kander were upper middle class, assimilated Americans "comfortable acknowledging the German aspect of their German Jewish background, but worried that their Jewishness... could undo their secure lives, because of growing anti-Semitism at the beginning of the twentieth century." At that time, "Kander saw no place for kosher dietary laws in the modern Jewish home."[199] Recipes and cooking courses stress American tastes. They also include several recipes of more traditional German dishes such as *kugels*, pies, cakes and *gefilte* fish. But the primary aim is to adopt the know-how of the host country so as to be able to entertain middle-class Americans in one's home.

Regarding eclecticism and the importance of a newly acquired identity, another book that deserves mention is the one written by Beulah Ledner, the pastry cook who became a caterer, the Queen of Doberge in New Orleans. She was born in 1894 in Sainte Rose, the daughter of Abraham Levy, from Duppigheim (Bas-Rhin, Alsace), and a German mother. In 1934, she was better known for her Austro-Hungarian cake, *dobo*, re-baptized French *doberge*, and her recipe for lemon meringue pie, than for her strudels, carrot cakes, cheesecakes, chocolate cakes, all the traditional Jewish pastries that are in her recipe book.[200] Her store, now Maurice French Pastry, has a sign that is tellingly multilingual: "Irish Cream, Doberge, Kugelhopf, Chocolate Delight, *et beaucoup plus*." The emphasis is on diversity, the juxtaposition of several languages, each referring to a specialty, with, at the end of the sentence, a small French touch. As for Holly Berkowitz Clegg's book, reprinted seven times since 1983, its objective is not to highlight a specific Jewish identity, but to offer a taste of Cajun cuisine, a spicier Creole cuisine from the bayous. In her introduction, the author, who was born in Texas and whose parents were from Central Europe, says she acquired Cajun roots from her husband's family, originally from Baton Rouge.[201] Her book includes traditional local recipes and other more classic French and American ones.

No doubt it is difficult to respect kashrut in the South; on the one hand, few stores are really kosher; on the other, the set of rural customs, as a whole, work against its rules. It is impossible to keep a store closed on Saturdays, which is market day in small towns, the day when the farmers and planters come to shop. "We were open on Saturdays because we did more business on Saturdays than the rest of the week. That's why the Reform movement has its roots in the South."[202] Nowadays, many families, whether they live in Texas, Virginia, Alabama, California or Florida, partake of traditional Jewish meals only on holidays. Few among them cook regularly. I was invited to restaurants where I discovered Creole cuisine and Southern cuisine. Creole dishes can be bought frozen or ordered for take-out in restaurants

The Invention of Kosher Creole Cuisine

A true work of invention, imagination and transcription, including wordplay, is presently being compiled thanks to the ingenuity of Mildred L. Covert and Sylvia P. Gerson, both from the Orthodox tradition. These two cooks settled in the South over twenty years ago and decided to adapt Creole cuisine and make it kosher. They have managed to be credible for the Jewish authorities while respecting Southern expertise and predominant tastes. They don't know if there is a link between cooking and hospitality:

Well I think it goes hand in hand. What I can tell you is that anyone can come to anybody's house in the South, and they accept you as a guest and invite you for dinner, whatever. They extend their hospitality but I don't know if you can connect that with cooking.

(Sylvia Gerson, New Orleans, September 27, 1997)

I spent a lot of time with Sylvia Gerson. Her mother had been a great cook, but she passed away with all her recipes. Sylvia herself became a cook because her husband respected the kashrut. She came from Pittsburgh and was not observant but after her marriage she began to keep kosher. She therefore had to re-learn everything. She kept kosher at home, but, like a number of families, she did not respect the dietary rules when she was outside the home. Indeed, many observant families, once in the United States, "renegotiated details of their religious practice, but few questioned their basic identity."[203]

The difficulty in respecting the dietary rules lies in the limited choice of kosher merchandise in New Orleans. For this food to be edible and conform to the norms, it was necessary to re-learn how to cook.

I arrived in New Orleans and there was no problem, I wanted to have a kosher household. And when I asked someone for a recipe, it was always with ham or shrimp. So, without realizing it, I converted these to kosher cuisine.

They said ham, I used corned beef or salami or sausage, whatever. They said shrimp, I took tuna, I substituted. That's how I became a kosher Creole cook without knowing it.

(Sylvia Gerson, New Orleans, September 27, 1997)

Cooks learned how to prepare kosher cuisine with a Creole slant, how to respect expertise and names by combining two cultures. Two books, Kosher Creole Cookbook and Kosher Southern-Style Cookbook, are the result. The first was published in 1982, the second in 1992. Shrimp, oysters and many pork dishes have been converted into kosher dishes. They have been given Southern culinary titles so they will be easily recognizable: Baked Cheese Grits; Oysters Moskawitz or Mockfeller are tuna combinations that respect the original preparation; Jambalaya, a sausage dish, is prepared with veal and becomes Veal Jambalaya; you get Jaffa Jazzy Beets; Spring Salmon Etouffée (a play on salmon and shalom, peace); Poor Boy, a market worker's shrimp or ham sandwich, becomes a corned beef sandwich with pickles. The traditional Jewish culinary specialty, gefilte fish, changes names and becomes Fish Balls with Encore Sauce. For Passover, these new cooks recommend Pass-over Yam Casserole, Exodus Spicy Squash, Afikomen Sparagus (matzo on the Seder platter); for Purim, Esther's festival, Pharaoh's Ears.

Initially no one wanted to believe that Sylvia Gerson's cuisine was kosher, so astonishing was the idea of kosher Creole cuisine.

The two cuisines, Creole and kosher, are completely different and seem very hard to reconcile. To do so, the two authors had to make substitutions. But they did more than mix foods; they also mixed languages, English and Yiddish. Sylvia Gerson had given thought to the question of combinations. Mixing two types of diet is not an easy thing; beyond food, there is the confrontation of two cultures. Their work and their books illustrate a desire to respect the rites of kashrut, but also to conform to the traditional food of the South and adapt to it. Lastly, my interlocutors make no distinction, in their work, between the Jewish cuisines from different countries-Alsace-Lorraine, Eastern Europe, Russia, Poland. For them, they all fall into the category of Jewish food. What separates Jewish communities is not their diverse European origins but rather the rites and affiliations of Reform Jews and those of Orthodox Jews. Changes have been taking place over the last twenty years; these days, there is greater tolerance between the two movements. My interlocutors performed a true work of invention combining two customs, Jewish cuisine and Creole cuisine, and intertwining two distant cultures. Cuisine, as they see it, mixes food and identity. The transformation of their Jewish cuisine into kosher Creole cuisine is a way of reaffirming two things simultaneously: their Jewish identity and their new sense of belonging to the American South.

Neo-Victorian Home of my hostess, Flo Geismar, on Washington Avenue, New Orleans

(*Photo by the author taken in 2000*)

Portrait of Isidore Newman, founder of Isidore Newman School.

Isidore Newman was born on February 28, 1837 in Kaiserslautern (Palatinate) Germany to Jacob Neumond and Clara Kahn

(Photo courtesy of Herman S. Kohlmeyer, Jr.)

Portrait of Rebecca Kiefer Newman, Isidore Newman's wife.

Rebecca Kiefer Newman was born on December 12, 1849 in Port Gibson, MS. Her parents, Louis Kiefer and Marie Roser were natives of Lembach, Bas-Rhin, Alsace

(Photo courtesy of Herman S. Kohlmeyer, Jr.)

Alice Wilson, born a slave, with Felix, Harriette and Emilie Fraenkel, in New Orleans, ca. 1903. These were the grandchildren of Felix Fraenkel of Rothbach, Bas-Rhin, Alsace *(Photo Courtesy of Albert Fraenkel)*

Great-grandson, Albert Fraenkel, at Felix Fraenkel's grave – Jewish Cemetery, Baton Rouge, LA

(Photo courtesy of Albert Fraenkel)

Félix, Jules and Emile Dreyfous, sons of New Orleans Notary, Abel Dreyfous, a native of Belfort, France

(Photo courtesy of Catherine Cahn Kahn)

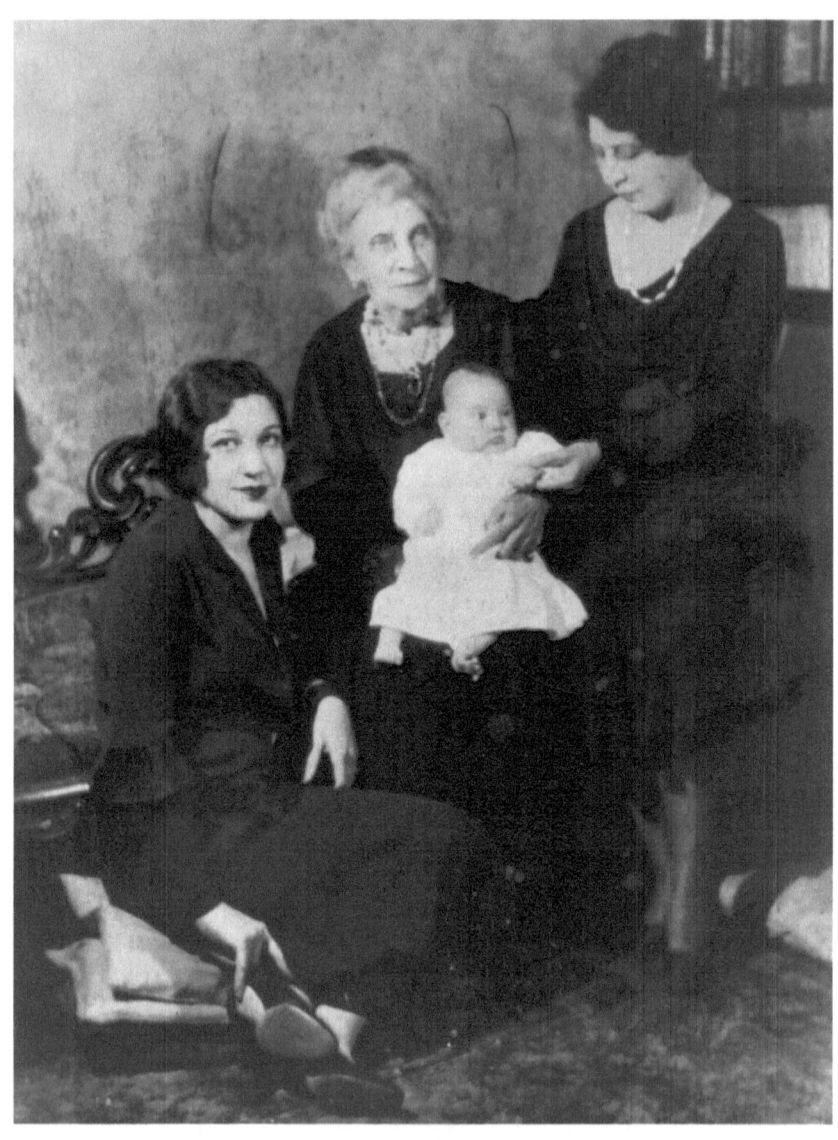

Four generations of Franco-German Women (1930):Great-grandmother Emilie Dreyfous Danziger (sister of Félix Dreyfous); grandmother, Jennie Danziger Jacobson; mother, Bertha Jacobson Cahn, wife of Leo Solis Cahn; baby, Catherine Cahn, future wife of Fred Kahn II

(*Photo courtesy of Catherine Cahn Kahn*)

Léon Fischel – Company A, 15th Louisiana Cavalry Battalion. (1861-1865) Léon was an aide to General Albert Sidney Johnston at Shiloh, and named his first son after the General.

(*Photo courtesy of Bert Fischel*)

Philip and Sophie Roos Sartorius circa 1913

(*Photo courtesy of Joel Sartorius*)

Page of autobiography written in Philip Sartorius's own hand ca. 1910. He made a copy for each of his children, writing with his left hand, account of a wound sustained at the Battle of Milliken's Bend on June 7, 1863.

(*Letter courtesy of the Scharff family*)

Picard & Geismar General Store, New River Landing, Ascension Parish, LA

(*Photo Courtesy of the Geismar Family*)

Geismar Plantation, New River Landing, Ascension Parish, LA

(*Photo Courtesy of the Geismar Family*)

Grave Marker of Louis and Seraphine Heyman Geismar, Hebrew Rest Cemetery #1, New Orleans, LA.

This cemetery has over 150 tombstones of immigrants from Alsace and Lorraine who came to Louisiana. Louis Benjamin Geismar, born on November 4 1857 at Grussenheim (Haut-Rhin, Alsace), died on March 17, 1934 at Geismar (formerly New River Landing), LA, where he had lived for 55 years. He was interred with his wife, Seraphine Heymann, (b. 10 December 1862; died 11 June 1940), whose father was a native of the Palatinate.

(Photo taken by the author in 2004)

Lemann General Store, founded in 1877 at Donaldsonville, Ascension Parish, LA.

(*Photo taken by the author in 1992*)

Marriage of Moïse Waldhorn to Albertine Löb

30 January 1884

(*Courtesy of Louisiana State Museum, Dept. of Archives*)

CHAPTER VI

Pledges of Fidelity to the New Country

The responsibilities taken by the first-generation immigrants of both sexes convey their strong commitment to their community. These responsibilities take the form of religious, charitable and educational activities. And they quickly transcend the community and extend beyond it. The objective of these associations is to welcome and assist new generations of immigrants, open places for prayer and meetings, and set up schools.

Community Action and Civic Action

Many members of the Jewish communities saw it as their ethical duty to take part in the social organizations that fulfilled the social and educational needs of their congregations. This commitment stemmed from *tzedaka*, one of the oldest, most sacred Jewish traditions, the Biblical commandment to help orphans, widows and the sick, and the obligation to respect justice and charity. *Tzedaka* can also take the form of aid to community organizations, including non-Jewish ones, in the Diaspora or in Israel. The members of the group do not confine themselves to solidarity within their own community. They are often solicited to manage the affairs in their cities. The wealthiest and most successful among them willingly take part in political life. Their activity takes place on another level; it reaches beyond the limited group of "one's own people," a familiar and emotionally close circle, and develops in a rational manner in the society at large. Initially a party to a religious community, the members start to make commitments in the secular world. Most of the newcomers want to participate fully in American society. However, usually only the prosperous families obtain recognition in the cities where they have settled. They form the "peddler aristocracy". Occasionally more modest figures are honored-such as Lazare Bloom in Jackson, Mississippi-and included as persons whose ethics and actions are irreproachable. The families of my interlocutors, and very often they themselves, American Israelites, have acted as connective links inside and outside their group. From the way they speak, they do not regard this transition from the community to the civic world as a rupture. They use the same term, "community," to designate both their congregation and their city. Peggy Blumberg, an active community and civic figure who was very involved in both worlds in Baton Rouge, was completely explicit on this matter:

> *We have always been an integral part of the Baton Rouge community. We participate in Baton Rouge's activities. When we do something for Baton Rouge, we don't do it as members of the sisterhood of a congregation. We do it simply as being an integral part of the community. The community is the community in general.*
> — *Peggy Blumberg (zal), Baton Rouge, September 15, 1997.*

These families have usually been living in the United States for several generations. Their commitment first occurs as integration into the Jewish community, and then later or concomitantly, as a civic integration. The biographical entries in *The Book of Israelites* and the life stories I collected often confirm this fact.

Community Solidarity

One of the goals of the Hebrew Benevolent Association is to assist Jewish immigrants and take charge of charitable activities. Given the recurrent epidemics of yellow fever between 1847 and 1853, and the frequent sudden deaths numbering a total of 98 persons in 1853, it became urgent to create and enlarge the

Hebrew Hospital in 1854, and found the Widows and Orphans Home to help destitute children and widows. Many immigrants supported the Home after the devastating epidemic of 1853. Between 1867 and 1878, one of the most active members, was Salomon Marx.[204] In 1921, Jonas Hiller and Joseph Loeb, of the second generation of immigrants, become its president and vice-president respectively.

On the other hand, in 1853, the Howard Association, a multi-faith aid association, also played a part in helping the first immigrants when they were hospitalized.

By focusing on some of the local figures we can illustrate how the immigrants organized community solidarity. David Wolbrette, a businessman in the stationery trade, was one of its eminent representatives. Born in Alsace in 1853, educated at the École commerciale of Strasbourg, he emigrated in 1872. After living in the small towns of Paincourtville and Plaquemine in Louisiana, he settled in New Orleans in 1889. He became a member of the Touro Infirmary, as did Hermann Kohlmeyer in 1877, Isidore Newman in 1892, and Julius Weis between 1880 and 1909.[205]

Julius Weis, a prominent figure in the New Orleans community, played a distinguished role in many charitable associations. His career, which seems surprising at first, is not really unusual. He arrived in New Orleans from Klingen (near Landau in the Palatinate) in 1845. He started out as a peddler in the Natchez area, as mentioned earlier. In 1853 he took over a store in the small town of Fayette, MS. In 1857, he sold this business and went to Natchez where he worked in a dry goods store. Finally, in association with two friends, Mayer and Deutsch, natives of the same village, he set up a dry goods business in New Orleans in 1864. He also traded in cotton in the back of the store. Plantation owners who were able to rescue their bales of cotton from being systematically destroyed by the Union Army sent their bales to him. He gradually shifted professions, from cotton merchant to cotton broker. Fifteen years after having opened his small town store and four years after his co-ownership of a new store in New Orleans, he became a full time cotton broker. At the suggestion of the Lazard brothers, with whom he had been working since 1846, he changed professions and became a stockbroker in 1891, creating the firm of Weis & Sons. This put him in contact with the business banks of Paris and London. He entrusted his cotton brokerage company to his son-in-law, Joseph Emanuel Friend, in 1890.[206] His temperate management as a businessman, which he called conservative, brought him prosperity and recognition. He was indeed very committed to the community on social issues as soon as he became prosperous in New Orleans. In 1843, he was on the executive board of the Rampart Street synagogue, in other words, the Ashkenazi Shangarai Chassed synagogue. He felt very strongly about this commitment. He wrote in his autobiography that he was very involved in the charitable work of his time. He participated actively in the development of the Reform community, Temple Sinai. In 1886, he was elected vice-president of the Jewish Charity Conference. He was a member of the committee that built the Jewish Orphans' home. Starting in 1880, he raised the funds needed to build a new hospital and he became its president. In 1884, he contributed to the purchase of forty locations in Metairie Cemetery for the members of the Temple Sinai congregation. In 1899, he made a sizeable contribution so a separate building could be erected at the Touro Infirmary as a home for the aged and infirm. In recognition, this building was named the Julius Weis Home for the Aged.[207]

Economic success often led to commitment in the community, as if this were a way of making success legitimate. Isidore Newman pursued a different path. His social commitment was on other fronts. A native of Kaiserslautern, he was close to Julius Weis. He arrived in New Orleans in 1853, at age 14. He became a talented financier and a city adviser, as well as a generous benefactor to Jewish and Christian charities. He was also the donor of a building that became the Manual Training School, the future Newman School. Julius Weis and Isidore Newman, both originally from the Palatinate, are cited in the first pages of the *Book of Israelites* of Louisiana. They are deemed dignified representatives of the city in the early twentieth century.[208]

Freemasonry, Clubs, Associations

Important are the Jewish and non-Jewish Freemason lodges that the newcomers soon became members of. Books on the first Louisiana Israelites mention this membership by the merchant, banking and medical elites. The biographical portraits of these dignitaries invariably end with the Masonic orders to which they belonged: Grand Lodge, Louisiana Lodge, Friends of Harmony, Foyer de la Persévérance, Germania Lodge, Houma Lodge and the Jewish lodges such as the Independent Order of B'nai B'rith. These biographies emphasize their status as Freemasons and comment on the great responsibilities held by the dignitaries in these lodges.[209] This membership is not secret; it is part of the Americanization process for eminent members of society. The lodges, influenced by the spirit of the Enlightenment, are concerned with man's progress and emancipation. They are founded on values that are close to those of Judaism: friendship, benevolence, honor and charity. They stress brotherhood, which binds the members through selection and the practice of well-defined rituals and stages (Masonic ranks: Entered Apprentice, Fellow Craft, Master Mason), which lead to different responsibilities such as Worshipful Master (president of the lodge) or State Grand Master, elected head of the State assembly, a position reached by the most dignified members. The various lodges across continents consider themselves as initiatory fraternities, who have the task of bringing a new wellbeing to society and help members' progress toward a spirituality aimed at brotherhood and equality. One of my friends described to me how she discovered that her grandfather had been a Freemason:

> *I didn't know my maternal grandfather was a Mason until his funeral, when a group of old men in white aprons and round hats (if I'm remembering rightly) performed some kind of ritual that I no longer recall precisely. I asked someone who they were and was told that my grandfather had been a Mason.[210] Years later, I found his ring in my grandmother's apartment. It*

must have been my father who told me it was a Masonic ring because I would not have recognized the symbols myself. My impression is that his being a Mason was never mentioned because it didn't have much meaning to anyone in the family. My grandfather was Jewish of course, though not at all observant. For him being a Mason no doubt had little to do with religion. I figure it was a social convention or a question of business contacts to belong to a lodge, and rather common at the time.
— Stephanie Golden, New York, September, 2007.

The issue of secrecy remains beyond the much older date of the first lodges. Even though American lodges seem much more open than lodges in France, rituals and projects are not divulged. However, families knew about their parents' lodge memberships. Their descendants. have their tombstones engraved not with Jewish symbols but with Masonic insignias, such as a compass and square, for example. This may mean, as this story shows, that the person was primarily attached to Masonry. But in America, religious affiliation can coexist very harmoniously with Masonic membership. Such was the case for Félix Fraenkel (1844-1888), Albert Fraenkel's great grandfather, buried in the Jewish cemetery in Baton Rouge; for Moses Rosenthal, born in Oberlauterbach (Bas-Rhin, Alsace) buried September 7, 1888 in Pineville (Alexandria); for Isaac Rosenthal, born September 1875, who died January 10, 1944 and was buried in the same cemetery. I counted almost twenty graves with Masonic emblems in that same cemetery.

Commitment to a lodge is a question of ethics and honor. It is not exclusive and does not conflict with belonging to a temple. Metz Kahn's grandfather, Salomon Marx, a founding member of Temple Sinai, boasted of being able to recite the Masonic ritual by heart in German. Masonic membership, which was very widespread for the first three generations of immigrants, leads us to believe that the population under study was guided by moral principles that coexisted with religious practice. This can pose problems to the religious authorities who are confronted with the multiple memberships of their co-religionists. It aroused bewilderment in Rabbi Stanley Dreyfus when he went to Shreveport during the Second World War.

> *He told me once I could only understand Judaism if I became a Freemason. That's stupid, I don't think it changes things much. In any way, it's an examination that evaluates honor and integrity. Some have reached the grade of Grand Mason, most have simply paid their membership dues to the organization. But the Jews thought it had a marketing impact.*
> *— Rabbi Stanley Dreyfus, New York, October 30, 2000.*

Stanley Dreyfus' remarks are not meant as an attack on Masonry but they warn against the strictly utilitarian and promotional aspect of lodge membership. American lodges are Deist, unlike the Lodges of the Grand Orient in France dating from the late nineteenth century; they honor the Great Architect of the Universe; take an oath on the *Book of Sacred Law* (Gospel, Torah or Koran) and therefore are not opposed to religious belief. They are a way of belonging to civil society, of being integrated and building social networks, of being recognized as part of the city's active elite, outside the strictly Jewish associations like the Hebrew Young Men's Society.

A wide social network also exists through the elite's various country clubs, clubs restricted to men. Clubs like the Harmony Club (for notables only) play a role of social cohesion; so does the Deutsche Company, a sort of early version of the Rotary Club, modeled on German clubs.[211] This prestigious club, the social center of New Orleans, included eminent professionals. "The intent and purposes of the Deutsche Company was to foster sociability, delve in science and art, all directed toward influencing traits tending to promote full fellowship." Salomon Marx, of German descent, was one of its founding members; the grandfather of one of my interlocutors, Joel Bert Myers, was a member as well. Men met among themselves, played cards, smoked and drank. For some members it was a way of staying faithful to the home country and its language. People belonged to the Union française founded by Abel Dreyfous in 1872, which included followers of all religions. The association's goal was to disseminate the French language and culture; it presented theater productions and later had schools for boys and girls in which French was taught. The Union did charitable work in its hospital during the yellow fever epidemic of 1878.

Professional associations like the Progressive Union included some Jewish dignitaries: Gustave Lehmann, who headed one of the most important firms of hardware products, was its executive director.[212] But this elite's activities was not limited to associations, it actually played a leading role in political life.

Civic Responsibility: Mayor, Legislator, Magistrate, Union Representative

The men who were most committed to public life began serving as General Postmasters, then as Mayors, and finally as Representatives on different levels-the parish, the State, the Federal government. Such was the case of Salomon Klotz, born in Reichshoffen, who left in 1874, and became mayor of Napoleonville, Louisiana. As for Léon Geismar, born in Grüssenheim, he served as a member of the Police Jury, which administered the parish's civil affairs, for a full forty-three years, from 1926 to 1969.[213] These distinguished citizens showed a true devotion to their place of residence; their commitment sometimes even led them to take on higher responsibilities on the State level. Félix Dreyfous, who was one Louisiana's most eminent attorneys, completed two terms in the Louisiana State Legislature between 1888 and 1892 and was on the municipal council between 1896 and 1900, where he fought against the prevailing corruption in the lottery system, an institution that brought a lot of money to the State of Louisiana.[214] His daughter Ruth Dreyfous, born in 1901, a psychologist who became very involved in the life of the city, described her upbringing as follows:

> The dinner table conversations were very important in

> *my upbringing and objectives, because my father was interested in the city of New Orleans and very devoted to it. We participated in political conversations and it was from my father's sense of responsibility that we inherited this strong attachment to values.*[215]

Other officials were committed on the national or international level. Michel Heymann took the position of President of the Board of Prisons and Asylums of the State and member of the Board of Free Kindergartens of New Orleans. Afterward he became a delegate to the International Prison Conference in Brussels, representing the United States. Finally, he prepared a special exhibit of the home he presided for the International Charity Conference of the Paris Exposition.[216]

Women and Charitable Associations

Women played a specific role in medical and educational charities.

They were also very active in their respective communities, first and foremost in the Ladies Hebrew Benevolent Societies but also in the sisterhoods for fundraising and organizing meals, meetings and fairs. It is thanks to the volunteer work of seventeen women that the Shaare Chesed Congregation of Baton Rouge, which was founded in 1857, was able to build a synagogue in 1877. "A great many of them," says Peggy Blumberg, "have descendants in that very temple." Not only did they fundraise to build the temple, they also continued their activity to furnish the building.

> *Despite financial obstacles, the ladies of the Congregation Shaare Chesed were determined to erect a permanent place of worship. They did not want to say their prayers in a dance hall forever. In January 1871, they organized as the Ladies Hebrew Aid Association. The preamble to their constitution states :We, the undersigned, have this day associated ourselves together for the purpose of building in the city of Baton Rouge a synagogue, for Jewish*

worship... The ladies undertook to equip the Temple and their records show that with a total membership of 17, they raised $139,935, a huge sum in those post-war days. After much investigation and debate, they invested the money in Torah covers, carpets, chandeliers, draperies, an organ and the Perpetual light.
— Peggy Blumberg, Baton Rouge, September 15, 1997.[217]

The women teach children Jewish history in the Sunday Schools. Their goal, according to the sisterhood of Temple Emanu-El in New York, is "to devote a certain fixed portion of their time to a definite task and attend to it herself; the chief object being the bringing together of the well-to-do and the poor — the haves and the have-nots."[218] The activities can also have a social side at Gemiluth Chessed in Port Gibson, Mississippi: "The Jewish ladies will organize a Japanese luncheon [...] The Luncheon is given for the purpose of having electric lights put in the temple."[219] Ruth Dreyfous, surrounded by her father and grandfather also cites the name of her grandmother for the role she played in the city. "Abel's wife, Caroline Kaufman, was called Charity Queen. She was very kind-hearted. She sewed linen at the time of the whooping cough epidemic. Every Thursday, she sewed for the Touro Infirmary. She went downtown to buy material, yards and yards, and gathered friends to sew together."

The Book of Israelites mentions two women's charitable associations that existed in many congregations, the Young Ladies Sewing Society created by Ruth Dreyfous's grandmother, Caroline Kaufman Dreyfous, and the Rachel Benevolent Association: "Material is purchased therewith and at intervals, they meet in a well-appointed room in the Touro Infirmary, dedicated to its purposes and with deft hands" sew the hours away, "for the time being devoting themselves to hallowed duties and turning away from social frivolities."[220] As can be seen, the women's associations were tinged with moralistic sentiments. Sewing kept them on the straight and narrow path. The objective of the Rachel Benevolent Association, founded in 1894, was to look after the city's indigent Jews, give them medical aid and medications and, if needed, pay for their burial. Another task was education. The Communal Hebrew School took over from the Sabbath school set up by prominent Jewish women in New Orleans. This school was opened to benefit immigrant children living in the Poydras and Dryades neighborhood near Liberty Street. We can assume these were Jewish children from Russia, Poland and Lithuania. "It is conducted by representatives of Orthodoxy and is recognized as a factor of Judaism in vogue in their special circle."[221] It was founded in 1902 and began offering classes in 1915. The school brought together families from different currents in Judaism until 1920. Then the Beth Israel Orthodox community, the second congregation in the city in 1910, founded its own school, separating itself from the Reform movement. Ephraim Lisitzky, a Yiddish poet, was its director. The ladies of New Orleans were present in initiating the first Jewish school but no mention was made of their role in the school that succeeded it. We can suppose that as they belonged to the Reform current they were not solicited, considering the cleavages between the two currents, Reform and Orthodox, at the time.[222] Finally, as soon as women received professional training, in the 1930s, they became involved helping schools and anti-poverty programs, and played a prominent role on educational boards. They initiated remedial courses and psychological testing and some women were in the forefront of progress in teaching reading skills and supporting difficult neighborhoods. Ruth Dreyfous worked as a psychological counselor at the Newcomb Tulane Child Guidance Center in the 1930s and in the New Orleans public schools in 1937.[223] Flo Geismar became involved in non-religious anti-poverty programs in black neighborhoods after the war, in the 1960s.

    The generation of Russian women, who arrived in the beginning of the twentieth century, were present in another area- social aid to Palestine. Rosalie Cohen's parents were Orthodox Russian Jews, peddlers who became furniture merchants. Her mother was a member of Hadassah, the first international association founded by Zionist Jewish women in 1912. Rosalie followed her mother's example. Born in 1910, she became active in the organization very early, seconded by women like Thérèse Abraham from the Reform tradition, in the Blue Box operation, in the 1930s, to help children with glaucoma in Palestine. Rosalie Cohen became the president of Hadassah. In 1959, she was the first woman appointed to the Jewish Federation, a sign of her great competence. When I met her in 2000, in her home, she answered my questions with a great deal of acumen and confidence, still displaying her political stature at age 90:

> *I must say that at the beginning Hadassah was a big part of my life and I created it, but now I no longer have to do it and this was before the establishment recognized Israel... My mother was at Hadassah and when I was a child, my mother was always going to meetings. I thought it had to be important (laughter) if my mother, a beautiful woman, went there so often. At the turn of the twentieth century it was a charity to help children in our Jewish community. Hadassah became famous and was imitated by other organizations. It was our contribution to sick people with funny eyes (glaucoma).*
> — Rosalie Cohen, New Orleans, October 10, 2000.

With time, I was able to observe how omnipresent volunteer women were in American society-helping the sick in hospitals, working as lecturers and guides in museums, as helpers in archives, at information desks in libraries; philanthropic women supporting the cultural and artistic activities of New Orleans, its opera, its orchestra, but also supporting activities that transcend affiliations: helping the Red Cross; giving educational aid to the Newcomb Nursery School; philanthropists such Mr. and Mrs. Edgar B. Stern and Percy Stern supporting Tulane University, the Dillard School or Loyola University.[224]

Furthermore, some of these women helped expand the art collections of cultural institutions. They donated works of American painters to museums and built collections that would later bear their names. Well-known women collectors and benefactors, they and their husbands are honored for their gifts to museums. Babette and Charles Wampold, for instance, donated their collection to the Fine Arts Museum in Montgomery and in 2006, the museum printed a catalogue of their donated works.

Women and Politics

As president of the National Council of Jewish Women, Ida Weis Friend (1868-1963) played a major role both nationally and locally. She was a member of the Democratic Party, a delegate to the Democratic Convention in 1921. She was very active in city affairs during the first half of the twentieth century. President of Hadassah in 1917, she was also President of the New Orleans Consumers League, the Voter's Registration League and the Urban League. She was chosen Woman of the Year by the Quota Club in 1946 and honored by the Urban League of New Orleans in 1960. While Ida Weis Friend remains emblematic for her influence in numerous associations, other women at the time worked for the emancipation of African Americans. They participated in the desegregation of schools through the Save our Schools programs. Mathilde Dreyfous and Ruth Dreyfous faced the violence of segregationists in order to keep the schools open, as in Plaquemine, Louisiana.[225]

The Limits of Social Commitment

The separations that existed in some circumstances between Jews and members of the old White Anglo-Saxon Protestant aristocracy, and the Catholic Creole families cannot be passed over in silence. Cultural, political and economic separations still exist. They are due to the exclusionary habits of the select clubs. One enduring barrier, according to one person I met, is that of "old money," money acquired generations ago. A dividing line still exists between Christians and Jews even though, to a large extent, these cleavages have been fading over the last twenty years. Anti-Semitism existed in the South but far less in small towns that counted fifty Jewish families or so. Jewish mayors were elected before 1900, in Natchez and Napoleonville, for example. Signs of hostility were more frequent in cities of more than 75,000 inhabitants, where there were a greater number of Jewish families. There was anti-Semitism in private schools, country clubs, political clubs, the Chamber of Commerce and the Rotary Club, according to a 1974 study conducted by David J. Goldberg in five Southern States. Harry Golden, the founder of the journal *Carolina Israelite* in 1941, to which he contributed until 1968, is quoted by David Goldberg as denouncing the anti-Jewish sentiment in big cities. In an article titled "Jew and Gentile in the New South: Segregation at Sundown," Harry Golden suggests that in large towns anti-Semitic sentiment was expressed by the failure of the leading Christian-dominated civic groups to invite a Jewish wife; often husbands themselves did not include a Jewish wife in civic affairs. "In the southern tradition the presence of the wife at an occasion is a symbol of the social union of the participants. By the same token, when on rare occasions a Jew was invited to meet his daytime community...the invitation was for himself alone — never did he bring his wife, nor was he expected to." There were Jewish merchants who had pleasant relations with their Christian colleagues, associates and competitors for fifteen or twenty years without ever meeting their wives. In other words, a Jewish wife, in the South, could not participate in occasions of social union and harmony. She bore the stigma of foreignness whereas her husband did not.[226] There were other forms of ostracism: Jews were not admitted in the New Orleans carnival, except the Rex Krewe, whose first king was Louis Solomon in 1872. "Elites in New Orleans kept Jews out of some of the prestigious krewes during Mardi Gras season in 1969 and these barriers remain intact today," says Leonora Berson.[227]

We have to nuance this statement. As Cathy Kahn, a sharp connoisseur of New Orleans society, explained it to me: "Bacchus and Endymion (krewes) are open to almost anyone who will pay the high price. Hermes has always taken some Jews, so has Rex. It is a little known fact, that the first king of Carnival — the first Rex, in 1872 — was Jewish. His name was Louis Solomon, (he was a banker and member of the Boston club). But you have to be invited. You can't just join. Fred (my husband) rode Rex for 50 years, because he was grandfathered in by his uncles, the Dennerys." The historian Karen Leathem adds, "Bacchus has Jewish members, and Orpheus and Muses have never discriminated against anyone. Muses is a women-only krewe". In the 2011 Carnival, two Jewish-themed Mardi Gras satirical groups paraded making fun of Jewish stereotypes — "the Krewe du Jieux" (of the Jews, founded in 1996 by L.J. Bernstein) and "the krewe du Mishugas" founded by Joel Nitzkin. "I think the Jewish community generally is very comfortable with Mardi Gras," said Cathy Glaser, the New Orleans regional director of the Anti-Defamation League. "It's fun, and there are plenty of opportunities for anyone to get involved." That's particularly true ever since the advent of Bacchus and Endymion, the "super krewes" that democratized and supersized Mardi Gras beginning in the late 1960s. The super krewes were founded by merchants and professionals, many of them Jews, who sought to capitalize on Mardi Gras' untapped tourist potential.

For many years, it was the custom for Jews to leave New Orleans at carnival time; this is what Oscar Levy explained to me when he showed me around the city. This situation was part of the accepted relationship between Jews and Christians "in a highly assimilationist and accommodationist mindset" as Justin Voigt's put it.[228]

The situation dates far back: Jews, like African-Americans, were only admitted to country clubs or other very select clubs like the Boston Club in New Orleans, on an exceptional basis.[229] Indeed, initially these clubs accepted wealthy Jewish industrialists like the Seixas, Weiss and Delgado families. Armand Heine, on the other hand, founded the Pickwick Club before the Civil War and organized the carnival bugle band. Rabbi Julian Feibelman points out that at first these clubs were open to Jews, but later they were excluded.[230] Today, according to my interlocutors, only about ten wealthy Jewish families have been admitted to the Boston Club.

In the 1920s, in a number of Southern cities, because of this exclusion, Jews founded their own country clubs, such as the

Montgomery Woodley Country Club. Nowadays, these clubs are open to the elite from all walks of life and every persuasion because members are in short supply. According to the sociologist Carolyn Lipson Walker, who conducted research on Southern Jews in the 1980s, in some communities Christians still harbor negative stereotypes regarding Jews. Contemptuous expressions and generalizations, such as "It's for the Jews," are common remarks in everyday conversation.[231]

The later survey I conducted in the South, between 1992 and 2000, reveals sensitivity to the problems of anti-Semitism in view of the actions of white supremacist extremists. People like David Duke, for instance, who revived the Ku Klux Klan in 1974, was the Republican candidate in a run-off with a Democrat, Edwin W. Edwards, for the Louisiana governorship in 1991 in spite of the Republican Party's disapproval. Edwards defeated Duke by a two to one margin. Some Evangelicals and Christian fundamentalists remain very present on American radio and television since Jimmy Carter's presidency in 1976, and exert a conservative influence on the Republican and Democratic Parties.[232] However, American anti-Semitism is rarely a subject of conversation. The Dreyfus affair was often mentioned in my presence, but not the Frank affair. Leo Frank was a Jew who was sentenced to death in Georgia after having been wrongly suspected of raping and killing a white employee; a black factory worker had testified against him. Mary Phagan had been found dead in the cellar of the company on April 27, 1913. Many petitions were circulated asking for Leo Frank's retrial. Though the governor finally commuted his sentence to life imprisonment in 1915, a band of "upright citizens" took him out of prison one night and hanged him in Marietta, the birthplace of his presumed victim. The case rocked Georgia, as well as the entire Jewish community, for two years. The historian Leonard Dinnerstein noted that "Many of his supporters believed that had Frank not been Jewish, the district attorney would not have put him on trial nor would a white jury have found him guilty, on the basis of a black man's testimony."[233] The latter was eventually tried as the murderer.

The "anxieties" and attacks that Jewish shopkeepers and

moneylenders had to endure in Louisiana and Mississippi, at the peak of the agrarian crises in the 1880s and during the populist movement in the early 1890s, seem forgotten. Let us recall that in Lawrence County, Mississippi, in 1893, Jewish shopkeepers were subject to "recurrent savagery"; they were "frequently attacked and terrorized" according to the weekly *American Hebrew*. As landowners they were accused, in 1893 by a man in Lawrence County, Mississippi, of being "the accursed Jews and others who own two-thirds of our land."[234] To my question about American anti-Semitism at the present time, one of my interlocutors replied that the United States was sufficiently large that if need be, refuge could be found in other States.

The comments of some of my interviewees are quite clear:

> **How would you describe the relations between Jewish communities and other communities?**
> Metz Kahn: They remain a problem with people like David Duke who continues to win votes. I've fought against him for twenty years. He was very powerful in directing the school system. I was in the French election committee and he wrecked our campaign. I fought against him for twenty years. From Baton Rouge he went to New Orleans. David Duke was a member of the Ku Klux Klan. He was a dangerous man. Most of the KKK members are ignorant, barely educated and not very intelligent. But they present a great danger.
> — Metz Kahn, New York, September 3, 1992.

Metz Kahn did not answer my question directly, except as it applies to the past, and dodged any reference to the present. It is true that in their interviews my interlocutors demonstrate how their families were part of the landscape of the region. In spite of obstacles and the vagaries of life, they succeeded in integrating themselves without closing their eyes on the cleavages existing in American society and Southern society in particular. There is still a boundary that has to be crossed, says Flo Geismar, a lucid observer of the cleavages in the South. Her daughter was allowed to join the New Orleans Junior League, a club for young girls from good families, after converting. "It's through individual will that frontiers are crossed: if you don't break the line, nobody will." But Flo Geismar herself did not convert.

Catherine C. Kahn, archivist of New Orleans Jewish community, who grew up in New Orleans in the 1940s told the journalist Justin Voigt about facing "the five o'clock curtain" as a girl in a very clear way: "You can be friendly and inseparable at school up to five o'clock [...] speaking about her relationships with Christians". "But when the five o'clock curtain came down, the Christian kids went to eight o'clock and nine o'clocks"-parties that marked one's entry into the debutante system-"and the Jewish kids didn't."

At the present time, three-fourths of the Jewish population in the South (800,000 people) is made up of newcomers from the North. The growth of the large Southern cities, their industrialization, the exodus of rural Jews and the range of opportunities for the university-educated younger generation have altered these different cleavages. The many interactions between Southern and Northern Jews and the return of a new Jewish consciousness in the South have gradually erased the separation between these two parts of the country. Furthermore, the "anxieties" of Southern Jews in dealing with the fundamentalists and the old Southern aristocracy have become more diffuse, even though they still exist.

Another way of asserting one's sense of belonging to a new country was to request to become an American citizen and to fight for the country. Was there a conflict between loyalty to the home country and loyalty to the host country? Are multiple fidelities possible? With time, the new country is chosen with greater and greater clarity. Over a few generations, attachment to the new country and to the South becomes combined with ties to the home country. The first generation maintains close ties with the home country. In the second generation these ties slacken, only to be reinvented in the third and fourth generations. Did the departure of emigrants mean a rupture in their fidelity to their former country? It was possible for the generation that came after 1918 to keep both nationalities. In these cases, one country was chosen over another.

The concept of fidelity is seen in different ways: fidelity to religious rites, to family, to the values of the country of origin. The term "fidelity" encompasses and surpasses the term "loyalty." Indeed, fidelity includes not just a political choice as in the notion of loyalty (loyalty to a country and its laws), it also implies an attitude to the past. Consideration of the past permits the elaboration of a memory with regard to the country of origin and does not create a rupture with the experience in the new country. It brings about continuity in a selective manner. It is therefore possible to talk about "fidelity" to the country of origin on the one hand, and "allegiance" to the host country on the other. Allegiance is interpreted as a pledge of fidelity, the act of submission and obedience that a subject pledges to his sovereign. Allegiance is a person's obligation of fidelity and loyalty to the political authority, the nation and the State involved.[235] Fidelity to the country of origin and allegiance to the new country, these two ways of belonging develop at different times.

Fidelity, Infidelity, the Heritage of the Home Country

When a country offers no employment, or possibility of promotion, when dignity is offended because of discrimination, the implicit contract between the nation and the citizen is no longer fulfilled. Is leaving the country really breaking the contract then? It was under such circumstances that a number of German Jews, like the ones in Ettingen (Hesse) immigrated to the United States after the failed revolution of 1848, when the outlook for economic development in their country looked dire and they were forced to pay heavy taxes. In Bavaria, their departure followed the defeated attempt, in 1846, of emancipating the Jews, as analyzed very persuasively by the journalist Philippson, the Bavarian correspondent for the weekly *Allegemeine Zeitung des Judentums*: emigration was a response to a legislation that failed to give citizenship to Jews, a response to a failed emancipation policy.[236] Throughout the 1850s the German Jewish press discussed the principles of belonging to a country and why Jews were led to emigrate. The question of emigration raised the question of indebtedness to a homeland. In 1846, community representatives, totaling thirty heads of family, attended the Assembly of the Bavarian States and discussed emigration. The answer was the following: "We belong to the homeland and this cannot be sold. Providence has placed us here. We are called on to love the country where we are born. If we offend our motherland by turning out backs on it, won't people say that we are selling our homeland for foreign material gains?" It was the absence of civil equality that forced Jews to leave their homeland "with a bleeding heart." "And leaving is not selling our homeland because if our future is somber, over there it is uncertain."[237] Furthermore, the United States was seen as the first country where complete freedom of belief was possible. Hence no distinction was made between Jews and other citizens and they would benefit from the civil service jobs accessible to all. It was therefore important for German Jews to attain equal citizenship and religious freedom.[238] Hence infidelity was not perceived as such. Most often it was seen as stemming from a lack of alternatives and necessity. Indeed, can it be said that they chose to leave, if they wanted to avoid poverty, cultural and political domination, a *numerus clausus* and French and German anti-Semitism in the nineteenth century?

What do the *émigrés* retain of the old continent, of old Europe, of the old world? Is there a fidelity to the values acquired in the former country, in lifestyle, marriage, religious practice. How do the styles of life change?

The question that arises concerns their tie to the country of origin: is there a break or continuity? In *The Uprooted*, Oscar Handlin strenuously upholds the principle of a clean break with the past, a commonly accepted idea that is now widely debated. The Jews of Alsace, Lorraine, the Palatinate, Baden, Württemberg and Bavaria became cotton planters, bakers, importers in New Orleans, cigar and liquor merchants, cotton brokers in Montgomery, clothes and china salesmen and bankers in San Francisco. They could only have pursued these professions thanks to previous experience, past role models, family examples, educational and professional training. It was not a clean break but there was an apprenticeship in new skills and adaptation to the customs of the host country.

Prior to 1863, immigrants living in the American South sometimes owned one or two slaves and they assert in their memoirs that they treated them humanely. They obeyed the rules of the country in order to be respected but with nuances and variations. Immigrants fought on the Confederate side, but did they have a choice if they wanted to defend the places where they lived? They became Southern patriots. A century later, their descendants-if only a small number-will be actively involved in the civil rights movement and put their lives in danger.

Though in their correspondence the first immigrants urged others to come to the land of the future, from 1871 to 1890 cultural and national causes triggered emigration. Paradoxically it was possible to remain a French patriot when leaving Alsace for the United States. In 1871, you could choose French citizenship from the United States. Hence, when asked by the French authorities, the Dennery family from Lorraine chose French citizenship in the presence of the vice-consul in St. Louis on July 2, 1872.

Acquiring citizenship implied giving up subservience to the German Reich. Allegiance to the new country included the required oath to give up German citizenship with the desire to acquire American citizenship, which usually took five years but sometimes much longer. The families I met stressed the obtaining of their new status with pride. When shown documents proving her family's German origin, one of my interviewees admitted, "Yes, so it seems. I was aware of it." The collective memory focuses only on patriotism. The fact of leaving after 1871 meant not wanting to live under the German empire, not wanting to do three years of military service, and generally wanting to escape from the Franco-German wars and Prussian militarism. Leon Geismar left at age fifteen in 1906. The family has proudly saved his certificate of American citizenship, the necessary document for belonging to the new country. Other families have done so too, such as the Fraenkels and the Metz Kahns in Baton Rouge.

Obligations and Adjustments to the New Citizenship

If infidelity was a departure pointing to the future, the new immigrant always found a new fidelity in his new country. Nostalgia for the old country was rare and very few immigrants returned, except for the obligation of national service. We found only three families who returned: the Weil families of San Francisco, both living in Strasbourg, and Alexandre Weil based in Paris for his work. Some certainly had plans to return but the Franco-Prussian War and especially the war of 1914-1918 in France and Germany quelled whatever vague desires they had.

Another form of patriotism was commitment to the Confederacy or the Federation during the Civil War. The "War between the States" was usually seen by these first Jewish immigrants who had settled along the Mississippi as a war in which they had to show loyalty to their host country. For this was their new promised land and they could hardly remain loyal to it if they failed to display patriotism. But the position of Jews was far from homogenous within the different immigrant groups or even within families. Indeed, though the newcomers took part in the war, they did not always support Secession. Their choice revealed their attachment to their new homeland, a sense of belonging and a certain freedom of opinion and critical mind. Very few families refused to fight on the Confederate side in 1861. Lucile Bennett's great grandfather, Salomon Hochstein, born in Alsace, joined the Home Guards in Louisiana at age thirty-six.[239] One of the immigrants originally from Alsace, Isaac Hermann, born in 1838, arrived in New York in 1859, settled in Georgia and enlisted in the Confederate Army in 1862. He wrote a book, Memoirs of a Confederate Veteran(1911). He enlisted instead of his friend, Mr. Smith. According to his biographer Sallie Monica Lang, Herman went up to the duty office declaring, "A Frenchman wishes to fight like an American." He was not alone. There were two Confederate Captains among the ancestors of my interlocutors: Bert Fischel's great-great grandfather Léon Fischel, originally from the Palatinate, who served in the cavalry of Wood's Regiment in Mississippi, and the Confederate Captain Simon Levy Jr.,[240]

Stanley Dreyfus' ancestor.[241] There was also Samuel Louis. Benjamin, Minette Cooper's great-grandfather, originally from Bouxwiller in Alsace, an immigrant living in Natchez, Mississippi, who was discharged from the Claiborne Light Infantry in Port Gibson on April 5, 1863. He reenlisted in the army in Natchez, on September 19, 1864.[242] He volunteered though he was not yet an American citizen. All the Confederates had to pledge allegiance to the Union at the end of the war. It seems that many Jews were far less enthusiastic than Isaac Herman in their attitude.

At the beginning of the war, Philip Sartorius, originally from Germersheim (Palatinate), reported in his *Memoirs* on the pitiable state of the Southern ships, the army's lack of preparation and each soldier's obligation to pay for all his supplies. He belonged to a cavalry regiment that had to provide everything-clothing, horses and food[243].

Not only did commitment to the Confederacy vary from State to State but also within families.

The first clear loyalty was to the place where one lived, and not to the political ideals of the Confederates.[244] The fifty-odd Jews of German and Eastern European ancestry who lived in Atlanta were divided in their response to the war. Some fought for Secession, others refused for various reasons. Some provided equipment for the war and others enlisted in infantry companies.

The Weil family, cotton merchants and exporters, who were natives of Otterstadt in the Bavarian Palatinate, operated cotton gins in Opelika and later in Montgomery. Jake, who lived in Montgomery, wrote to his brother Josiah Weil in Munich, on May 16, 1861 in very moderate terms. This letter offers an interesting testimony on the range of positions with regard to slavery and the war. It also raises ethical values and recalls the biblical proscriptions in Exodus that Jewish families are supposed to abide by: no man has the right to own other men over a long period of time. According to the Deuteronomy, Jews must free slaves after six years: the first verses of the *Mishpatim* (laws) state that no Hebrew should be held in slavery for more than six years and that he will go free "automatically" in the seventh year-in other words, without having to be bought or having to pay his master for his liberty. Also, the master is not to let slaves perform degrading tasks and must give them sufficient funds to support themselves when they are freed.

These principles are stated in a letter from the pioneer Jake Weil in his letter to his brother Josiah Weil :

> My dear brother Josiah,
>
> This shall be the last letter I shall write to you for a long time, for I once more take arms to serve my country. I have been assigned to the Home Guard and our duties are to protect the City... He [President Davis] made a speech most impassioned and I find him a man both imposing and impressive but I fear he has not the stomach nor the verstandt (comprehension) to lead us through the struggle that ensues. Our friends Lehmann and Durr tell me that I am unwise to involve myself in this.

He already expresses reservations, like others:

> I think you know my feelings. We set free our slaves other than our body and household servants as soon as there were enough settlers to lease our lands. In truth one man never has a right to own another man. But one man has no right to sell property to another and after he has invested the proceeds claim that the buyer is evil and should divest him from his property. Yancey and the other fire-eaters I do not hold with also. In this dispute for a man of reason is no place left. Of two evils I choose the one more familiar. The land has been good to all of us. We shall not be deprived of rights or property without the course of law which our constitution granted. I shall fight to my last breath and to the full extent of my fortune to defend that in which I believe.
>
> Our brother Henry has taken a view more moderate. He has bought bonds of the Confederacy, as have I, but that is all. I fear they may prove

worthless [...].
Signed Your little brother, Jake.

Another example confirming this lucid, critical view of the government of the Confederacy comes from Philip Sartorius. In his *Memoirs* written in 1910, he describes the Secession process and makes the following retrospective comment: "The Governor called the Legislature and they in turn called constitutional conventions and the states seceded in quick succession." Then he adds, "A large number of prominent wealthy citizens were opposed to secession depicting in graphic pictures the ruin that would result in a contest with the U. S. their description was almost prophetic."[245]

But in spite of their attachment to the Confederacy, the Weil, Marx, Dreyfous and Sartorius families changed allegiances for reasons of survival. Philip Sartorius, after having been gravely wounded in the Confederate Army, saw the cotton fields burn not far away, in Mississippi. He was present for the arrival of the army and during the epidemic. He left his home and took refuge in St. Louis. In order to save his family, he pledged allegiance to the Union as he mentioned in his Reminiscences written for his son in 1910: "After that [the epidemic and the absence of a physician], we concluded to leave and to go to St Louis [...] and in order to get a permit from the military authorities I pledged allegiance. It was the latter part of August 1863." In St. Louis he started a new business, cigar manufacturing, until the end of the war in 1865.

The obligations of the war and the national service weighed heavily and did not leave citizens much choice. In moments of crisis, of war, enlistment was required: for bi-national citizens military service in France was required during the Second World War and after being demobilized in France they could also be drafted and serve in the American army. Those families I met in the South who arrived much earlier and who became American citizens in the nineteenth century had no choice but to serve.

Alsatian families were German between 1871 and 1918, French until 1940, German until 1944, and French again in 1945. The last two generations had to serve two different countries, before and after their arrival in America. Bi-national in America, they had to fight under the French and American flags while their brothers and fathers had fought in the German and French armies.

Flo Geismar's father was a German national when he arrived in 1909. He thought he would return to France and did not immediately become an American citizen. He was suspected of espionage during the Second World War. Yet he always felt French and American. His daughter, on the other hand, who was born in the United States, feels no ambivalence. She maintains ties with the family, with a village, but not with a country. Her response reflects the opinion of many descendants. I met, such as the Fraenkel, Kahn and Myers families.

> **Do you have the impression of belonging to two countries and what is your feeling on this subject?**
>
> *Flo Geismar: I feel I have bonds, but the ties are not to the country but to individuals. The family has always been important for the Picards, the Geismars, all the relatives.*
>
> **You told me that your father was always loyal to the United States even if it wasn't the country of his birth. How did he handle that?**
>
> *The United States was always good to my father. There's a lack of understanding because when he arrived in 1909, he came with a German passport. He sent a telegram to Mexico to his cousin Simone; he was not explicit about a child born during the Second World War. The Germans were our enemies and there were many posters and almost all Germans were suspicious until they were checked. He was born in Alsace when it belonged to Germany. He never felt German. French, yes. German, no. My uncle, after the First World War, wouldn't let him return so he wouldn't be sent to the front.*
>
> — Flo Geismar, New Orleans, October 23, 1997.

There were strong displays of solidarity for the families back in Europe: money and packages were sent, not to mention the contribution of women, such as Ruth First in New York who joined the Red Cross, or the role of the Société israélite française de New York and the Association pour le Rétablissement des Institutions et des Œuvres israélites en France (ARIF)founded by French immigrants in New York, associations that collected considerable funds at the time ($25,000) for the reconstruction of community buildings and synagogues in France after the war. Both associations also played an essential role in supporting families and Jewish institutions on the old continent.[246]

CHAPTER VII
The Relation to the Other

Very involved in the economic, social and political activities of their cities, Jews met the Christian majority and, regardless of the religious factor, the other minority groups-Irish, Italian, German and French. But it was the relations between African Americans and Jews in the South that were most often mentioned in my interviews.

What kind of image did Jewish immigrants have of their neighbors? From my repeated sojourns in the South (from 1992 to 2006) I was able to gather the testimonies of people belonging to different religious traditions. Relations with the surrounding society seemed to unfold in an atmosphere of mutual acceptance. This was true in small and medium-sized towns, because Jews and Christians were close neighbors and the percentage of Jews was small. However, after extended conversations and establishing mutual trust, another vision of the Jew emerges, as stigmatized and belonging to a world apart.

Spatial Proximity Living Together

Jewish families were extremely scattered and isolated. In the 1880s there were about one hundred families in the cities of Shreveport and Baton Rouge, Louisiana, and Natchez, Mississippi. Two hundred families lived in Alexandria and Rapides Parish in Northern Louisiana. They had started organizing into communities in the 1860s.[247] It is hardly surprising that the religion of those around them, whether Catholic or Episcopalian in Louisiana, Baptist and Presbyterian in Jackson, or Methodist in Montgomery, became included in the world of Jewish families. They had Christmas trees up until the Second World War, exchanged gifts and celebrated Thanksgiving. Interfaith relations, as recalled by my interlocutors, seemed perfectly cordial.

Children played together and went to the same schools-public school when they existed, parish schools for young girls of the first and second generations. Indeed, these were the only places where girls could receive an education.[248] Arrangements were easily made to excuse Jewish children from Catechism class. On the contrary, children of different religions helped one another out. But this harmonious climate also underscored the isolation of my interlocutors in a predominantly Christian society.

> *I didn't see any other Jewish children aside from my cousins and my brother and sister, except in Sunday school or Saturday at temple. Everyone was Catholic. It was so Catholic that they taught Catholicism in the public school and we would sit under a tree waiting for Catechism to be over. My best friends were Catholic and we couldn't go out to play until my best friend had learned her Catechism. Therefore I knew the Catholic Catechism better than my Jewish Sunday school because no one helped me learn it.*
> — *Flo Geismar, New Orleans, October 22, 1997.*

Quite logically, in a minority position, Judaism tended to filter into the social fabric where it took root. As I traveled through the small towns, I spotted Jewish names on the signs of the stores on the main streets: Weil, Levy, Wolff, Cohn, Simon, Lorman, and the Lemann general stores. A former Lexington resident confirmed this harmonious atmosphere to me. It is true that he was the child of a mixed marriage and tried to reconcile the Jewish and Christian worlds in his remarks:

> *How do I perceive the South? Jews became assimilated to the Gentile culture much more easily than in the Northern cities because they were not as numerous. The cities needed store owners and they filled a need. They were accepted and fitted into the community completely. In the Northern cities they remained separate in a way and maintained their old identities. But in the South, there weren't very many*

Jews. They sent their children to Sunday school, to Protestant churches. My mother is Christian and my father is Jewish. I'm the product of a perfect union. My parents have been married for forty years.
— *Leroy H. Paris, Jackson, October 17, 1992.*

The question arises of whether one should lose one's identity and be integrated in the small towns, or if one should remain separate and maintain it. Are there no other alternatives? The testimonies of small-town residents show that the practice of Judaism was not easy; though it was neither denied nor concealed. Such is the case for Abraham Kahn's family who had first settled in Raceland, Louisiana, and then moved to New Orleans in the 1880s:

Why did they choose Temple Sinai?
Joel Bert Myers: I think that at the time it was the most liberal synagogue. When they went to live in New Orleans, it was the first time my great-great grandparents had a place to pray. At that time, they were part of Christian society, even if they were Jewish, they were not prepared to be traditional Jews.
— *Joel Bert Myers, New Orleans, October 18, 2000.*

For this family, fitting into the Southern landscape was facilitated by the fact that they had no apparent dissimilarities from the Christian world. The Jewish affiliation remained private and the family had to conform to Christian norms. In the big cities of New Orleans and Montgomery, relations were easily established. There were no Jewish neighborhoods or ghettos properly speaking. Jewish and Christian families lived side by side. Initially immigrants settled in the shopping districts, in the lower middle class neighborhoods. Then the prosperous second generation moved into the neighborhoods of the American Protestant elite, such as the Garden District in New Orleans. Indeed, by the end of the nineteenth century, families moved out of the shopping districts to the more residential neighborhoods uptown — Jackson Avenue, Audubon Avenue — where they were joined some thirty years later by Jews from Eastern Europe. The more affluent had houses built for themselves. Such was the case of the Dreyfous, Dennery, Weil, Kohlmeyer and Switzer families. The first synagogues were built near the city's shopping district. Later, in the 1920s, new ones were built in the residential neighborhoods, and most recently, synagogues have followed the residents into the outskirts, to Metairie.

Jewish families gravitated to Canal Street, Rampart Street, Esplanade Avenue, streets marking off the boundaries of the French Quarter in New Orleans, or Commerce Street, the shopping district in Montgomery. The situation is entirely different in the big Northern cities, as Julie Grant Meyer points out, a native of Detroit who has been living in New Orleans for about twenty years. People lived in neighborhoods that were entirely Jewish:

> *In Detroit, where I grew up, the neighborhood was one hundred percent Jewish. There was an invisible frontier and beyond this frontier it was one hundred percent Catholic, and beyond that, one hundred percent Protestant. And why? Because the parishes were nearby. My neighbors walked to the church and we walked to the synagogue. My public school, a few blocks away from my house, was one hundred percent Jewish and my teachers were Jewish and they could have closed during the holidays because there was no one in school. Just the principal and a few teachers. I went there from kindergarten to my sophomore year and only after seven years of schooling was there a Christian girl in my class for the first time. I had no real contact with non-Jews.*
> — Julie Grant Meyer, New Orleans, September 24, 1997.

Religious Coexistence: An Expression of Democracy

Interfaith relations are seen as necessary to keep tensions in check. These relations show that beyond differences, the common core of religious affiliation, unity in faith is the pivot of American democracy. Will Herberg stresses this "harmonious" aspect of the three religions, Protestant, Catholic and Jewish, to which Islam should lately be added. A European may be surprised by this openness, but this attitude is completely accepted in the United States:

> *Interfaith in this country is the device that American experience has elaborated for bringing some measure of harmony among the religious communities and in some degree mitigating their tensions and suspicions. It is made possible by their common grounding in the American Way of Life and their feeling that despite all differences of creed "brotherhood" and "affirmative cooperative action" among Protestants, Catholics, and Jews is not only possible and desirable. But in a sense mandatory if American democracy is to function properly.*[249]

The Pittsburgh platform of Reform Judaism in 1885 recognized the necessity of dialogue with other religions and interfaith relationships in order to further the Americanization of minority groups. It stressed the necessity of crossing ideological and geographic frontiers. Interfaith relations exist at all levels of society: The American kind of interfaith is "operative at all levels of civic life, but carefully steering clear of religious or theological discussions [...] it stressed commitment to the shared values and ideals of the American Way of Life," and is opposed to controversial discussion of religion, according to Will Herberg.[250] Affinities depend on the local context, the distinctive characteristics of each city, and on personalities. Some religions are more open than others. In general, relations are good between the Episcopalian and Jewish religions.[251] As for the other faiths, relations vary according to circumstances. On the local level, different forms of exchanges have been taking place since the 1880s: loans of churches or synagogues when in need; exchanges of organists from church to synagogue; participation of

Christians in Jewish choirs in small towns like Vicksburg. This also occurs in cities like Natchez and Jackson, cities where religious cleavages are more acknowledged that in more tolerant cities. The Lutheran church and the Gates of Prayer temple in New Orleans share the same organist. In Jackson, Baptists use a former synagogue.

When one or another religious group is in difficulty, solidarity sets in. In Natchez, a synagogue is loaned while a Protestant church is being built. When disasters strike people help one another. Sometimes synagogues become houses of worship for other religions, such as the old synagogue in Montgomery that was sold and became a Methodist church; at other times churches are purchased and become synagogues, such as the Dispersed of Judah in 1850. These places remain places of worship. There is a space for exchange between churches. Which churches are involved? Catholic, Episcopalian, Methodist, Presbyterian. Relations are infrequent with the Baptist church, according to one of the active members of the Jackson community.

> *Flo Lehmann: Let me explain our relationship with the non-fundamentalists, the Baptists, it's unusual. In fact, they came together after we had built our new synagogue. We still had the old one. They requested permission to use our temple until they were organized. It's unusual because most Baptists don't have contact with us. Here in Jackson we're on very good terms with them. With the Catholics we've always been. The Episcopalian school has a new principal who is Jewish and his wife comes to temple. His wife is young and pretty.*
> **And with the Presbyterians?**
> *FL: I wouldn't say they're bad, but not very close.*
> — *Flo Lehmann, Jackson, September 19, 1992.*

Georges Simonnot, a French Cajun and friend of Metz Kahn's, who knows the families of Donaldsonville and the surrounding area, stresses the absence of conflict between the Catholic and Jewish milieus. In fact, Abraham Klotz, a Jew of Alsatian descent, was elected mayor of nearby Napoleonville several times.

> *There was no religious controversy. The Jewish children went to public school or private schools. The Sternfels went to Catholic school. They married in the church. We wouldn't have meals with Jewish families, only coffee.*
> — *Georges Simonnot, Baton Rouge, September 29, 1997.*

It is harder to imagine this type of exchange in the big cities of the Northeast where groups live more closely together. Indeed this seems obvious for two of my interlocutors who have been living in the South for two or three generations.

> *Grace Zelman: Oh you know, these people in New York think they're very cosmopolitan, but that's not really the case. They stay among themselves. They live in a closed circle. Jews are Jews and they let you know it.*
> **Do the Jews live together here?**
> *Flo Geismar: No, not here. I think we're more assimilated, more protected.*

Very often the rabbi is very close to the faithful. He is also very much a part of Southern society. As such, he is invited to interfaith ceremonies, just as he himself invites Baptist and Methodist ministers at least twice a year. In addition to exchanges of buildings, priests, pastors and rabbis sometimes address congregations of different churches or participate in their rituals. This is in the tradition of Reform Judaism. Reciprocal invitations are extended and Christian members of the neighboring church are invited on high holy days and for the Seder. I was personally invited by a relative to a women's day among black Baptists. I went to the Sunday school at the Benjamin Franklin Church. I felt I understood the spirit of the place and the meaning of Negro spirituals. I was struck by the mystical relationship with God and the warm relationship between the believers. No one was surprised by my presence.

For the sake of mutual understanding, some synagogues open their doors to the public every year.

> *Flo Geismar: It's called "operation comprehension." We open the synagogue to non-Jews who want to learn about Judaism. First, they come into the synagogue, are given a history of Touro and a brief history of the Jews. Then we visit each room. And in each one, we showed a different holiday with an exhibit on how the holiday is celebrated at home and in the synagogue.*
> *— Flo Geismar, New Orleans, October 23, 1997.*

Social Coexistence

Interfaith action also exists in the area of social rights. In institutions that are predominantly Jewish, Christian employees are given days off for Christian holidays. Collaborations take place in order to implement specific outreach programs: indeed, one of my interlocutors supported the creation of small black Baptist churches and the implementation of neighborhood anti-poverty programs. In 1965, at the initiative of Catholic nuns, Flo Geismar worked for a program that helped provide schooling to black children and alleviate the impoverishment of certain neighborhoods. She offered some of her houses as living quarters for families. Flo's parents were of two different religions, her father was Jewish and her mother Catholic. She doesn't erect barriers between different religious beliefs, but, on the contrary, makes these into an asset in her work. This anti-poverty program was later exported to other countries, including Israel.

Interfaith associations are established in Montgomery at the time of the civil rights movement: Catholic women, Jewish women and black associations come together for charitable causes to help the black community.[252] Other actions are more political and are aimed at countering extremist leaders.

This was the case during the Million Man March held in

Washington on September 23, 1995, organized by Black Muslims and their leader Louis Farrakhan, whose discourse was both anti-women and anti-Jewish. On this occasion, members of the most moderate Baptist black churches joined the Jewish congregations in protest.

Yet there are limits in the images and language of my interlocutors.

The Boundaries between Jews and Christians

The terms used to designate one or another group already indicates this separation. Indeed my interlocutors refer to "Jews and non-Jews" or "gentiles" and "Jews." The boundary is inscribed in the language used by my interlocutors. The boundaries between the two milieus, Christian and Jewish, as well as the sporadic instances of anti-Semitism during the election campaigns of racist candidates, cannot be overlooked. But many of my interlocutors believe that "assimilation" guarantees protection and safety.

> *Grace Zelman: We've never had the ugliness of swastikas, only once or twice, a long time ago. This was when David Duke was here. His supporters used to draw swastikas on temple doors and in cemeteries. But to a very small extent. We were very lucky. As Jews, we were assimilated to Christians, even our rabbis...*
>
> *Flo Geismar: We assimilated but nevertheless we're still separate. We're assimilated in many ways but there's an old separation. I call that the old business, the organizations founded by Christian milieus.*
>
> — *Grace Zelman, Flo Geismar, New Orleans, July 8, 1992.*

Though the middle and upper classes in large cities are seldom ostracized, separations do exist. Malvina Balogh was born in 1906. She was educated in New Orleans and lived in New York in

1992. She wrote her reminiscences for the ninety-fifth birthday of her aunt Emilie Fraenkel: "During my early and later adolescence I was clearly troubled by the north/south, Jewish/Christian extravagant/frugal dichotomies that seemed to pervade my life."[i] Other witnesses are more positive and say they never felt excluded in their social life. In the 1940s, Jacky Toledano's mother was on excellent terms with Catholic circles and with the bishop, an important figure in New Orleans. However Jacky Toledano does not deny that a separation exists between the Christian milieu and the Jewish one but she accommodates to it, being invited by other elite clubs. She knows that no young Jewish woman, unless converted, can come out as a debutante in Southern high society.

> *I never at any stage of my life felt that I couldn't be a member of a club that I wanted to join. I never felt left out of anything. In school I was always invited, I was on the list of people that Christians felt they had to invite. I truly think that I was never excluded in any way. I can't go to the Boston Club here, but I have no desire to. I'm invited to the Lions Club, and have been invited to the Yacht Club by my girlfriends for years. There is a Christian aristocracy and a Jewish one. The Jewish one is at Touro synagogue where I've always felt comfortable. I was a member and still am. My friends went to public school with me, or to Newman, which is a private school, and a prominent place.*
> — Jackie Toledano, New Orleans, September 18, 1998.

Today, these separations persist in a more diffuse manner and manifest themselves differently. In New Orleans, fundamentalist Evangelical churches were expanding their presence and gaining followers in many institutions. A Jewish friend of mine who had resigned from the private non-denominational Waldorf School told me about a remark that had been made about her. A colleague had reported: "She's an excellent teacher, and she'll be a great loss. But anyhow, she teaches values that are not Christian."[ii]

The Jew, a Sorcerer in the Small Towns of Louisiana

The following story was told to me by Carol Mills, who found she had Jewish and mulatto ancestors in Avoyelles parish in central Louisiana, a poorer and more isolated region than the cities located on the banks of the Mississippi. She told me about things she had heard. She explained that Jews were seen as similar to voodoo practitioners. The term "voodoo" is the name given to the religious rites and practices prevalent in Creole culture.[iii] This meant that Jews, like African Americans, were sorcerers in a way. And the two stigmas, Jewish and African American, were very close.

> I think that being Jewish meant being a bit "voodoo," out of the mainstream, and [my mother] didn't want me to be that. A woman whose name is Hirsch called me the other night. She is not Jewish, but her last name is Jewish and she told me that her ancestors were called 'voodoos' because they were Jewish. They were different, they spoke differently and acted differently. My ancestors were from Avoyelles parish, a very poor agricultural parish, essentially made up of farmers and storekeepers.
> — Carol Mills, New Orleans, June 24, 2004.

This story should be viewed with reservations. Indeed, it is the only account of its kind. After hearing it, I asked other families if they had heard of the term "voodoo" being applied to Jews. They all answered in the negative. But one person, whose great grandparents had immigrated to Louisiana and Mississippi, told me the story of a peddler whose head people used to feel to see if he had horns:

> Rumors went around about Jews. For instance, white Baptists thought that there were little horns on

Michelangelo's Moses. When the Jewish peddler stopped by, the buyer would ask if he could touch him to see if horns were growing on his head: "Would it bother you if I touched your head to see what your horns are like?"
— *Metz Kahn, Baton Rouge, September 26, 2004.*

Stephanie Golden whom I met in New York confirmed this belief: "It is quite true that commonly in the South people believed that Jews had horns. My mother spent the war years in Richmond, Virginia, and Charleston, South Carolina, and she described to me how someone — I think it was her landlady in one of those cities — wanted to know where her horns were. And a college friend of mine — exactly the same age — told me that her father was drafted during the Korean War and sent somewhere in the south — possibly one of the Carolinas. So she lived there for a few years and went to school there. This would have been in the early 50s. She told me how the other children in her elementary school were surprised that she had no horns. This was at the other end of the South from Louisiana. I believe it was a widespread belief."

Was this a way of seeing Jews, as persons who practiced sorcery and who could be diabolical figures, figures of evil? Indeed, Michelangelo did sculpt Moses with symbolic horns and clouds around his head, but this was due to a misunderstanding of the word *qaran* in Exodus, chapter 34, verse 29: "rays of light reflected from a polished surface," the literal meaning being "to shine out, to dart forth, as horns on the head" with the verb *garan* coming from *degeren* (horn). These representations are not new and have existed as part of the image of the Jew since the Middle Ages.[iv] The demonizing of the Jew has persisted throughout the centuries: is it surprising that it also existed in this region? Judaism was a foreign religious practice for this rural Catholic population, as foreign as voodoo.

Jewish families in a rural context seemed to have been isolated. The inhabitants were not strict in obeying Jewish religious practices. Devoutness weakened because it was unsupervised by religious authorities. Priests and rabbis were traveling clergymen. Hence the population organized itself as best it could. Crossovers from one religious group to another were tolerated, transcending prejudices, because the inhabitants lived in such close proximity.

During my interviews in the South, the question of the relations between Jews and African Americans often came up spontaneously. What can be said of these relations?

A Gulf between Southern and Northern Jews

Non-Jewish culture has affected Southern Jews more than Northern Jews. Southern Jews strove to adjust to their Southern environment, to its rhythm, values, lifestyle and the obligation of adapting to the Christian world. They also wanted to champion models of Jewishness that were different from those in the North. North and South mutually accused one another of provincialism and insularity, of withdrawing into their Jewishness within a circumscribed and narrow milieu, under the influence of the surrounding lifestyles.

Carolyn Lipson Walker, in her 1980 survey, spoke with a young Jewish woman from Alabama, who had just moved to New Jersey and who was surprised that Northerners were so ignorant of what was going on in the South: "The children of my mother's best friend wanted know if I lived on a plantation, if I had slaves. She couldn't believe that I was Jewish because there are no Jews in Alabama."

I personally came across similar reactions when I was among Jews on Long Island. My friends were surprised to hear there were Jews in the South. The tone was condescending as if Jews could only live in New York, Chicago or Florida. These are age-old conceptions. Carolyn Lipson Walker uses the term "uncivilized world" for the South referring to the work of Louis Schmier: Either Southern Jews are seen as living in dreadful conditions, or in an excessively romantic style, an impression largely derived from films and literature.

"Max Friedmann moved to Birmingham in 1918, his family in

Cincinnati thought he had moved out of civilization. The first segment of the Friedmann family came to Birmingham in 1937 for the bar mitzvah of Karl B. Friedmann. 'Apparently they were amazed to find civilization here.' Karl Friedmann relates, 'My father invited his sisters and brothers for the bar mitzvah to view a Saturday night lynching in downtown Birmingham. Some were appalled. All believed it was going to happen.'"[257]

Within the Jewish Diaspora, the estrangement and ignorance of Southern and Northern Jews therefore seem great, reflecting the conceptions of all the inhabitants of these two large regions. Some of my interlocutors, recent newcomers to the South, wonder about this region, their ways of doing things, their Southern accent, their exceedingly discreet ways of being Jewish. But it is mostly around the black issue that differences set in.

Slavery is not mentioned publicly. Nowadays it is an issue that causes embarrassment in Jewish milieus, for historical, ideological and identity reasons. The dispute weighs heavily, even if it is over a century old, between the few Jewish abolitionists who expressed themselves during the fight against slavery and the pro-slavery supporters.

These cleavages mirror the geographical location of the respective groups, Southern and Northern, the divisions within each group, their exegesis of the Bible (Exodus, Leviticus), and their socio-economic status. The complication was manifest during a recent exhibit, *From Alsace to America* organized by the Museum of the Southern Jewish Experience in Jackson in the summer of 1998. The event, which many families took part in, attracted 70,000 visitors. The fact that there was no mention of slavery in this marvelous exhibit was striking.

Indeed, a range of documents were on display shedding light on the emigrants' religious life in Alsace as well as on the different stages of immigration and integration in the South: departure, lists of immigrants on ships and in houses, the offices of cotton merchants, synagogues, Sabbath evenings, marriages and family histories. There were video interviews with families of Alsatian and German origin, the differences between the two being barely noticeable. Nothing controversial was shown. Nor was slavery alluded to, or Jewish mulatto families. A few Jewish children may have been mulatto, though they were very rare. An archivist friend of Alsatian ancestry in New Orleans told me that when she was a child, in 1930, she noticed that some mulatto children had the same name as her relative, Isidore Danziger. An 1860 slavery census shows that he owned three black slaves, three women, aged 64, 42 and 40.[258]. It is highly plausible that mulatto children were born later on or that Isidore had a relationship with one of these slave women. "We thought the children had died," my interlocutor said. This is one of the reasons why it is hard to raise the issue of race relations between Jews and African-Americans.

Slavery is still a prickly subject in different communities and among Jewish families. During my conversations with families, a small number among them knew, wanted to know or remembered that their ancestors owned slaves. These facts can only be found on the census lists of slave owners and on notarized bills of sale. The archives of the Jewish communities (those of New Orleans, the Gates of Prayer founded in 1850 and the Touro Synagogue in 1848) show nothing, nor do those of the Beth Or Jewish community in Montgomery, founded in 1858. The Civil War and its impact aren't mentioned either, though in 1861 Montgomery was the capital of the Confederacy.

Denial, embarrassment, shame, social pressure. It is hardly pleasant to refer to the reality of the past. The accusations of "Jewish slave-owner" come from all sides. There are Internet sites titled "Jews and the Black Holocaust" complaining that historians do not clearly denounce the role of Jews in slavery. There is a growing demand that the former colonial and slave-owning countries, including France, recognize their debt to the descendants. of slaves. As far as the United States is concerned, the situation must be qualified given the pre-established relations at work, in neighborhoods, and during the common struggles against poverty. For instance, Flo Geismar and I were warmly received in September 1997, at the Franklin Avenue Baptist Church in New Orleans for women's day. We were invited by a choir member with whom Flo Geismar has had a long-standing acquaintanceship. Similarly, St. Peter the Apostle Catholic Church in Moss Point, Mississippi, part of the diocese of Biloxi, whose congregation is primarily African-American, welcomed me very cordially in December, 2010. The service was conducted by a white priest. He was a member of the order of Josephites who are dedicated to preaching to African Americans. I was accompanied by the district judge, Robert Krebs who is very highly regarded by the parishioners for his program of probation and re-schooling of young delinquents.

The most prosperous Jews, small in number, did indeed own slaves. They were not the initiators of slave-ownership, nor its defenders, but were usually caught between two conflicting worlds.

In *antebellum* times, slavery was mentioned as a necessity, a system the immigrant had to subscribe to. He could be very shocked by the dreadful treatment they were subjected to and the hunting down of runaway slaves, but he did not oppose slavery and he adopted it when his financial situation permitted it. Domestic slaves, nannies or home employees, play an important part in family life and childhood.

Jewish merchants and peddlers often included the African-American population among their customers because many Jewish stores extended credit, had affordable prices and were cordial with African Americans. On plantations, after peddlers had sold merchandise to the owners, it was customary for them to ask for permission to sell to the African Americans on the property. The peddlers exchanged merchandise for molasses, cotton and sugar, which they would later resell.[259]

As for the relations between Whites and Jews, the comment of a Metz Kahn whose family has been living in the South for four generations is completely explicit: "My grandfather used to say, 'Every night I pray for the African Americans because if there were no Blacks, they would be picking on Jews.'"[260] This kind of humor is an indirect but clear denunciation of the bigotry that prevailed in the South until the 1960s.

The Emancipation Proclamation was met with mixed feelings. The plantation owners in Louisiana, a State that was liberated by the Northern forces in 1862, had always been haunted by the fear of a slave uprising. In the May 8, 1862 entry of her diary, Clara Salomon, a young Jewish woman of Sephardic descent living in New Orleans, expressed the following thought after the prisons were opened and the African Americans were freed: "I fear more the negroes to be released. An insurrection is my continual horror." The writer Elliott Ashkenazi comments, "Many in the South had feared a slave insurrection, even before the Civil War. Planters in rural Louisiana, the principal slave-owners, were the most concerned. Clara, an urbanite from a mercantile family, had the same fears."[261]

The Position of Immigrant Jews: A Halfhearted Commitment to the System

The paternalistic relationship between Jews and slaves in the Memoirs of the period is confirmed by the oral testimony of the descendants of these families. One of my interlocutors from Pascagoula emphasized the point that "slaves were the most valuable asset a man had, and worth much more than his land. It does not make sense that most would mistreat the most valuable asset they had ... In my mother's family slaves stayed as paid employees for generations and we still wrote to their families and visited with them into the 1960s". "Jews owned slaves-never very many-they usually treated them well," this observation is confirmed in many Southern States. The historian Leonard Rogoff, in his study of the relations between Jews and African Americans in Durham, North Carolina, emphasizes the fact that the history of Jews, their familiarity with poverty and discrimination, made them sensitive to the situation of African Americans though they were prudent in expressing it.[262]

The descendants of the notary public Abel Dreyfous also explain that Irish servants were preferred over slaves who were too expensive. The register of notarized sales from his office show thirteen bills of sale of slaves in 1845. There were fourteen bills of sale between 1851 and 1852, four of which were to Jewish families. This distinguished citizen, who was very respected in the city, participated in the slave society. But neither his correspondence nor the biography of his son, Félix Jonathan Dreyfous, allude to this "singular institution."

The Jews tried to improve the cruelest aspects of segregation but their foremost attachment was to the States that had welcomed them. During anniversary dinners of the communities, they clearly asserted their loyalty "to father and grandfather and the lost cause."[263]

By owning slaves, Jews showed their desire to perpetuate Southern antebellum norms. Therefore Jews were not seen as a threat to established models. Being a slave owner contributed to the consolidation of the status of Jews. Oscar Solomon Straus, who settled in Georgia, said the following in his memoirs: "As a young boy brought up in the South I never questioned the rights or the wrongs of slavery. Its existence I regarded as matter of course, as most other customs and institutions."[264] The institution was adopted by a small minority of Jewish immigrants who prospered as wholesalers and retailers in the garment, wood and cotton trades in various States. I was able to check this with greater precision by consulting the slave censuses in the Special Collections in Louisiana and Alabama.

In Alabama, the prosperity of prominent merchants like the Weil family, originally from Oberlustadt in the Palatinate and settled in Opelika, occurred only after the Civil War, in 1865. However in Montgomery, the 1860 census already lists some slave owning families: Abraham, 36 years old, originally from Oberlustadt, owned two slaves, and Isaac Abraham, six. The latter was a businessman and owned nine thousand acres of land. E.C. Hausman, 38 years old, a garment merchant, owned twenty thousand acres for private and professional use. He was a native of Saverne and owned five slaves. Acreage in personal and business property, and the number of slaves a person owned, were usually the criteria for determining wealth. A Mr. B.G. Levy owned 45 slaves, including 28 children. He was a cotton merchant. According to my informers, he sold construction boards. We can assume that he owned a plantation and was also a merchant.

According to this same census, out of the two thousand Jews listed in the 1860 census in Alabama, fourteen owned a total of seventy-five slaves in 1860.[265] They were storeowners or wholesalers of merchandise. Their properties ranged in size from ten thousand to forty thousand acres. The great majority were of German origin; only three were from Alsace, connected to families from the Palatinate.[266]

In Louisiana, the *Code Noir* of 1724, which regulated the status of slaves, prohibited Jews from settling in Louisiana. Merchants, traders and trappers conducted business in the state but really only started settling in the early nineteenth century. A small fraction of the Jewish population were slave owners. In 1850, 32 slave owners owned 113 slaves. In 1860, out of 8,000 Jews in Louisiana, 96 owned a total of 225 slaves. The slaves were employed as domestic servants or worked in the stores. Hence, in 1860, the Bavarian Samuel Kahn, a merchant living in Jackson, LA, married to Augusta Kiefer, originally from Durkheim, Germany, owned six slaves. The merchant Philip Sartorius owned one slave. Léon Godchaux[267], the owner of a clothes store, was listed in the New Orleans census of slave owners as having one slave, the mother of three children. Mr. Heine, a relative of Heinrich Heine, had one female slave; N. Newman had two; Theo Danzinger had three.[268]

It was shocking to mistreat them, as Julius Weis points out in his autobiography. Some Jews felt they could not reject a system that was part of their environment and in which they constituted a minority. The post-Civil War period was one of suffering, destruction, poverty and hunger for the families I studied, a time when everything had to be rebuilt anew. But it does not seem, from what we heard from our interlocutors that their relationships with their African American servants changed. The families kept their African American employees over several generations. The latter even followed them in their peregrinations, to St. Louis or California, even if they sometimes ran away after making the trip. Many remained where they were, having no other place to go. Immigrants then had to pay their employees.[269]

Some families were embarrassed when we broached this

subject, because of the difficult present-day climate between Jews and African Americans.

The Ambivalent Relations between Jews and African Americans

From the beginning of my interviews, the idea kept recurring that Southern Jews established a more familial and personal relationship with African Americans than non-Jews. Even if they led separate lives, black and white families were in daily contact for social and economic reasons. Black personnel in Jewish families were omnipresent and indispensable. They attended the children's weddings. They were included in family photographs, from the late nineteenth century to the 1990s. Most surprising was their length of service until very recently. The parents of my interlocutors were very often helped by black cooks. They brought the traditions of Creole cuisine into Jewish homes. They also learned to cook Jewish dishes, as previously mentioned. They were also children's nannies. Metz Kahn gives a good description of the affectionate relationships between nannies and children:

> *My nanny remained with us and left us only when my family decided to return to New Orleans and she stayed with us until she found another job. I was 16 years old and she was almost 90 and every time I went to see her in Shreveport, for Christmas, or her birthday, she had something for me. She had worked from 1946 to 1986. She was part of the family. Now she is dead.*
> — Metz Kahn, Baton Rouge, September 30, 1997.

The people I met had often been brought up by black governesses when they were children, and so had their parents. Albert Fraenkel II described Alice Wilson, born a slave, who came to New Orleans to work at his grandmother Carrie Switzer's house in 1899.[270] She was employed for fourteen years and helped raise the three children: she was an important member of the family. No one called her anything but "Mammy." She was a marvelous cook who addressed Albert as Boss and called Carrie "Madame". Mammy wore impeccably clean linen, the finest quality apron, a lace collar and a white hat. She was very neat looking. She lived in her own "quarters," a room in the backyard behind the house. Among her possessions she had a beautifully framed portrait of a man. When questioned she would admit that the handsome man was her husband, Dr. Cotta. She had been "placed" at his house when she was fourteen.

Closer to us, after having lived through the very troubled period of desegregation in Martin Luther King's city, Babette Wampold, whose family was Franco-German, justifies herself, in Montgomery, against the prejudices of Northerners. As a child she lived in the small town of Demopolis in Alabama. She walked around the countryside all by herself without any problem. Her father hired black workers very early on, years before desegregation. She points out how strong the intimacy could be between white children and their nannies. The nanny sometimes replaced the mother. She fed the children and educated them. She had assimilated the educational codes of whites and taught the children the conventions and rules that the mother had sometimes not handed down. She could sometimes be stricter than the mother. In those days, each class and each race was assigned its place:

> We are frightened by the way the racism of Montgomery is viewed, but no one is all that brutal. They [the people in New York] don't understand at all. Even among Whites there's not physical feeling (of prejudice) toward black skin. We work together, we kiss one another; Blacks and Whites speak the same way and eat the same soul food. We eat soul food all the time. And everyone's been educated by a black nanny and, in some families, everyone considers their nanny almost as a mother. She used to spend the whole night with us, I slept next to her; I'm attached to her. It's a sensual and sentimental relationship; she protected me and gave me rules, much stricter ones:

which boys I should date. She was aware of the social classes. She wanted me to go out with people from the same milieu as mine, that were socially suitable for me. Even if my mother agreed to the company I kept, Roberte did not.
— *Babette Wampold, Montgomery, November 4, 1998.*

On the whole, Jewish families claim that they treat African Americans better than Christian families and that they show respect and consideration for them.[271] The length of service in their homes is an indication of the ties that unite them. Nor is it unusual for families to take an interest in the children of their employees. Today, young African American women cook, drive and accompany wealthy elderly people in their outings. It should be emphasized that in spite of this closeness, they do not usually share meals with their employers. In Baton Rouge, there is an early morning bus service for African American employees going into the residential neighborhoods. In New Orleans, there are some black employees who are over seventy and have been working for the same family for years. African American women servants advise their employers on how to organize their households.

Jews and African Americans rubbed shoulders outside the home, on roads and plantations, and later in stores. The first business contacts were established by peddlers on the plantations or in town in the stores. Clive Webb[272] studied the relations between Jewish merchants and African Americans during segregation. He points out that Jews sold second-hand, inexpensive products that were accessible to African Americans and that merchants were often kind to them.

The writer Eli N. Evans stresses the fact that the prevailing image of the Jewish peddler after the Civil War was positive. The peddler, too, was a foreigner with an accent who owned no slaves; he smiled at African Americans and was ready to serve them.[273] Yet Clive Webb quotes Harold Cruise in his well-known 1984 book, *The Crisis of The Negro Intellectual: A Historical Analysis of the Failure of Black Leadership*: "It is from the Jewish storekeeper and trader that the Southern Negro got his latent anti-Semitism."[274] Other historians see things differently. Louis Schmier establishes a tie between the peddler and the black customer, the first offering low, negotiable prices and respecting the customer's dignity, and the latter, the black client, guaranteeing a regular source of revenue. Business ties were thus reinforced by loyalty and affection.[275] But actually, as shown by the experience of Aaron Bronson, a Russian Jewish immigrant who set up his business in a small town in Tennessee in 1920, the relationship was very ambiguous, as Stella Suberman wrote in the *Jew Store* in 2001: "I'm here to earn a living, not for a crusade"[276] explains Braunstein, one of his colleagues in Savannah. Yet Aaron Bronson was far from prejudiced or racist. African Americans were not allowed to try on clothes in the fitting rooms and Aaron Bronson "would at least meet a Negro customer at the back door and arranged there for a return or an exchange." From the standpoint of African Americans, the Jewish storeowner was nonetheless White, even if his religion set him apart. He benefited from the privilege of being white. The tensions between African Americans and Jews stem from the inequalities between the two milieus. But in some cases merchants maintained very good relations with African Americans. Lazare Kahn, for instance, the great grandfather of one of my interlocutors, was very much liked.

> *Lazare Kahn was born in Mommenheim in Alsace and settled in Jackson, Mississippi before the Civil War. Blacks called him Mr. Honey because he was so sweet. There wasn't much money in the family and if he met someone in need he would give them his coat and belt.*
> — Metz Kahn, New York, September 3, 1992.

The climate between Jews and African Americans could be tense. Clive Webb in his meaningful article, "Jewish Merchants and Black Customers" published in the *Southern Jewish History* in 1999, mentions that Matthias Block was killed by an African American in Waco, Texas in 1906. His murderer, Jesse Jones, was hanged. This climate in the late nineteenth century and early twentieth century can be explained by economic factors-the relations between borrowers and lenders-but also by older factors: rivalries, hostilities and stereotypes that were rooted in the mentalities of the two minority groups. In rural stores, Jews were often moneylenders. They lent to sharecroppers, not just to landowners. They lent money before the harvest and were reimbursed later with interest. According to Louis Schmier, the interest rates were considered too high. Yet he gives no exact figure. He justifies these rates by the poverty of the borrowers, the small sums that were lent and the high risk taken by the lender.[277] We all know the conflicts and tensions such situations can create. Whereas the African Americans didn't trust the Jewish merchants and disliked them in many ways, they admired their keen business acumen and economic success. It was hard to start a black business in the 1920s because of lack of capital. "If there was a Jewish store on the corner and a Negro store around the block, or vice versa, and the Jew store sells for two or three cents less, the Negro will go to the Jew store because he can get the same thing for less money," according to the newspaper *Atlanta Independent* of July 8, 1923. Indeed the thrifty management of the Jewish manager is also impressive. He knows how to reinvest all his profits in his business. The stereotype of the Jew who will do anything to earn money became a positive model. This was no longer a vice but an example to be followed.

Accepting African American customers in department stores that observed Southern laws and traditions raised problems. Restaurants and lavatories, when they existed, were segregated. Black employees did not work in sales but in maintenance and upkeep. This discrimination greatly destabilized Jewish activists who supported desegregation, writes Clive Webb. Actually Jewish merchants were very dependent on the goodwill of their white customers. Berney Strauss, president of the L. Hammel Dry Goods Co. in Mobile, Alabama, was ready to fulfill the demands of the NAACP in 1938 and include toilets for his employees and black buyers.[278] But then he backed down immediately, saying that "it was not a custom of department stores in the South to have comfort facilities for colored shoppers." It is not surprising therefore that in 1959 CORE organized a series of direct actions against Jewish department stores. Indeed, in Florida, CORE organized a sit-in movement against a specific Jewish store with the target "get the Jew first."[279] Yet conflicts between African Americans and Jewish storeowners were not as violent as in the ghettos of Chicago and New York. African Americans, disappointed that they did not obtain stronger support from the Southern Jewish population, classified the Jews as being on the side of Whites and oppression. Relations between Jews and African Americans were made more difficult thereafter.

However, for a great majority of African Americans, the only Whites who viewed their African American customers with compassion and respect were the Jews.[280]

Desegregation: The Dilemma of Southern Jews

There were some precursory actions prior to the desegregation movement itself. Some activist belonging to the enlightened bourgeoisie of New Orleans took part in the movement along with a few rabbis. The Louisiana League for the Preservation of Civil Rights rose up against the denial of rights to African Americans in public spaces. The New Orleans chapter led a fight in 1939 to give African Americans access to Pontchartrain Beach and swimming pool. The League worked with the city's only African American lawyer and invited him to their meetings. On April 12, 1941, they wrote to the mayor urging the recruitment of African American policemen in the city. The League was vigilant about the violation of the rights of African Americans in small towns, for instance in Natchitoches, working to obtain "a semblance of civil rights" for African Americans throughout the South. It launched an intensive campaign in public education and civil rights, and organized demonstrations where they gave speeches and distributed leaflets. Among the most active members were George Dreyfous, president of the League, and his wife Mathilde Dreyfous, president of the New Orleans League of Women Voters. She would later become head of the Save our Schools association.[281]

A few years later, on December 16, 1949, Ralph Bunche, head

of the NAACP and former United States mediator on Palestine, was welcomed by Rabbi Julian B. Feibelman at the Reform Temple Sinai, at the request of the city's Interracial Committee because no other public auditorium was available. He anticipated criticism from both sides, from the community in general and from his own congregation. He was proud that the synagogue's administrative board supported him.[282] It was feared that the anti-Semitism, though not ostentatious, that existed in the large cities would resurface when there would be demonstrations in favor of desegregation. "This was considered as an integrated event unprecedented in the city's history."

The desegregation of buses, restaurants and, above all, schools, supported primarily by Northern Jews, undermined the relations between Northern and Southern Jews. Southern Jews were caught in the crossfire. Out of self-protection they kept their distance. Their leaders, the rabbis, who didn't want to be seen as agitators, stayed silent for the most part, in contrast to their Northern colleagues who were very active.[283]

A survey made in 1974 in small Southern communities showed that 16% of Jews saw themselves as progressives. That group stated they had been publicly active during the struggle for civil rights. In this respect it was possible to talk about the "dilemma of the Southern Jew."[284]

Babette Wampold clarifies the position of Jews in Montgomery, the city that was at the center of the movement:

> *The Temple was afraid of having problems. White Christians were more active. They passed a motion. They were very intelligent and wealthy and in a solid position. They had nothing to lose. Jews thought it was dangerous, whether true or not. The Jewish community didn't have that kind of courage and lucidity. Up until 1998, the Country Club of the city didn't accept Jews, nor did the Magnet ball or the carnival.*
> *— Babette Wampold, Montgomery, September 30, 1998.*

But there were several more discreet actions. All the employers drove their employees. Cars served as collective taxis. And some associations joined others:

> We joined with the National Jewish Commission, the Negro Women, the Black Committee and the Catholic Women's Committees to help young people philanthropically, to collect clothes. This was so successful that the federal government created its own initiative.
> — Babette Wampold, Montgomery, September 30, 1998.

In Louisiana, most Jews had a natural sympathy for the aspirations of African Americans whom they saw as a minority group whose struggle was the same as theirs. But they didn't want to disassociate themselves from the dominant white majority after the enormous efforts they had made to get accepted. The historian Murray Friedman notes: "Because the thoughts they harbor on the race issue differ from those of the majority of their white neighbors, they feel "disloyal" to Southern attitudes and institutions.[285] And in the same trend of ideas, Albert Vorspan,[286] remarks: the Southern Jew is not seeking martyrdom, but acceptance. Like most other "nice" people, he has no great relish for social ostracism and economic reprisals. It is already evident that some Jews are taking great pains to dissociate the bombings of synagogues from the assaults on Negro churches and Negro homes, or on integrated schools in Clinton and Nashville."[287]

The inhabitants of Baton Rouge described the need for this integration and the difficulties in achieving it given the violent climate that prevailed at the time:

> The dialogue between Blacks and Whites focused on school integration. We had three groups of parishes here that tried to facilitate school integration. Integration was seen as inevitable, a factor of peace and order and in large part, of dignity. But there were riots in Baton Rouge.
> — Bettie Atkin, Metz Kahn, Baton Rouge, Sept. 3, 1997.

Bea, Flo and Celeste Lehmann, from the third generation of Alsatian immigrants, were active during the civil rights movement. They point out how divided the Jewish communities were. The Jackson community, for instance, didn't always follow their very active rabbi, Perry Nussbaum. He arrived in the South on May 17, 1954, called "Black Monday" because it was the day the Supreme Court ruled that segregation in public schools was unconstitutional. He joined many associations in the city. He was inspired by interfaith work and according to Rabbi Zola, "One of Nussbaum's priorities soon became, as he phrased it, 'to storm the thick and high walls of Protestant fundamentalism in the Bible Belt.'" He wished to establish ties with the politicians and the moderate churches and fight against the influence of the extreme right. In 1955, he delivered sermons in which he took a position publicly, teaching that African Americans, like Jews, were by nature entitled to share God's gifts, improve themselves, offer their children the best possible education, and had a right to economic security and political equality.[288] He took part in the CCAR forum on the problem of desegregation in the South pointing out that he and his colleagues were trying to defend the fundamentals of Judaism under very difficult circumstances. These positions frightened his congregation to such an extent that some members wanted to withdraw from the United American Committee, the B'nai B'rith and other organizations that had fought for the civil rights cause.[289] Indeed some other congregations, most notably in Florida, did withdraw their affiliations. Furthermore, the president of the New York chapter of the NAACP was Jewish and this greatly troubled the Southern communities.

They also had to fight against fear and entrenched racism. There were obstacles to integration throughout all of Southern society. Cohabitation and making all public places accessible were particularly hard to implement given that an inbred prejudice against African Americans was deeply rooted in people's upbringing.

Bea Lehmann and her sisters supported desegregation unequivocally and actively. They described the telephone threats they received and the bomb that damaged their synagogue.

> *Students were killed; we talked and distributed food. Perry Nussbaum, the rabbi, called on the State to put the guilty in jail. The Jackson synagogue was bombed. We received phone threats. Integration gave us bad publicity. Now we have a few black members in our congregation. There was a time when they were not wanted. There was a group that didn't want them against a group that did. Of course, among Christians it was the same. They didn't want to admit Blacks. Some took a long time accepting them and still don't. I don't think this is due to education, it goes with the milieu and is typical of some people; it's ingrained. We have Jews that bring up this question. You can't do anything about it. And this situation exists in other places, not just among Jews.*
>
> *Fortunately the situation is different now. We go wherever we want...*
>
> — Bea, Flo, Celeste Lehmann, Jackson, September 19, 1992.

Vicki Stamler's mother, who came from an old Southern family, fought a courageous and dangerous battle, according to what her daughter says:

> *For my mother it was different. But my father was educated in a very progressive way. She had been educated in the traditional and privileged Southern manner.*
>
> *She came from a very wealthy family with ideas about Whites and Blacks and segregation. When she met my father she had different ideas. She later became a very active champion of the civil rights movement. It was in Decatur Carrollton. She spoke out for civil rights and the Ku Klux Klan set fire to my father's office. The FBI followed us for several months and tried to protect us. For many years she lectured for*

> the Anti-Defamation League and collected information about the Klan. But she never spoke very much about her activities because her life was in danger. She also wanted to protect us. My father supported her.
> — Vicki Stamler, Strasbourg, July 30, 1998.

There were conflicts between the generations and estrangements. The generation prior to desegregation found it hard to accept equal rights for African Americans. In the years of the civil rights movement, most of the Jewish population was silent for fear of reprisals. The Jewish population was confronted with its precarious status and its fear of the murderous violence of racist organizations, the White Citizen's Committee such as the Ku Klux Klan.

> Our generation understood, but the previous generation couldn't accept it. Many people of our generation had problems because they had been educated by their parents. Essentially the change came from our generation.
> — Bettie Atkin, Baton Rouge, September 30, 1997.

> My father had always had black servants in the house. The Blacks took care of the children but when integration came, the first time a black person sat next to my father in a bus, he was so upset, he was 70 years old, that he got up and walked 7 miles along Canal Street rather than sit next to a black person. I had a lot of conflicts with my father and I used to say to him, "You had Blacks working in your home and you entrusted them with my life." It was a question I could never discuss with my father.
> — Metz Kahn, New Orleans, September 24, 1998.

Badly-Healed Wounds

My interlocutors have kept a vivid memory of the civil rights struggle. They feel that the desegregation of the schools enforced in the 1960s was badly organized and ended in failure. It still leaves wounds among most of them. The Southern Jewish population had to confront their vulnerable status again, fearing both the murderous violence of racist organizations and the reprimands of black associations. They did not really like the fact that Northern Jews had come down South to show them how to behave on their own terrain. There was a real gap between the national Jewish organizations, supporters of the NAACP, and the Southern Jewish population. Many Southern Jews feel that desegregation was conducted in an awkward and brutal manner, and they accuse the federal army.

> When they began the process of integration, they didn't start with the lower grades so as to build integration year by year. They started with the higher grades. You couldn't mix people who had been brought up in completely different ways at the start. They had already formed their opinions. I have never understood the law that was applied throughout the entire country… It made no sense to start with the upper grades and not with the lower ones.
> — Bettie Atkin, Metz Kahn, Baton Rouge, September 30, 1997.

And according to Leroy Paris, both much more critical and very "Southern":

> There was a huge difference between the Blacks at the time and the white elite that forced the doors to equality open, if I may express myself in these terms. It was an absolute shock to the cultural system. It was so remote from the Southern way of life that it was hard to accept. The U.S. government forced them. At first the Southern population rejected equality but it had no choice. It was simply something they had to accept. During the years 1960 to 1970, and including the early 1970s, the refusal to accept integration persisted. But the Blacks came to be more and more numerous as

> *part of the system and they were integrated into the White culture. In the 1980s, we got there and I would say that today there are no more prejudices but...*
> — *Leroy H. Paris, Jackson, September 18, 1992.*

As for the effects of desegregation, it created new separations as it caused "white flight" — white families moving into other neighborhoods or cities when they couldn't afford private schools.

> *Whites deserted the school system. They moved to private schools because they didn't want to support the public schools. But we're the people who helped to organize magnet schools, mixed schools, of Blacks and Whites, selected by tests. The Whites didn't want to vote for tax increases. The Blacks requested a million dollars in order to upgrade the schools or tear down the old ones and build new ones so as to offer educational opportunities, a team of teachers, smaller class sizes per teacher and review the entire educational system. In New Orleans the money is controlled by the Whites, but politically, the Blacks have the power.*
> — *Metz Kahn, Baton Rouge, September 30, 1997.*

The Enduring Separation Between African Americans and Whites

Gaps still exist in other forms. They are particularly visible in the school system. There is a majority of African American students from disadvantaged families in the public schools whereas the well-to-do white children attend private schools. This trend has become less clear-cut in recent years though the level of public schools does not seem adequate. Parents who can afford it send their children to religious or secular private schools where they are more likely to receive a good education.

But there are many differences, depending on the cities and

the states concerned, as one volunteer, who helps children with learning difficulties in New Orleans, points out:

> *In New Orleans, the tuition in Catholic schools is very low and private schools give scholarships to help families. The public schools are a disaster. The teachers I work with all agree. And this whole business of equalizing brings down the level.*
> — *Jo-Ellyn Kuppermann, New Orleans, September 24, 1998.*

Efforts are being made to strive for excellence for all as in the magnet schools that select the best students regardless of their origins. They offer new opportunities to disadvantaged minority groups. But here too opinion is divided between supporters of public schools and private schools. It is a fact that the public schools are regaining ground and are not as deficient as they were. A great deal of progress has been made since hurricane Katrina (August 29, 2005).

According to the Schools for New Orleans report, in 1995-2005, public school enrollment in New Orleans decreased by 25%, while non-public school enrollment increased by 5%. By 2004, one out of three students in New Orleans attended a private or parochial school-a rate three times higher than the national average for private school enrollment. In 2004-2005, the public and private schools were divided along racial and class lines. While 65% of New Orleanians were African-American, 94% of New Orleans Public School students were African-American and 77% of New Orleans Public Schools (NOPS) students lived below the poverty line. By 2008-2009, the report New School for New Orleans notices the great improvement brought to the educational public school system: "48 schools in New Orleans are public charter schools, serving 56% of the student population", independently controlled with limited oversight by either the New Orleans Parish School Board or the Recovery School District (RSD), or the Louisiana Board of Elementary and Secondary Education (BESE).[290]

One of my interlocutors who has long supported Newman

School, the leading private school comments: "Public schools are in better shape after Katrina, thanks to the charter school movement which becomes an attractive alternative." Charter schools, according to the journalist Grace Chen, "fit in a niche between private and public schools. They are funded with public money (except for their facilities) and they are an alternative to regular public schools systems. Charter schools receive waivers from public school districts in exchange for promising better academic results." And one of my interviewees emphasized the part played by the two universities, Tulane University and the University of New Orleans: "One major player in the schools is Tulane, which determined that they could not attract faculty and administrators without there being a good public school for them. So they are running three levels of public schools, lower, middle, and high school, and with fine results. The University of New Orleans is also involved with one or two projects. Lots of citizen groups have gotten involved in other failing schools, with mostly good results."

Another New Orleans resident, who presided over women's Jewish associations for many years clearly compares the two systems and highlights the attractiveness and the commitment of the greatest part of the Jewish population for public schools:

> *When I was growing up, kids went to private schools if their parents could afford it, and if they cared. Newman was just about the only private school that Jewish kids would go to, so many more were in the public schools. There are a few more private schools available, and as the public schools became almost 100% black, they [the public schools] became less attractive to the community of whites, much less Jews, who traditionally went there. The top public school, a city-wide magnet school, always attracted a good Jewish following, from those who couldn't afford Newman and from those who didn't want to spend the money and from those who wanted to support public education.*

The tensions between the African American and the Jewish milieus have to be seen in the context of a much larger movement. The return to tradition among Jews and their assertion of identity is matched by African American identity politics that is creating a real transformation. The African American minority, as recent events have shown, seeks recognition of its history and a greater emphasis on the teaching of slavery as part of the American history curriculum. This implicates the Jewish minority, which they see as having played a major role in their oppression. There is a current movement to review the history of the relations between Jews and African Americans and to question the collaboration between the two groups during the civil rights movement.[291]

The Jewish population living in the South found itself at the heart of contradictions that were hard to surmount. In the eyes of African Americans, they had the privilege of being white even if their religion was different. They could be slave owners and conform to the social norms of segregation in the South. Yet Jews are eager to show that, in their relations with African Americans, they had been kind and had tried to temper the slaves' oppression by treating them properly, taking care of their children, freeing them, and even sometimes making them beneficiaries of their assets. They employed African Americans in their stores years before desegregation. Though close to the African Americans because they too were a minority group and victims of oppression and discrimination, they had nevertheless not wanted to cut themselves off from the white majority with whom they lived on a daily basis. They maintained good neighborly relations with that majority, welcoming their religious officials and collaborating with them.

The Jewish population was not itself untouched by prejudice. Just like in the other faiths, in the Jewish communities, prejudices against African Americans were deeply ingrained and were the result of an environment founded on separation and inequality. If courageous Jewish leaders and lucid activists fought for civil rights in the South, they endangered themselves, their families and their group by their commitment. The great fear among Jews was that their integrated status, as Jews, could be called into question. The Jewish population in the South feared the murderous violence of white racist organizations and a resurfacing of anti-Semitism.

Furthermore, they were faced with the ways in which militant action was carried out and the integration process implemented. It was difficult for Southern Jews to accept the fact that Northern Jews had come down to give them lessons in ethics and behavior. Occasionally they felt betrayed by their co-religionists from the North, the NAACP officials who collaborated with black leaders and challenged their daily status quo. The "Black Revolution" changed Southern mentalities in depth even if the process took almost thirty years.

However, significant inequalities still exist between African Americans and Whites.

CONCLUSION

Can the term Diaspora be applied to the group of immigrants from the Rhine valley who settled in the South of the United States in the nineteenth and twentieth centuries?

If the Jewish Diaspora is defined as a group of exiled immigrants, some of whom still have a feeling of belonging to a common history, and have maintained a loyalty to their country of origin and to transnational networks, then it is possible to say that this group of Jewish immigrants constitutes a Diaspora. Indeed, solidarity among the Jews of the Rhine valley was an essential factor in their decision to settle in the South of the United States. The immigrants from this frontier region were supported by their relatives and acquaintances. Their shared languages played an important role in their first contacts abroad and their network of acquaintances. Yet this solidarity did not mean that the national and cultural differences between France and Germany vanished entirely. The differences between the two groups became apparent during the First World War, for instance. But transplanted in a new environment, whatever distinctions might have existed became less marked. Indeed, in the context of a new national entity, the former cleavages transmuted into economic, family and community alliances. This is why it is possible to speak of the acculturation of this common Diaspora. Indeed, adjusting to the new country required balancing past and present in a variety of ways. The Americanization process was not immediate; it took place in stages, with "assimilation" being a constant concern as well as the desire to settle successfully.

The most observant immigrants were initially attached to an Orthodox Judaism imported from the old continent, but this changed in the 1870s with their adoption of Reform Judaism. The immigrants responded to the demands of modernity. They also conformed to the dominant Christian models in their midst. As a result, their commitment became primarily charitable, helping their co-religionists in their primary needs, such as schools, hospitals, homes for widows and orphans and the purchase of burial grounds in cemeteries. The building of religious edifices occurred at different times; synagogues in cities such as New Orleans and Montgomery were built in the 1850s while synagogues in the small towns of Mississippi, Louisiana and Alabama, where the majority of the immigrants went to live, were built later.

As soon as they settled in the 1850s, the German and French groups formed genuine ties of solidarity. Daily mutual aide took place more slowly between the Jews from Western Europe and the Jews from Eastern Europe, who began to settle in the United States in great numbers in the 1880s. The relations between these two Diasporas, whose histories and habits were different, remained somewhat uncomfortable for one generation. The first group showed a desire to belong to the new country as quickly as possible, while the latter group wished to preserve the characteristics of the old community, such as the use of Yiddish and an assertive, conspicuous religious practice. Though relations improved greatly due to the financial success of some Eastern European Jews, the frequent conjugal alliances between the two Diasporas and the rapprochement in the 1940s between religious institutions, a fine separation still exists between the two groups.

For the Rhine Valley immigrants, the central reference, initially, was the native country: France or Germany. Ties to the home country slackened in the second generation. The central focus of Jewish identity then became the country where they had settled, America and more specifically, the South. The focus on the host country, which became the "only home" appeared as one of the foundations of Reform Judaism at its beginnings, and shaped the American Israelite.

Starting in the 1920s, the position of Reform Judaism became more open to the land of Israel. And following the tragedy of the Holocaust and the birth of the State of Israel in 1948, the position of the group changed. It unanimously supported the new Hebrew State in 1967, during the Six-Day War.

Sporadic relations with the ancestral lands, France and Germany, were restored and more clearly asserted with the third generation. These relations are no longer superimposed on relations with Israel — the "historical land" — but complement them. Indeed the two countries embody two different reference points: one stands for the founding, mythical history of a people over the long term; the other represents the roots of family history, a continuity of family ties, a heritage to be handed down. Hence the third generation's visit to the place of origin of the first pioneer marks a stage in the reconstruction of group identity. The ties between the different members of the Jewish Diaspora living in the South are growing stronger thanks to united actions of trans-territorial solidarity. For example, many of my interlocutors were very active, before 1989, in supporting Russian Jews and later helped them immigrate to the United States or Israel.

A minority among minorities, the Jewish population in the South barely makes up one percent of the population. Indeed, of essentially rural origin, when these immigrants opted for the South-a number totaling 12% to 20% of the Jewish immigrant population-they settled in the small towns along the Mississippi river and its tributaries. They were a population of poor people; they left overpopulated villages where they had virtually no future prospects and where they were exposed to discrimination and national conflicts. They began as peddlers and after about ten years managed to settle in one location.

Having worked as small merchants, secondhand dealers and artisans in their home countries, they rapidly occupied the position of an intermediary class, adapting to the new climactic and agricultural environment, providing necessary merchandise to farmers and planters at a time when sugar was in full expansion.

The originality of the Jewish immigrants, compared to the majority, was their ability to move merchandise around and their aptitude at setting up general stores in small towns. With the money they earned, or the mortgages they secured on the local lands, they managed to acquire plantations, which they learned to manage. From tradesmen they became plantation owners.

Their ability to move from one small town to another, and after about fifteen years, to larger cities, was a sign of their success. The proximity of ports, as places of exchange and resources, was an asset, and contributed in diversifying their professions, which included cotton sales, business ventures, import-export, and the sale of cigars and valuable objects.

The upward mobility of this population can be gauged by their migration from small towns to the large cities of Louisiana, Mississippi and Alabama. The small towns of Alexandria, Monroe and Plaquemine, Opelousas and Donaldsonville, saw their Jewish populations increase until 1927. After that, the rural exodus began in favor of bigger centers-medium-size cities at first, such as Shreveport, Louisiana, which had 2,000 Jews in 1927 and Montgomery, which had 3,000-or New Orleans which had 9,000 Jewish inhabitants, and Birmingham, which had 4,000. These four cities saw their population increase at the expense of small towns whose populations were shrinking. There were only a few Jewish inhabitants in Natchez, Port Gibson (Miss.) and Donaldsonville (La.), towns that had attracted between fifty and two hundred Jewish families at the beginning of the century.

Not all the immigrants who moved to the big cities became prosperous. It sometimes took two generations. The majority of immigrants typically faced tribulations, insecurity, successive setbacks in "accommodating" to the new country. For all the well-known families-the Newman, Godchaux, Weis, Dreyfous, Marx and Loeb families-legendary figures of prosperity and charitable service-there were countless employees and owners of anonymous stores just managing to make ends meet.

In the South, regardless of financial success, commitment to the community as determined by religious affiliation, is an obligation: "You have to belong."

In the United States, it is not unusual for a stranger or foreigner to be greeted with a question about his or her religious affiliation. This is not considered indiscreet. It is an introductory step in a relationship and shows that religious affiliation is one of the foundations of American culture.

Frontiers between religions exist but they are not as rigid as in Europe, nor is the separation between public and private space. Interfaith relations sometimes lead to conjugal cohabitation. In a more general way, affiliation is a subjective choice, a matter of the heart and the emotions that transcends established institutions:

"The idea of religion is from your heart." This position is linked to a fluctuating itinerary made up of twists and turns. "People who have converted to Judaism can come and go," noted Julia Marcus in New Orleans. What stands out is a wide range of situations in community and extra-community affiliations: priority is granted to individual choice.

From this choice we can distinguish three large categories: the first represents the minority, Jews who are affiliated with a community and are observant Jews for whom Judaism is a religion. Another category, and the largest, consists of Jews who are affiliated to a temple and its activities but who do not consider themselves practicing Jews. The second group in this category is made up of Jews who are not affiliated with a community and who identify themselves as "cultural Jews;" they belong to no institution but they see themselves as belonging to Jewish culture, either because of their family history or by choice. Non-affiliated Jews claim to belong to a cultural or universal Jewishness; they meet with mutually cooperating minority groups, with people of mixed ancestry, and are in the vanguard as active social critics. Finally the third group is made up of Jews who have distanced themselves from Jewishness or have converted to other faiths.

But within these three large categories, there seem to be many different configurations of belonging, as varied as life itself. Individual choice prevails over institutional pressure. Forms of belonging, of bipolarity, Jewish and Christian, affiliation due to memory, or a Jewish genealogy, take on meaning through distinctive narratives and personal experience. A new generation mixes religions and marries into other faiths, spanning every possible variation, from conversion to the balancing of two religions, to the abandonment of all expressions of religious identification.

Parallel to this scattering of religion, in response to the process of assimilation, there is a return to tradition that greatly influences the temple rituals currently observed. This strengthening of the religious can be explained by a need to identify with a Judaism that differs from other affiliations. The younger generation insists on distinguishing itself from the general current. There is a clear-cut generation gap between people 60 to 80 years old, who are attached to a cultural and charitable Judaism, the Israelite's Judaism, and the Judaism of the younger set, who desire greater rigor, spirituality and observance. According to them, Judaism opened itself excessively to outside influences. At present, a process of de-assimilation from the majority current is taking place, the sign of an intensified expression of identity.

Political and social commitment is reflected in the struggle against anti-Semitism and against openly racist political figures. As far as relations with the African-American community are concerned, the position of this group is sharply different from that of Northern Jews. There is a great closeness to African-Americans due to the history of the region. Every family maintains personal relationships with their black neighbors, employees and friends. But demands calling for a greater recognition of slavery and accusations against Southern Jews for being pro-slavery, have changed these good relationships and made them harder to sustain.

Beyond minority interrelations, class distinctions reflect racial differences. The public schools in the big cities are attended by the most disadvantaged populations, who are mostly black. Beyond minority interrelations, class distinctions reflect racial differences. Many Jewish children were enrolled in private schools because of the mediocre level of the public schools. The quality of public schools as compared to private schools, the commitment of cities to improve them, is a major concern. Public schools failed to fulfill their promise of giving minorities access to the middle class. Presently the alternative of charter schools and the profound changes brought about in public schools after hurricane Katrina give new hope and opportunities to minorities. Disparities still exist. The quality of education is of great importance. A public school education enabled my Jewish interlocutors to rise to the middle or upper classes.

The families I met gave me a warm welcome. They were most willing to answer my questions; they accompanied me on my discoveries and were curious about my work, so much so that I felt an obligation to meet their strong expectations. Indeed, my presence as a researcher, my questions and interviews, sometimes sparked independent initiatives on the part of my immigrant informers. Some interlocutors wrote their Memoirs, others began their own research. My work with them operated on three levels.

The first was geographical and historical. I explained to my hosts the meaning of the geographical locations (Alsace, France, Germany) mentioned on their ancestors' tombs. Why did a particular German village become French at a specific date? The distinction between Alsace, Germany and France and the proximity of the families in the border areas were difficult to understand on the American side of the Atlantic Ocean; they saw national frontiers as fixed once and for all. My informers had an unchanging view of their country of origin. For them, the "old continent" remains a land of misfortunes and regression, a land of incessant conflicts, characterized by an absence of liberty and equality. By and large these negative images of the original homeland remain rooted in their minds. They look upon the old continent with critical distance. The country that was left behind is of little importance; priority is given to the adopted country, as though their first aim was to conceal the memory of a difficult past. Indeed the host country is seen as more open and more democratic than the country of origin. For my interlocutors, the legitimacy of their ancestors' departure is never questioned.

The second level involved the family histories of my interlocutors. During our meetings, I was insistently asked to clarify the reasons for the emigrants' departure, the socio-economic and political context of the home country, the complexity of the different regional affiliations (Alsatian, Mosellan, French, German).

The third level was to welcome the descendants. in France and Germany when they made the return trip on the tracks of their ancestors. Indeed, they returned to precise locations, to specific villages, not in order to discover the country as a whole, but motivated by their tie to the original pioneer and his family and from a desire to understand. The return trip was a way of creating a continuity between past and present, of rebuilding ties, but also a way of comparing the imagined country with the real country.

A dialogue took place between informers and researchers thanks to tools, maps, genealogical trees, and the translation of French texts into English. By my research I helped contribute to the memory and understanding of family events, while I myself was helped by a number of my interlocutors who served as go-betweens in my work. The research conducted by the sociologist can bring about an updating of family histories and can lead to new questions on the research subject. The researcher became, over my years of investigation, the intermediary between the Old Continent and the New, a position, which, because of its fluidity, permitted freedom of movement and thought. Scientific knowledge is a work of mediation on distance and difference.

The singular American experience that was recounted highlighted the adaptation and quick Americanization of this immigrant group, but also the proximity and complexity of the relationships between the black and white worlds. While accommodation, defined by the sociologists of the Chicago School, as the second stage in immigrant assimilation, did effectively take place with this particular population group, it was not preceded by a conflictual phase, nor did it lead to marginalization or withdrawal into a community. This group strove to adapt to the norms of the host country. Beyond the big port cities, it scattered for the most part in rural areas. It did not form ghettos but settled on shopping streets.

In order to contribute to the history of immigration it is necessary to be aware of the subtle differences in each of the countries studied and, beyond that, to accept being out of step with some of the preconceptions and ideological assumptions of insufficiently traveled theoreticians. The terrain is a means of discovering truth. A long acquaintance with it is required in order to master the complexity of reality.

ENDNOTES

[1] The Rhine valley: the regions and Länder bordering the Rhine river. On the left bank, Alsace (Bas-Rhin and Haut-Rhin) and the French department of Moselle; on the right bank, the Länder of Rhineland-Palatinate and Baden-Württemberg.

[2] Avraham Barkaï, *Branching out, German Jewish Immigration to the United States, 1820-1914*, (New York, London, 1993), 8-9; John F. Nau, *The German People of New Orleans, 1850-1900*, (Hattiesburg, 1960), 11.

[3] "The Study of Ethnic Relations", *Dalhousie Review*, 27, January 4, 1948, 480.

[4] *Les Diasporas, 2000 ans d'histoire*, edited by Lisa Anteby-Yemini, William Berthomière and Gabriel Scheffer, (Rennes, 2005).

[5] Chantal Bordes-Benayoun, Revisiter les Diasporas », *Diasporas, Histoire et Sociétés*, 1, 2002, 11-21.

[6] Dominique Schnapper, « De l'État-nation au monde transnational, du sens et de l'utilité du concept de diaspora » , *Revue européenne des migrations internationales*, 17, 2, 2001, 9-36. This idea goes back to the first pioneers and settlers, who were sold land at a low price in exchange for clearing it, farming it, and pushing back the frontier of the American West.

[7] Richard Marienstras, *Être un peuple en diaspora*, Paris, Maspéro, 1975, 180-181

[8] Chantal Bordes-Benayoun, *op. cit.*, 2002, 11-21.

[9] Interviews with Rosalie Cohen, Joel Bert Myers, and Abraham Metz Kahn.

[10] Nicole Lapierre, in her book *Pensons ailleurs*, (Paris, 2004), 107, quotes the German historian exiled in the United States, George L. Mosse, (*Confronting History, A Memoir*, Madison, 2000, 217). Mosse describes his relationship to knowledge before his departure to Mannheim: "I remained filled with restlessness 'a travel fever' which was never to leave me while its roots lay no doubt in the experience of statelessness during my formative years with 'The free floating intellectual' of the Weimar years played its part."

[11] Freddy Raphaël, « La haine est clôture », *D'une frontière à l'autre: migrations, passages, imaginaires* (ed. Colette Zytnicki, Anny Bloch-Raymond, Jean-François Berdah), (Toulouse, Éditions Méridiennes, 2007), 13-18.

[12] Chantal Bordes-Benayoun, *op. cit.*, 20.

[13] Interviews with Jackie Toledano, Metz Kahn, Jo Ellyn Kupermann and Julie Grant Meyer, New Orleans, 1992-1995.

[14] Dominique Schnapper, *La Compréhension sociologique, démarche de l'analyse typologique*, (Paris, 1999), 58-59.

[15] Nicole Fouché, *L'Émigration alsacienne aux États-Unis*, 1815-1870, (Paris, 1992), 157.

[16] Avraham Barkaï, *Branching out, German Jewish Immigration in the United States, 1820-1914*, (New York and London), 8-10; Hans G. Reissner, "The German American Jews (1800-1850)", *Leo Baeck Institute Yearbook*, 10, 1965

[17] Nicole Fouché, *op.,cit.*, 157

[18] A.D. B-R, 3M 703, Emigration en Amérique, 1828-1837.

[19] *300 Jahre Pfälzer in Amerika, 300 years, Palatinates in America* (ed.Roland Paul), (Landau, Pfällzische Verlagsanstalt, 1983), 86.

[20] Alfred Wahl, *Confession et comportement politiques dans les campagnes d'Alsace et de Bade 1871-1939*, (Strasbourg, 1980), 311.

[21] Avraham Barkaï, *op cit.*, 8.

[22] Reissner, *op. cit.*, 61.

[23] Préfet du Bas-Rhin, 23 mars 1817 (ANF 6138, préfecture du Haut-Rhin 29 mars 1817, quoted by Paul Leuilliot, *Essais d'histoire politique, économique et religieuse, l'Alsace au début du 19° siècle*, t. II, *Les Transformations économiques*, (Paris, 1959), 33.

[24] Nicole Fouché, *op. cit.*, 56.

[25] A.D. Haut-Rhin,Émigrants vers l'Amérique 1800-1870, list established by D. Dreyer, secrétaire général des Archives.

[26] The following section is based on the *Registre des procès-verbaux du*

Consistoire du Bas-Rhin, 14 mars 1853, 10 juin 1858 et 1858-1863; and on David Cohen, *La Promotion des juifs de France*, 2 parts, Doctoral Dissertation, (Aix-en-Provence, 1980), 101.

[27] Procès verbal du Consistoire du Bas-Rhin, May 24, 1853.

[28] Procès verbal du Consistoire du Bas-Rhin, May 24, 1853.

[29] Procès verbal du Consistoire du Bas-Rhin May 24, 1853.

[30] Aristide R. Zollberg, « La révolution des départs », *Citoyenneté et Émigration*, (ed. Nancy Green, François Weil), (Paris, 2006), 60, and François Weil, « L'État et la migration en France », *op. cit.*, 119-135.

[31] Instruction dated April 28 and October 8 1832, préfet de la Moselle.

[32] Gustave Chandèze, *De l'intervention des pouvoirs publics dans l'émigration et l'immigration au XIXe siècle*, (Paris, 1828), 8.

[33] AD Bas-Rhin 414 D 2154, Départs vers Le Havre, Agences d'émigration vers l'Amérique et l'Algérie, 1855-1870.

[34] Louis Chevalier, « L'émigration française au XIXe siècle », *Etudes d'histoire moderne et contemporaine*, C. Bloch, L. Chevalier *et al.*, (Paris, 1947), 148.

[35] A.D. Bas-Rhin, 3M704, Passagers étrangers en Amérique, Le ministre de l'Intérieur au préfet du Bas-Rhin, le 9/06/1854.

[36] The paragraph is based on accounts given by Philip Sartorius and Rosine Cahn, and interviews with Stanley Dreyfus and Flo Geismar.

[37] American Jewish Archives, Vital Statistics, Family Record, Léo Cahn.

[38] My thanks to Cathy Kahn, archivist at the Touro Infirmary, New Orleans, for having shown me the documents of her maternal ancestor.

[39] American Jewish Archives, Vital statistics, Family Record, Léo Cahn

[40] A.D. Bas-Rhin, 3M 704, Passagers en Amérique, préfecture du Bas-Rhin, 7-9 novembre 1854, préfecture du Bas-Rhin aux commandants de la gendarmerie, commissaires des cantons de Brumath, Bischwiller, Haguenau.

[41] Daniel Levy, *Les Français en Californie*, (San Francisco, 1884); *Le Guide franco-californien du centenaire*, (San Francisco, 1949), 67-79; Annick Foucrier, *Le Rêve californien. Migrants français sur la côte Pacifique, XVIIIe-XXe siècles*, (Paris, 1999).

[42] AD Bas-Rhin, 3M 668,État numérique des passeports à l'étranger, département du Bas-Rhin.

[43] Diary written in German by Isaac Levy, born December 16, 1870 in Lembach. The original manuscript is owned by his son, Ernest Levey and his granddaughter Lauren Levey. It was sent to me by the historian Pierre Katz and translated, in 1990, by Maurice Wolff, a member of the Cercle de généalogie juive in Paris.

[44] Julius Weis, *Autobiography of Julius Weis*, (New Orleans,1903), 5-6.

[45] Edmund Uhry, *Galleries of Memory*, (Leo Baeck Institute, NYC, Typescript, 1946), 146.

[46] Avraham Barkaï, *op. cit.*, 1-14.

[47] Autobiography of Julius Weis, *op. cit.*, 1-6.

[48] Philip Sartorius, *Reminiscences of my Father Sartorius...*,12.

[49] *Memoirs* of Rosine Cahn, her recollections of Alsace, Paris, New Orleans and San Francisco from the 1790s to the 1860s (b. Paris August 18, 1837, d. San Francisco, April 21, 1909), unpublished.

[50] American Jewish Archives, Family Record, Vital Statistics, Léo Cahn, France.

[51] Louis Chevalier, *op. cit.*, 148.

[52] "The story of Geismar," Bernard Postal, New York, July, August 1976, vol 4, 4, 350.

[53] Daniel Soyer, *Jewish Immigrant Associations and American Identity in New York, 1880-1939*, (Cambridge, 1997).

[54] John F. Nau, *The German People of New Orleans, 1850-1900*, (Hattiesburg, 1960).

[55] Carl A. Brasseaux, *The Foreign French, 19th Century French Immigration to Louisiana, 1840-1848*, (Baton Rouge, 1992), 17.

[56] Jacob Rader Marcus, *To Count People, American Jewish Population, data 1584-1984*, (New York, London, 1989), 11-55.

[57] *The History and Legacy of Louisiana's Free People of Color* (ed. Sybil Klein), (Baton Rouge, 2000) 172, 173. Due to this institution, the image of the Creole woman, or "woman of color", is very ambivalent. Because of her status as a "placed" woman she has been stereotyped as loose and immoral, which is hardly compatible with the group's desire for emancipation.

[58] Mary Gehman, *op cit.*, p. 37

[59] Mary Gehman, *op. cit.*, 71, 72.

[60] New Orleans *Times Picayune*, October 1, 1853, quoted by Nau, *op. cit.*, 8-12.

[61] Ronald Creagh, *Nos cousins d'Amérique, Histoire des Français aux États-Unis*, (Paris, 1988), 241-242.

[62] This is the case of the Dreyfous, Switzer and Cahn families.

[63] Recollections of Rosine Cahn..., *op. cit.*, 31-32.

[64] For this part of my analysis I have relied on the work of Cathy Kahn, archivist at the Touro Infirmary, unpublished proceedings of the Colloquium on Southern Jewish History in New Orleans, 1994. Memoirs of Rosine Cahn, *op. cit.*, Reminiscences of Philip Sartorius, *op. cit.*

[65] Howard N. Rabinowitz "Continuity and Change, Southern Urban Development, 1880-1890"; *The Growth of Urban Development*, B. A. Browell (ed. D. R. Goldfield), (NY & London, 1977), 103.

[66] François Weil, *Naissance d'une Amérique urbaine, 1820-1920*, (Paris, 1992); *The City in the Southern History, Port Washington* (ed. Blaine Brownell, David R. Goldfield), (London, Kennicat, 1977); Moses Rischin, *The Promised City, New York Jews 1870-1914*, (Cambridge, 1962).

[67] Read Lewis, "Americanization", *Encyclopedia of the Social Sciences* (Max Lerner, Edwin, A. Seligman and Alwin Johnson ed.), 1942, 33.

⁶⁸ Robert E. Park, "Assimilation", *op. cit.*, 281-282.

⁶⁹ Jane Godchaux Emke, Commentary written for the Léon Godchaux exhibition, (1828-1899), October 16, 1995.

⁷⁰ Freddy Raphaël, *Judaïsme et Capitalisme*, (Paris, 1982); Elliott Ashkenazi, *The Business of Jews in Louisiana 1840-1875*, (Tuscaloosa, London, 1988).

⁷¹ Jacob Rader Marcus, *op. cit.*, 11-109.

⁷² *op. cit.*, 9.

⁷³ Elliott Ashkenazi, *op.cit.*, 14.

⁷⁴ Philip Sartorius, *op. cit.*, 22-60.

⁷⁵ Autobiography of Julius Weis, *op. cit.*, 11. *The Book of Israelites of Louisiana, Their Religious, Civic, Charitable and Patriotic Life*, (New Orleans, 1904), 89.

⁷⁶ Lucile Aron, *The Peddler*, American Jewish Archives, Cincinnati, Ohio, Series Small Collection, Abraham Simon, received November 15, 1935.

⁷⁷ Bennet H. Wall, "Léon Godchaux, and the Godchaux Business Enterprises", *American Jewish Historical Quarterly*, 16, 1, 1976, 52-53, including the unpublished comments of his great-great granddaughter, Jane Godchaux Emke, October 16, 1995, 10-11.

⁷⁸ Edwin Adams Davis, *Louisiana* (Baton Rouge, Third edition, 1970), 203.

⁷⁹ Bennet H. Wall, *op.cit.*, 60; Elliott Ashkenazi, *op. cit.*, 117.

⁸⁰ Autobiography of Julius Weis, *op. cit.*, 11.

⁸¹ Hasia Diner, "Wandering Jews: Peddlers, Immigrants, and the Discovery of New Worlds", Colloquium of the Southern Jewish Historical Society, Charleston, 28-31 October 2004. It seems that in Alsace Jews usually worked as peddlers only temporarily. Freddy Raphaël and Dominique Lerch point out that of the 54 peddlers listed in the census between 1854 and 1870, only 16 were permanent, the others worked as peddlers only exceptionally, or for one or two years.« Enracinement et Errance: le colportage juif en Alsace au XIXe siècle », in Freddy Raphaël et Robert Weyl, *Regards nouveaux sur les juifs d'Alsace*, Strasbourg, 1980, 220.

[82] Stella Suberman, *The Jew Store, a Family Memoir* (Chapel Hill, 2001), 8.

[83] Lerch point out that of the 54 peddlers listed in the census between 1854 and 1870, only 16 were permanent, the others worked as peddlers only exceptionally, or for one or two years. "Enracinement et Errance: le colportage juif en Alsace au XIXe siècle", in Freddy Raphaël et Robert Weyl, *Regards nouveaux sur les juifs d'Alsace*, Strasbourg, 1980, 220.

[84] Leo E and Evelyn Turitz, Early Jews in Mississippi, Jackson, Miss, 1983, 26 in Hasia Diner, « Entering the Mainstream of Modern Jewish History: Peddlers and the American Jewish South », *Southern Jewish History*, 8, 2005, 16.

[85] Edward Cohen, *The Peddler's Grandson, Growing up Jewish in Mississippi*, (Jackson, 1993), 8.

[86] Hasia Diner, "Entering the Mainstream of Modern Jewish History: Peddlers and the American Jewish South", *Southern Jewish History*, 8, 2005, 16.

[87] Hasia Diner, *op. cit.*, 5.

[88] Hasia Diner, *op. cit.*, 19.

[89] Hasia Diner, *op. cit.*, 19, ref. Léonard Rogoff, *Homelands: Southern Jewish Identity in Durham and Chapel Hill, North Carolina*, (Tuscaloosa, 2001), 95.

[90] Actually there were seven plantations.

[91] Ashkenazi, *op. cit.*, p. 13.

[92] Brenda S. Babin, *op. cit.*, Dr Jean Kohn, "Benjamin (Louis) Geismar, trader and industrialist in Geismar (USA)", *Judaica Philatelic Journal*, V, 4, dec. 1969, 721.

[93] Autobiography of Julius Weis, *op. cit.*, 22-23.

[94] Interview with Jackie Toledano, New Orleans, September 18, 1998.

[95] Bennet H. Wall, "Léon Godchaux, and the Godchaux Business Enterprises", *American Jewish Historical Quarterly*, 16, 1, 1976, 53. Such is the case of Julius Weis.

[96] American Jewish Archives, Cincinnati, Manuscript Collection, n° 114, Lazard Kahn Papers, 1821-1961, Lemann Bernard Brothers, Correspondence to Lazard.

[97] Interviews with Jackie Toledano and Benny Toledano, New Orleans, September 18, 1998.

[98] This is true of the following families: Kiefer, Port Gibson (Miss.), Kohlmeyer, Lazarus, New Orleans, Bloom, Opelousas, Jackson (Miss.), Weil, (Opelika, Montgomery), Loeb, (Montgomery, Alabama); George S. Bush, The American Harvest, the Story of Weil-Brothers Cotton, (N.J., 1982).

[99] Information given to me by Herman Kohlmeyer. He is a cotton broker on the New York Stock Exchange and lives in New Orleans, His father had been a cotton broker as well.

[100] Elliott Ashkenazi, *op. cit.*, 21-23. I have based my account on Elliott Ashkenazi's study and information given to me by Herman Kohlmeyer. He is a cotton broker on the New York Stock Exchange and lives in New Orleans. His father had been a cotton broker as well.

[101] A remarkable illustration is the foundation of a small Judeo-Alsacian Museum in Bouxwiller (Alsace) opened in 1998 thanks to the involvement of the architect Gilbert Weill and the AMJAB. A day of celebration of Jewish Heritage has occurred every September since then.

[102] Michel Bandry, Le Sud, (Nancy, 1992), 140-146.

[103] Weis, *op. cit.*, 27.

[104] Isabelle Richet, "Religion et politique, une pas si sainte alliance", *Hérodote*, 106, 3, 2002, ref. *The American South in Twentieth Century* (Graig S. Pascoe, Karen Trahem Leathem and Andy Ambrose ed.), (Athens, Georgia, 2005).

[105] Interview with Fred Kahn on 24/09/1998. Fred Kahn died in 2005.

[106] I was able to interview Charles Dennery II in 1992 and Fred Kahn in 1998. They have both died since then.

[107] Elliott Ashkenazi, *The Business of Jews in Louisiana*, 1840-1875, Tuscaloosa and London, 1986, 21-23. I have based my account on Elliott Ashkenazi's study.

[108] Interview in September 1992 with Gaston Hirsh (zal), Donaldsonville and the website of the Goldring/Woldenberg Foundation, History of the Southern Jewish Life, Digital Archive, Donaldsonville

[109] Elliott Ashkenazi, *op. cit.*, 51.

[110] Reminiscences of Philip Sartorius, *op. cit.*, 14.

[111] *Habits of the Heart* (Norbert Bellah ed.), (1986, new. ed), 227.

[112] Norbert Bellah, *op. cit.*, 220; Denis Lacorne, *De la Religion en Amérique. Essai d'histoire politique*, (Paris, 2007), 178-188.

[113] Norbert Bellah, *Beyond Belief, Essays on Religion in a Post-Traditionalist World*, (Berkeley and Los Angeles, (1970, 1991), 179.

[114] Arthur Hertzberg, *The Jews in America, Four Centuries of an Uneasy Encounter*, (New York, 1989), 116-117.

[115] Kenneth Hoffmann, 100th Anniversary Celebration Gemiluth Chassed Synagogue, Sunday October 20, 1991, the Jews of Port Gibson, Mississippi, Gravestones in the Jewish Cemetery.

[116] Oscar Handlin, *A Pictorial History of the Immigration*, (New York, 1972).

[117] Patrick Cabanel, Chantal Bordes-Benayoun, *Un modèle d'intégration, juifs et israélites en France et en Europe, XIXe, XXe siècles*, (Paris, 2004).

[118] In 1983, a hundred Reform rabbis refused to officiate at interfaith marriages, The American Reform Reader, Michael A. Meyer, (New York, 2001), Rabbinical Opposition to Officiation, 1983, 163.

[119] The complete title is: *The Book of Israelites of Louisiana, Their Religious, Civic, Charitable and Patriotic Life*, (New Orleans, 1904).

[120] Elliott Ashkenazi, *op. cit.*, 105.

[121] For the development of the different synagogues, their transformations, reconstructions and fusions in New Orleans, see Irwin Lachoff, Catherine C. Kahn, *The Jewish Community of New Orleans*, (Arcadia, 2003).

[122] Eliott Ashkenazi, *op. cit.*, 75-76.

[123] Touro Synagogue in Newport, Rhode Island, is the oldest synagogue in the U.S, dating from 1754.

[124] Lee Shai Weissbach, "East European Immigrants and the Image of Jews in the Small-Town South", *American Jewish History*, 85, 1997, 231-232.

[125] John Higham, *Strangers in the Land: Patterns of American Nativism, 1860-1925*, (Wesport, first edition 1963, 1980), 63-67; *Send these to me: Immigrants in Urban America*, (Boston and London, 1984), 117-152.

[126] *Daily Picayune*, April 18, 1906

[127] *Jewish Ledger*, August 26, 1898, 19.

[128] Kenneth Hoffmann, *100th Anniversary Gemiluth Chassed Synagogue*, op. cit., unpublished. During my trips I made a point of visiting the temples and Jewish cemeteries in every city, often on the high holy days, such as Rosh Hashanah and Passover.

[129] Michael A. Meyer, W Gunther Plaut, "The Status of Children (1988)", *The Reform Judaism Reader*, (New York, 2001), 170.

[130] op. cit., 172, 170.

[131] Joel Bert Myers, Interview in New Orleans, October 18, 2000

[132] Kaufman Kohler, *Jewish Theology* (New York, 1928), 445-446, quoted by Nathan Glazer, *American Judaïsm*, (Chicago and London, 1957, new. ed. 1989), 54.

[133] In 1983, a hundred Reform rabbis refused to officiate at interfaith marriages, *The American Reform Reader*, Michael A. Meyer, (New York, 2001), Rabbinical Opposition to Officiation, 1983, 163.

[134] Sometimes, in the nineteenth century, the child of a Christian father and Jewish mother was excluded on both sides and could not find a husband even if she had received a Jewish education: "Her misfortune was that her father was Christian. It was an obstacle to her marriage with Jewish men", ref. *Memoirs* of Rosine Cahn..., 33.

[135] Interview June 2, 1996, in New York with Ruth First (zal).

[136] Interview October 5, 1997, in Montgomery with Rhoda Abraham Dreyfus

[137] Interview with Julia and Sylvia Marcus, New Orleans, March 9, 1994.

[138] Interview with Vicki Lazarus, New Orleans, October 20, 1995.

[139] Sometimes exceptions were made and Jews were accepted into these clubs, such as the eminent cotton merchant and broker, Julius Weis

[140] Hanna Arendt, Rachel Varnhaghen, *La vie d'une juive allemande à l'époque du romantisme. Lettres de Rahel (1793-1814)*, (Paris, 1986, first edition 1933), 15.

[141] Danièle Hervieu-Léger, "Le Converti, une figure de description de l'ultra-modernité religieuse", *Diasporas, Histoire et sociétés*, 3, 2003, 15 and Danièle Hervieu-Léger, *Le Pèlerin et le Converti, la religion en mouvement*, (Paris, 1999).

[142] *op. cit.*, 13, and Danièle Hervieu-Léger, *La religion pour mémoire*, (Paris, 1993).

[143] My interviewee does not refer explicitly to a messianic Jewish group even if it is relevant to think of a Judeo-Christian category.

[144] Interview with Carol Mills in New Orleans, June 2004.

[145] Isabelle Richet, *La Religion aux États-Unis*, (Paris, 2001).

[146] France Culture, *Les Nouvelles guerres culturelles aux États-Unis*, August 21, 2006, « La religion ».

[147] See the positions of Reform rabbis and a few dissidents in Fred Rosenbaum, *Visions of Reform, Congregation Emanu-El and the Jews of San Francisco, 1849-1999*, (Berkeley, 2000); Michael A. Meyer, *Response to Modernity, A History of The Reform Movement in Judaism*, (Detroit, 1995).

[148] Bobbie Malone, *Rabbi Max Heller, Reformer, Zionist, Southerner, (1860-1929)*, (Tuscaloosa, 1997), 92.

[149] Michael A. Meyer, *op. cit.*, 293-294.

[150] Flo Geismar, Interview October 20, 2000, New Orleans.

[151] Bobbie Malone, *op. cit.*, 109-138 and more specifically, 124-125.

[152] Bobbie Malone, *op. cit.*, 92.

[153] Edward Cohen, *The Peddler's Grandson, Growing up in Mississippi*, (New York, 1999).

[154] Reminiscences of my Father Philip Sartorius, *op. cit.*,13, 18.

[155] Recollections of the Weil and Cahn Families, *op. cit.*,34.

[156] Recollections of Rosine Cahn…, *op. cit.*, 38. The original text had been slightly modified because of her uneasy English writing.

[157] Reminiscences of my Father Philip Sartorius, *op. cit.*, 24.

[158] Autobiography of Julius Weis, *op. cit.* , 6-7.

[159] Benoît Fromenthal, 147 lettres, Center of Jewish Archives, Cincinnati, Only manuscript collection, 461.

[160] Reminiscences of Rosine Cahn…, *op. cit.*, 38.

[161] Most plantation women were not ladies of leisure according to Ann Firor Scott in her study on elite women, *The Southern Lady*. Most of them worked hard. A handful of privileged women lived in luxurious affluence. See Sally G. McMillen, *Southern Women, Black and White in the Old South*, (Wheeling, 1992), 107.

[162] Laura Locoul Gore, *Mémoires de la vieille plantation familiale*, (Vacherie, Louisiane, 1936, 2000).

[163] Anne Muxel, *L'Individu et la mémoire familiale*, (Paris, 2002), and more specifically "Un infini désir de reviviscence, des images souvenirs", 23-28.

[164] Irwin Lachoff and Catherine C. Kahn, *op. cit.*, 48.

[165] Irwin Lachoff and Catherine C. Kahn, *op.cit.*, 94.

[166] The opposite is true among the orthodox families we visited whose houses contained paintings, souvenirs of their trips to Israel, and religious objects for the Sabbath. Solomon Klotz (born in Uhrweiler, Alsace, June 15, 1854, died in Napoleonville, May 10, 1931. He was the husband of Fanny Wolf. He was the

elected mayor of Napoleonville from 1922 to 1931, followed by his son, Samuel Klotz, from 1939 to 1945

[167] Anne Muxel, *op. cit.*,17.

[168] My thanks to Max Warchavski (zal) for the translations.

[169] Interview with Jean Meyer, Strasbourg, October 7, 1997.

[170] Elliott Ashkenazi, *The Business of the Jews of Louisiana*, *op. cit.*,38.

[171] Benoît Fromenthal, 147, letters, Center of Jewish Archives, Cincinnati, manuscript collection, n° 461.

[172] American Jewish Archives, Lazard Kahn, Miss Col no 174. Correspondence from Bernard Lemann and Bro, to Dear Lazard and Coralie, Jan. 9, 1887.

[173] Interview with Rosalie Palter Cohen, New Orleans, September 10, 2000.

[174] Interview with Rosalie Palter Cohen, New Orleans, September 10, 2000.

[175] Sylvia P. Gerson, Midred Covert, *Creole Kosher Cookbook*, (New Orleans, 1989).

[176] Codofil, Linguistic Policy on the Net.

[177] Interview with Moise Dennery, New Orleans, September 9, 1992.

[178] Bobbie Malone, *The Life of Felix Jonathan Dreyfus: The Life of Integrity and Service (1857-1946)*, (New Orleans, 1995), 10.

[179] According to the German Society archives in New Orleans, 227, 247 Germans arrived in the port between 1848 and 1858 of which 60,000 remained in the city: *One Hundred Years in New Orleans, Louisiana Centenary Souvenir, Redemptorist Fathers*, New Orleans, 1944, quoted by John F. Nau, *op.cit.*.

[180] Nau, *op. cit.*, 84-85. Beth or Congregation Records, Montgomery, Alabama; Congregation Beth Elohim, Records, Brooklyn, founded September 29, 1861. These archives are in cursive German up until the 1870s.

[181] Anne Rochell Koenigsmark, *Isidore Newman School, One Hundred Years*, (New Orleans, 2004).

[182] Interview with Fred Kahn, New Orleans, September 24, 1998.

[183] About the Acadians, French exiles form Acadia who settled in the Northwest of Louisiana, ref. Carl Brasseaux, *Acadian to Cajun: Transformation of a People, 1803-1877*, (Jackson, 1992), and Carl Brasseaux, *French, Cajun, Creole, Houma*, (Baton Rouge, 2005).

[184] Claudine Fabre-Vassas, *La bête singulière. Les juifs, les chrétiens et le cochon*, (Paris, 1993); Anny Bloch-Raymond, "Ce que nos mères et grand-mères nous ont transmis de la cuisine juive alsacienne", *Regards sur la culture judéo-alsacienne, des identités en partage*, (Strasbourg, 2001), 227-236.

[185] David Goldfield and Blaine Brownell, *Urban America: A History* (Houghton, 1990), 92-122; Rima and Richard Collin, *The New Orleans Cookbook*, (New York, 2004), 3-6.

[186] John W. Blassingame, *Black New Orleans, 1860-1880*, (Chicago, 1973), quoted by Arnold Hirsh and Joseph Logson, *Creole New Orleans, Race and Americanization*, (London and Baton Rouge), 206. John Blassingame, *The Slave Community, Plantation Life in the Antebellum South*, (New York, Oxford, 1972, 1979).

[187] Mary Gehman, *op. cit.*, p. 85; Caryn Cossé Bell, *Revolution, Romanticism and the Afro Creole Protest Tradition in Louisiana*, (Baton Rouge and London, 1994).

[188] S. Frederick Starr, *Inventing New Orleans, Writings of Lafcadio Hearn*, (Jackson, 2001), 191-198.

[189] Rima and Richard Collin, *The New Orleans Cookbook*, (New York,1989), 3-6.

[190] Bethany Ewald Bultman, *New Orleans, Compass American Guide*, (Oakland, Ca, 1996).

[191] Leon E. Soniat Jr, *La Bouche créole*, (Gretna, Louisiane,1981); *Jambalaya, Official Cookbook*, (New Orleans, 1983).

[192] Now, after Hurricane Katrina, these sentences should be written in the past.

[193] Interview with Sylvia and Julia Marcus, New Orleans, September 23, 1994.

[194] Marcie Cohen Ferris, "From the Recipe File of Luba Cohen: A Study of Southern Jewish Foodways and Cultural Identity", *Southern Jewish History*, (1990, 2), 152-153. I was present at this commemoration and I never felt any dissension among the local participants, who had come from different States and had diverse affiliations. I want to thank Marcie Cohen Ferris who was so helpful when I started my research in Jackson in 1992.

[195] Marcie Cohen Ferris, *op. cit.*, 129-164 and her book *Matzo Ball Gumbo: Culinary Tales of the Jewish South*, (Chapel Hill, 2005).

[196] I met with Leah Chase on June 14, 2004. The Dooky Chase Restaurant gets the following recommendation: "Elegant black Creole food. The crabmeat farci, shrimp Clemenceau, the fried catfish, the sweet potatoes and the bread pudding are exceptional", Bethany Ewald Bultman, *op. cit.*, 843. Chase Leah, *Dooky Chase Cookbook*, (New Orleans, 1990).

[197] Marcie Cohen Ferris, *op. cit.*, 146.

[198] Kramer, *op. cit.*, 99.

[199] Barbara Kirshenblatt-Gimblett, "Kitchen Judaïsm", *Getting Comfortable in New York: The American Jewish Home, 1880-1950* (Susan L. Braunstein and Jenna Weissman Joselit ed.), (New York, 1990); Anne L. Bower, *Bound Togetether: Recipes, Lives, Stories and Reading, Recipes for Reading: Community Cookbooks, Stories*,(Amherst, 1997), 3, quoted by Marcie Cohen Ferris, *op. cit.*,146.

[200] Maxine Wolchansky and Beulah Ledner, *Let's Bake with Beulah Ledner. A Legendary New Orleans Lady*, (New Orleans, undated), III. My thanks to her son, the architect Albert Ledner, for having shown me Beulah Ledner's pastry shop, built by him, and which is now the French Maurice Pastry.

[201] Holly Berkowitz Clegg, *From a Louisiana Kitchen*, (Memphis, Dallas, San Antonio, 1983, 1991).

[202] Interview with Metz Kahn, New York, September 3, 1992.

[203] Regarding the subtle divisions between outside and inside the home for observant immigrant families, see Hasia R. Diner, *Hungering for America, Italian, Jewish, Foodways in the Age of Migration*, (Cambridge, Mass., 2002), 180.

[204] *The Book of Israelites of Louisiana...*, *op.cit.*.

[205] Touro Infirmary, (Baton Rouge, 1979).

[206] I met Joseph Ernest Friend, Joseph Emanuel Friend's son, in September, 2004. He is a lawyer in New Orleans and could be considered as a member of the peddler aristocracy described by Metz Kahn, in the beginning of my trip.

[207] *Autobiography of Julius Weis*, (New Orleans, 1908), 27.

[208] *The Book of Israelites, op. cit.*; Julius Weis, Isidore Newman, 75-79.

[209] *The Book of Israelites..., op. cit.*, "Solomon Marx", 89, "Alfred Hiller", 87.

[210] During the funeral of a Freemason, after the priests have departed, it is not unusual for the brothers to hold hands, arms crossed, making a chain around the tombstone. The deceased is the missing link but the chain must be welded together again in spite of his absence.

[211] *The Book of Israelites, op.cit.*, 60.

[212] *The Book of Israelites, op. cit.*, 90.

[213] Let us recall that Louisiana is divided into parishes, not counties like the other States.

[214] Felix Jonathan Dreyfous, *The Life of Integrity and Service (1857-1946)*, (New Orleans, 1995), unpublished.

[215] Ruth Dreyfous, *It has been interesting my life*, 1995, unpublished. Interview, New Orleans, September 23, 1995.

[216] *The Book of Israelites, op. cit.*, 78, *op. cit.*, 101. No date is given for these two events. I suppose they took place in the late nineteenth century.

[217] Jewish Roots in Baton Rouge, information gathered by Peggy Blumberg in Treasurer's Book of Ladies Aid Association, Mrs Richard Goldberger, 100 years of Reform Judaïsm, 1858-1958, Yearbook of Liberal Synagogue, 1977, Archives of the synagogue Shaare Chesed, Baton Rouge.

[218] Hyman and More, *Jewish Women*, 1343, quoted by Hasia R. Diner and Beryl L. Benderley, *Her Work Praises her. A History of Jewish Women in America from Colonial Times to the Present*, (Cambridge, 2002), 233-234.

[219] Jewish Roots in Baton Rouge, information gathered by Peggy Blumberg in Treasurer's Book of Ladies Aid Association, Mrs Richard Goldberger, 100 years of Reform Judaïsm, 1858-1958, Yearbook of Liberal Synagogue, 1977, Archives of the synagogue Shaare Chesed, Baton Rouge.

[220] *The Book of Israelites*, op. cit., 101. No date is given for these two events. I suppose they took place in the late nineteenth century.

[221] *The Book of Israelites*, op. cit., 61.

[222] Irvin Lachoff, Catherine C. Kahn, op. cit., 68.

[223] Ruth Dreyfous, *It's been interesting my life*, (New Orleans, 1995), unpublished, 27-29.

[224] Rabbi Julian B. Feibelman, *The History of The Jewish Community in New Orleans*, Tulane University, Dixon Hall, April 22, 1968.

[225] op. cit., 88.

[226] David J. Goldberg, *A Study of Small-City Jewry in Five South Eastern States*, Paper, Columbia College, Professor Rosenstock, 1975, 26, Harry Golden, quoted by David Goldberg, 27. Harry Golden, "Jews and Gentlemen in the New South: Segregation at Sundown," Commentary, 18 (1955), 403-412.

[227] Leonora E. Berson, *The Negroes and the Jews*, (New York, 1971), 8-9, quoted by Leonard Dinnerstein, *Antisemitism in America*, (Oxford, New York, Toronto, 1994), 195.

[228] Interview with Oscar Levy, New Orleans, September 18, 1992 and *Tablet Magazine*, "A New Read for the Jew" by Justin Voigt, February 16, 2010. See also James Gill, *Lords of Misrule, Mardi Gras and the Politics of Race in New Orleans*, (Jackson, 1996).

[229] This exclusion was confirmed by many people I spoke to: Oscar Levy (New Orleans), Babette Wampold (Montgomery), Ray Rozolsky (Natchez), Flo Geismar (New Orleans), Carol Mills (New Orleans). The exclusion of Jews from elite clubs in big cities was also true in the North and West up until the 1960s. See Leonard Dinnerstein, op. cit., 156.

[230] Rabbi Julian B. Feibelman, *The History of the Jewish Community in New Orleans*, (New Orleans, 1968), 7.

[231] Leonard Dinnerstein, *Antisemitism in America*, op. cit.,194.

[232] On the influence of Evangelicals and their political power, see Douglas Kennedy's *In God's Country* (London, 1996); Sébastien Fath, *Militants de la Bible aux États-Unis : Evangélistes et fondamentalistes du Sud*, (Paris, 2004); Isabelle Richet, "Religion et politique, une pas si sainte Alliance", *Hérodote*, (2002), 151-166; "Les Evangélistes à l'assaut du monde", *Hérodote*, (2005),

[233] Leonard Dinnerstein, *Antisemitism in America*, (New York, Oxford, 1994), 184-185.

[234] Leonard Dinnerstein, *Antisemitism in America*, op. cit., 182.

[235] *Trésor de la langue française informatisé*. Internet website.

[236] *Allgemeine Zeitung des Judentums*, 1839, 159, quoted by Glanz Rudolf, *Studies in Judaica Americana*, chapter "The Immigration of German Jews up to 1880", (New York, 1970), 92-95.

[237] The Proceedings of the Bavarian State, 1846; *Allgemeine Zeitung Des Judentums*, 1846; cf. the debates on emigration in the years 1853, 1854. Debate on emigration: Philippson's editorials are quoted by Olbrisch Gabriele, *Les États-Unis, terre d'émigration pour les juifs allemands 1837-1882*, French translation, Master's thesis, supervised by Doctor Peter Alter, Cologne, 1993, 15.

[238] Glanz Rudolf, *op. cit.*, 85-103.

[239] Correspondence with Lucile Bennett, September, 1992.

[240] Isaac Hermann, letter dated June, 1926, American Jewish Archives. Interview with Bert Fischel in Dallas; Isaac Herman, *Memoirs of a Confederate Veteran*, (Lakemont Georgia, 1911, 1973). Also, Anny Bloch-Raymond, "L'émigration juive alsacienne aux États-Unis (1830-1930)", *Archives juives*, (1999) 32, 2, 91. Interview with Stanley Dreyfus (zal) (New York).

[241] Cf. Bertram William Korn, *American Jewry and the Civil War*, (Marietta, Georgia, 1995). *Jews and the Civil War* (Jonathan D. Sarna and Adam Mendelsohn ed.), (New York and London, 2010).

[242] Correspondence with Minette Cooper October 20, 1995.

[243] Sartorius Philip, *Reminiscences of my Father Philip Sartorius written by him for me*, (Port Gibson, 1910), 34.

[244] Abraham J. Peck, "Sharing the Agenda, African Americans and Jews in the post-Civil Rights, An American Historical Perspective", (Saint Louis, Missouri, 1993), 102.

[245] Sartorius Philip, *op.cit.*, 34.

[246] Interview with Ruth First, New York, June 2, 1993. Philip Baumann Archives, New York. The Comité de l'Association pour le Rétablissement des Institutions et des Œuvres israélites en France et dans ses possessions d'outre-mer included: Rabbi Langer, Henri Baumann, Philippe Baumann, Marcel Belmont and Nadine Greilsamer. Interview with the Société israélite française de New York, November 10 1991. Members included Paul Levy, Julien Weil and René Loeb.

[247] Rabbi Martin I. Hinchin, *Four Score and Eleven*, ed. Martin I Hinchin, 1984.

[248] Interview with Joel Bert Myers, New Orleans, October 18, 2000.

[249] Will Herberg, *Protestant, Catholic, Jew*, (New York 1960), 245.

[250] *op. cit.*, 244-245.

[251] The Episcopal Church is very tolerant of Judaism. It welcomes Jewish families and interfaith marriages and it appeals to the upper classes. Interfaith marriages between Episcopalians and Jews are not unusual among the youngest generation in the Jewish families I met. These marriages are often a path to upward mobility. Episcopalians also encourage interfaith relations.

[252] Interview with Babette Wampold, Montgomery, November 4, 1998.

[253] Quoted by Albert Fraenkel II, *A backward Look, Felix Albert to Felix to Albert: the many Generations of our Family from Rhine to Mississippi Rivers*, (San Francisco, 2004), 111.

[254] Interview with Vicki Stamler, Strasbourg, June 18, 2004.

[255] Voodoo was adopted by the African Americans of Santo Domingo and later Louisiana. It is a syncretic African and Catholic form of worship that includes witchcraft, sorcery and magical practices, as resistance to the oppression of slavery. Marie Laveau (1794-1881) was recognized as the high priestess of voodoo in New Orleans. Offerings are still left on her grave.

[256] Exodus Chapter 34, verse 29: "the skin of his face shone" hence the physical representation of Moses' head surrounded by clouds. (The Bible, American King James Version). The presence of horns is due to a misinterpretation of the word *quaran*. This term figuratively signifies. The

resulting error can be seen in the Jerusalem Bible, based on Jerome's Vulgate translation of verses 29-35, depicting Moses' shining face with the verb *qaran*, derived from *deqeren* (horn): "et ignorabat quod cornuta esset facies sua" (and he did not know that his face was horned). The subsequent *Nova Vulgata* abandonned these horns with its rendering, "ignorabat quod resplenderet" (Moses knew not that the skin of his face shone).

[257] Mark H. Elovitz, *A Century of Jewish Life in Dixie: The Birmingham Experience*, (Tuscaloosa, 1974), 85-86, quoted by Carolyn Lipson Walker, *op. cit.*, 17.

[258] Census, New Orleans, Special Collection 1850-1860. It includes slave owners and a list of their slaves: age, sex, color, black or mulatto. New Orleans Historic Collection, Williams Center of Research. Interview with Cathy Kahn, New Orleans, October, 1998.

[259] Rosine Weil Cahn Memoirs..., *op.cit.*, 42.

[260] Interview with Metz Kahn, Baton Rouge, June 26,2004.

[261] Elliott Askenazi, *The Civil War Diary of Clara Salomon. Growing up in New Orleans, 1861-1862*, (Baton Rouge and London, 1995), 355.

[262] Leonard Rogoff, "Divided together: Jews and African Americans in Durham, North Carolina", *The Quiet Voices, Southern Rabbis and Black Civil Rights 1880-1990s* (Mark Bauman and Berkley Kalin ed.),(Atlanta, 1997), 190-212.

[263] Temple Beth Or de Montgomery 100 years, 1952. The Lost Cause is an interpretation of the American Civil War (1861-1865) that seeks to present the war, from the perspective of Confederates, in the best possible terms. Developed by white Southerners, many of them former Confederate generals, in a postwar climate of economic, racial, and gender uncertainty, the Lost Cause created and romanticized the "Old South" and the Confederate war effort, often distorting history in the process. For this reason, many historians have labeled the Lost Cause a myth or a legend. On line Encyclopedia Virginia.

[264] Mark I. Greenberg, "Becoming Southern: The Jews of Savannah, Georgia, 1830-1870", *American Jewish History*, 62-63; *Memoirs of American Jews, 1775-1865* (Jacob Rader Marcus ed.), 3 vol., (Philadelphia, 2), 95.

[265] 1860 Census, Special Collection, Archive Department, State of Alabama.

[266] I encountered no difficulties in consulting the archives and census information in New Orleans, excluding the periods of flood or of evacuation due

to the threat of fire on the wood building of the New Orleans Historic Collection. In Alabama, even though I was with a city resident, the 1852 Black Code of Alabama was given to me only reluctantly, fearing the use I would make of it in 1998.

[267] For a long time, the Godchaux family claimed not to have owned slaves. Leon Godchaux's great-great granddaughter, Jane Godchaux Emke, corrected this legend: "Family legend and several written sources claim that Leon Godchaux never owned slaves [...] But he and his family did own several slaves in New Orleans during the 1840s and 50s. They were probably household servants", *op. cit.*,3.

[268] New Orleans, 1850 Census; 1860 Census, Special Collection

[269] This is a very positive image, bordering on propaganda. It is true that some former slaves stayed on the plantations as sharecroppers. But the conditions of work were so difficult, the wages so low, and the living conditions so wretched, that many former slaves fled to the neighboring towns or migrated to the big cities in the North, such as Chicago. According to Nicholas Leman about five million Blacks left the South between 1940 and 1970, a mass emigration that led to the growth of ghettos in Chicago, New York and Washington. See Nicholas Lemann, *The Promised Land, the Great Black Migration and How It Changed America*, (New York, 1992).

[270] Albert Fraenkel II, *Backward Look*, *op. cit.*, 92-95.

[271] On the domestic women, see Susan Tucker, *Telling Memories Among Southern Women: Domestic Workers and Their Employers in the Segregated South* (Baton Rouge, 1988) and Kathryn Stockett, *The Help*, (London, 2009).

[272] Clive Webb, "Jewish Merchants and Black Customers", *Southern Jewish History*, (1999), 2; 55-75.

[273] Eli N. Evans, *The Lonely Days were Sundays, Reflections of a Jewish Southerner*, (Jackson, 1992), 7.

[274] Harold Cruise, *The Crisis of the Negro Intellectual: A Historical Analysis of the Failure of Black Leadership*, (New York, 1967, 1984).

[275] Louis E. Schmier, "Helloo Peddleman ! Helloo", Jerrell Hofner and Linda Ellsworth, "Ethnic minorities in Gulf Coast", Pensacola, Fl, Gulf Society and Humanities Conference, 1979, 75-88.

[276] Stella Subermann, *op. cit.*, 26; 63.

[277] Louis Schmier, "For Him the Schwartzers Couldn't Do Enough", *American Jewish Historical Quarterly*, (September 1983), 73, 83.

[278] Clive Webb, "Jewish Merchants, and Black Customers, Southern Jewish History", 2 (1999), 73-74.

[279] Raymond A. Mohl, « South of the South? Jews, Blacks and the Civil Rights Movement in Miami », 1945-1960,Journal of American Ethnic History, 18, 1999, quoted by Clive Webb, *op. cit.*, 74.

[280] Cheryl Greenberg, "Southern Jewish Community and the Struggle for the Civil Rights", *African Americans and Jews in the Twentieth Century* (V. P. Franklin, Nancy L. Grant, Harold Kletnick *et al.*), (Columbia, 1998), 130-131.

[281] Mathilde Dreyfous, Papers, 1952-1971, Tulane University, Howard Tilton Manuscript Department.

[282] "New Orleans Temple gives Bunch Hall for Unsegregated Audience", *Times Picayune*, November 16, 1964.

[283] Leonard Dinnerstein, *Antisemitism in America*,, (New York, Oxford, 1994),191-194.

[284] David J. Goldberg, *op. cit.*, 19; Albert Vorspan, "The Dilemma of the South Jew", *The Jews of the South* (Leonard Dinnerstein and Mary Dale Palsson ed.), (Baton Rouge, 1993).

[285] Murray Friedman, "Virginia Jewry in the School Crisis, Antisemitism and Desegregation", *The Jews of the South, op. cit.*, 343.

[286] Albert Vorspan, *op. cit.*, 388.

[287] Quoted by Rabbi Zola in his article "Perry Nussbaum in Jackson", (Tuscaloosa, London, 1997), 239.

[288] Perry Nussbaum, High Holiday Sermon 1955, Nussbaum papers, Sermon File, AJA. "The Essence of Brotherhood", Sermon delivered May 14 1958, Nussbaum papers, Sermon File AJA, quoted by Gary Philip Zola, *"What Price Amos? Perry Nussbaum's Career in Jackson, Mississippi"*, Mark Bauman and Berkely Kalin, *op.cit.*, 242.

[289] Gary Philip Zola, *op. cit.*, 244

[290] My source is the New Orleans Public Schools Website.

[291] Abraham J. Peck, "Sharing the Agenda? African Americans and Jews in the post-Civil Rights, an American Historical Perspective."

APPENDIX I- TABLES

Immigration tables to America
(Bas-Rhin, Haut-Rhin)
Number of Passports, Bas-Rhin, Alsace (1846-1856)

Delivery Date	Total number of travelers	North America	California	South America
1846	936	207	-	-
1847	1006	243	-	-
1848	1047	126	-	-
1849	1110	190	-	-
1850	952	189	-	-
1851	971	189	-	-
1852	1481	573	-	-
1853	1573	545	76	95
1854	1442	580	98	76
1855	1485	505	81	115
1856	1406	445	63	141

List of emigrants from the sub-prefecture of Haguenau (1874-1881)

Year	Total number of migrants	Number of Jewish migrants
1874	49	8
1875	43	7
1876	22	1
1877	14	1
1878	189	41
1879	49	9
1880	33	8
1881	52	11
Total	451	86

Number of passports issued in the Bas-Rhin, Alsace (1846-1856)

Date	Total	North America	South America
1846	936	207	-
1847	1006	243	-
1848	1047	126	-
1849	1110	190	-
1850	952	189	-
1851	971	189	-
1852	1481	573	-
1853	1573	545	95
1854	1442	580	75
1855	1485	505	115
1856	1406	445	141

Professions of the Jewish heads of families requesting passports (Bas-Rhin, Alsace, 1827-1837)

Total	Primary sector	Secondary sector	Tertiary sector	Artisans	No profession	*Undeclared*
45	3	2	24	10	3	3

Professions of the Jewish heads of families requesting passports (Haut-Rhin, Alsace 1800-1870)

Total	Primary sector	Secondary sector	Tertiary sector	Artisans	No Profession
82	4	1	M :47 F :9	11	10

List of Jewish emigrants from the Haut-Rhin, Alsace 1800-1870 according Daniel Dreyer

Family name, first name	Age	Profession	Birthplace (Residence)	Date of request for passport	Destin-ation
Meyer Aron	18		Uffholtz	26/07/1865	N.Y.
Baumann Louise	17		Mulhouse	1//06/18/62	N.O.
Blum Henri	16		Bergheim	9/12/1861	Saint Louis
Bloch Bernard	29	Butcher	Guebwiller	23/12/1863	N.Y.
Bloch Joseph	28	Butcher	Soultzmatt (Thann)	0/10/1869	N.Y.
Bloch Marc, his sister	-		Seppois le Haut	April 1826	N.Y.
Bloch Jean, Dollfuss (spouse) 5 children	38 37		Lutten	December 1831	N.Y.
Bloch Alphonse	24	Wholesaler	Durmenach (Berne)	14/09/1864	
Bloch Anthelme	21	Tailor	Lutten	18/06/1869	N.Y.
Bloch Aron	24	Lithographer	Rixheim (Mulhouse)	25/01/1868	N.Y
Bloch Joseph	22	Cartwright	Lutten	10/05/1859	Canada
Bloch Georges	24	Day laborer	Lutten	28/02/1862	MN
Bloch Aron	25	Butcher	Seppois		N.Y.
Bloch Aron	23	Peddler	Horbourg	26/01/1857	N.Y.
Bloch Théodore	21	Pelt tradesman	Cernay	24/04/1857	N.Y.
Bloch Sarah	22	Milliner	Guebwiller	12/09/1856	N.Y.
Bloch Jeannette	23	Seamstress	Guebwiller	12/09/1856	N.Y.

Bloch Léopold	25	Tradesman	Guebwiller	12/09/1856	N.Y.
Bloch Reine	25	Seamstress	Guebwiller	16/09/1586	N.Y.
Bloch Louis	27	Baker	Soultz	03/11/1854	N.Y.
Bloch Salomon	16	Tradesman	Guebwiller	10/07/1852	N.Y.
Bloch Charles	21	Textile merchant	Foussemagne	21/01/1849	N.O.
Block François	23	Stonemason		16/10/1865	N.Y.
Block J.P.	22	Stonemason		08/11/1862	N.Y.
Block Catherine	20			08/05/1863	N.Y.
Blum Agnès	18		Uffholtz	27/07/1866	Reading PA
Blum Thiebaut	26	Wine grower	Uffholtz	06/08/1863	Montevideo
Blum Judith	19	Chambermaid	Thann	15/06/1864	N.Y.
Blum Joseph	36	Day laborer	Steimbach	31/12/1856	N.O.
Blumstein Emma and Brunette					
Blumstein H. + brother in law	22	Laborer	Sainte Croix aux Mines	31/05/1854	N.Y.
Blum Chrétien and family	57	Weaver	Angolsheim	17/02/1853	N.Y.
Blum Jacques	31	Merchant	Muttersholtz	May 1849	N.Y.
Blum Madeleine, born Pierçon three children and daughter in law	41		Bretagne (Thann)	23/09/1847	N.O.
Blum Jacques	24	Horse trader	Bergheim	17/08/1849	N.O.
Braunschwig Samuel	20	Tradesman	Durmenenach	29/081854	N.Y.
Brunschwick Cécile	26		Belfort	12/07/1844	N.O.
Coblentz Samuel	17	Assistant trader	Lixheim (Mulhouse)	30/07/1869	San Francisco
Dietisheim Isaac	18	Peddler	Hegenheim	18/07/1866	N.Y.
Dreyfus Félix	33	Butcher	Sierentz	01/08/1857	N.Y.
Dreyfus Charles	24		Mulhouse	14/02/1863	N.Y.
Dreyfus Elie	26	Livestock broker	Uffholtz	24/02/1868	N.Y.
Dreyfus Samuel	24	Tradesman	Sierentz	19/09/1857	N.Y.
Dreyfuss Paul	24	Tradesman	Altkirch	13/08/1849	N.Y.
Dreyfus Lehmann spouse and 4 children	40	Baker	Rixheim (Mulhouse)	16/07/1847	N.Y.
Dreyfuss Benjamin	19	Livestock merchant	Soultzmatt	13/07/1852	N.Y.
Dreyfuss Benoit and family	53	Tradesman	Altkirch	08/06/1854	N.Y.
Friedmann	27	Spinner	Altenstatt	20/09/1865	N.Y.

Georges			(Mulhouse)		
Gassmann Joseph Simon Catherine and 2 children	28	Printer	Lutterbach	17/08/1864	San Francisco
Gintzburger Théodorine	19		Vieux Thann (Sierentz)	20/05/1865	N.Y.
Gross Joseph	31	Peddler	Colmar	29/10/1856	N.Y.
Hirsch Charles, Léopold	17	Engraver	Hattstat (Neuchâtel)	30/06/1866	N.Y.
Jacob François	22	Weaver	Thannenkirch	03/10/1861	Mexico
Isaac Pauline and sister	32	Seamstress	Soultz	11/10/1854	N.Y.
Kahn Goetschel	22	Broker	Seppois le Bas	27/04/1863	Rio de Janeiro
Katz Joseph	24	Tailor	Cernay	11/08/1851	N.O.
Lang Léopold	26	Tradesman	Durmenach	23/06/1856	Rio de Janeiro
Lang Baruch	20	Merchant	Durmenach	25/10/1853	N.Y.
Lang David	21	Wholesaler	Durmenach	29/06/1853	N.Y.
oseph	15		Altkirch (Colmar)	02/05/1860	N.Y.
Lévy Abraham	16	Matttress maker	Hirsingen (Durmenach)	04/06/1857	N.O.
Lévy Baruch	-	Butcher	Seppois	31/03/1857	Philadelphia
Lévy Henriette	17		Cernay	31/03/1857	Philadelphia
Lévy Pierre	17		Mertzen (Seppois le Bas)	20/01/1857	N.Y.
Lévy Samuel	23	Merchant	Kembs	28/08/1863	Washington
Lévy Aaron	23	Livestock merchant	Seppois le Bas	21/09/1867	N.Y.
Lévy Emile	18		Pfastatt (Mulhouse)	28/11/1865	N.Y.
Lévy Lehman	28	Tradesman	Durmenach	11/05/1866	N.Y.
Lévy Aron	17	Cap maker	Cernay (Mulhouse)	05/08/1870	N.Y.
Lévy Marie	27	Ironer	Thann	27/03/1867	N.Y.
Lévy Marc	25	Commercial traveller	Thann	09/04/1867	N.Y.
Lévy Julie	39	Cleaning lady	Thann	29/10/1866	N.Y.
Lévy Florine	30	Cleaning lady	Thann	29/01/1866	N.Y.
Lévy Edouard	23	Travelling salesman	Mulhouse	30/08/1850	N.Y.
Lévy Aron	24	Merchant	Thann	18/07/1854	N.Y.
Lévy Moïse	28	Butcher	Soultzmatt	03/07/1852	N.Y.
Lévy Rosalie	23	Seamstress	Biesheim	14/07/1852	N.Y.
Marx François	19	Textile merchant	Urbeis	28/08/1966	San Francisco

Marx Joseph and spouse	14	Wine grower	Ribeauvillé	08/02/1855	N.Y.
Marx Marx	42	Tradesman	Ribeauvillé	20/07/1857	N.Y.
Meyer Joseph	22	Merchant	Bernandorf (Altkirsch)	01/02/1849	N.Y.
Metzger Jacques	20	Assistant trader	Mulhouse	06/02/1854	N.Y.
Metzger Joseph	41	Merchant & tailor	Kintzheim (Mulhouse)	21/01/1852	N.Y.
Meyer Louis	19	Livestock merchant	Durmenach	08/10/1860	N.Y.
Meyer Isaac	19	Horse merchant	Horbourg	15/07/1862	Rio de Janeiro
Meyer Gustav	22	Assistant trader	Ribeauvillé (Colmar)	07/11/1855	N.Y.
Nordmann Jacques and Sarah, spouse	69	Tradesman	Hagenthal	11/02/1865	N.Y.
Nordmann Joseph	23	Watchmaker	Hegenheim	11/02/1865	N.Y.
Netter Isaac et Ullmann Fanny				06/08/1866	N.Y.
Rauscher Catherine, born Lehmann and 2 children	49		Oberlauter-bach (Mulhouse)	21/08/1854	N.Y.
Rein Aron	24	Painter Photographer	Sierentz	15/05/1865	N.Y.
Rosenkranz Charles	29	Farmer	Wolschwiller	21/04/1862	N.Y.
Roos Arthur	17	Assistant trader	Mulhouse	15/05/1867	N.Y.
Roth Jacques, Louis, Eugène	22	Farmer	(Belfort)	23/01/1860	N.Y.
Roth Michel			Wahlbach	Janv. 1827	USA
Roth Jean	24		Durslinsdorf		America
Roth Henri, spouse and 3 children	39	Weaver	Bourbach le Bas	27/11/1847	N.Y.
Roth (13 people			Colmar		N.Y.
Samuel Henriette	29	Milliner	Bischeim	01/07/1852	N.Y.
Samuel Thérèse	29	Seamstress	Fontaine (Bergheim)	12/08/1854	N.Y.
Sager Thérèse	22		Oberhergheim	21/02/1856	N.O.
Schwob Charles	18	Clerk	Pfastatt	15/03/1854	N.Y.
Schwob Joseph spouse and 3 children	42	Shoemaker	Manspach	29/03/1948	Buffalo
Schwob Paul et son épouse	54	Farmer	Manspach (Mulhouse)	01/10/1846	N.Y.
Schwob Jacques	30	Farmer	Waltenheim	09/12/1858	N.Y.

Schwob Moïse	23	Assistant trader	Hegenheim	09/12/1864	N.Y.
Schwob Sébastien	22	Household servant	Hindlingen	20/101865	America
Schwob Victor	33	Merchant	Melisey-Foussemagne	15/10/1855	N.O.
Sichel F. Joseph spouse and 2 children	40	Weaver	Memel-shoffen (Werentzhouse)	03/06/1840	N.Y.
Silbermann Blaise	27	Butcher	Bernwiller		San Antonio TX
Silbermann Simon + 2					San Antonio TX
Ulmann Lehman	19	Second-hand dealer	Sierentz	28/10/1860	N.Y.
Ullmann Fanny	27	Seamstress	Soultzmatt (Helrningen)	24/10/1865	N.Y.
Ullmann Abraham	21	Farmer	Sierentz	17/09/1857	N.Y.
Ullmann Judas	20	Tradesman	Sierentz	18/05/1857	N.Y.
Ullmann Nathan	24	Merchant	Durmenach	12/05/1857	N.Y.
Ullmann Salomon	19	Second-hand dealer	Durmenach	19/04/1851	N.O.
Ullmann Nathan	21	Merchant	Durmenach	09/04/1847	N.Y.
Wahl Joseph	28	Assistant trader	Rixheim (Mulhouse)	07/12/1866	N.Y.
Wahl Salomon	40	Wholesaler	Durmenach (Mulhouse)	23/08/1866	N.Y.
Wahl Aloyse	18	Weaver	Lutten (Bettlach)	20/02/1860	N.O.
Wahl Henriette	40		Blotzheim	14/10/1865	Brooklyn
Wahl François Joseph	30	Farmer	Bettlach	25/10/1856	N.O.
Weil Salomon	17	Merchant clerk	Biesheim	14/07/1852	N.O.
Weil David	23	Butcher	Wattwiller	30/11/1854	N.Y.
Weil David	54	Carpenter	Mulhouse	30/11/1854	N.O.
Weil Suzanne	21	Schoolteacher	Wattwiller	07/11/1854	N.Y.
Weil Léopold	18	Merchant	Cernay (Mulhouse)	31/10/1854	N.O.
Weil Benjamin		Livestock merchant	Soultzmatt (Dornach)	09/08/1848	N.Y.
Weinmann Auguste	19	Baker	Waldscheid (Masevaux)	17/03/1854	N.Y.
Weinmann Jean	23	Household servant	Gummersdorf	17/02/1844	N.Y.
Weinmann François Joseph, spouse and 2 children	39	Tailor	Thann	29/03/1847	N.Y.
Wertenschlag	24	Bookbinder	Cernay	29/10/1847	N.Y.

Jacques, his brother			(Soppe le Bas)			
Weill Abraham		Tradesman	Dornach			

Immigration to America 1871-1918
Alsatian nationality relinquished by young people from the six Haut-Rhin, Alsace districts

Name	Age	Profession	Origin Birthplace	Destination	Guarantee	Date of request for passport
Bacharah Constant	25	Tradesman	Thann 12/08/1867	San Francisco	1 uncle San Francisco	1892
Bauer Ernest	43	Draftsman	Morschwiller 12/04/1849	America		1892
Bauer Eugene	24	Butcher	Ranspach le Haut	America		1893
Bloch Emile, Hermann	19	Mechanic	Grettling, Suisse, 12/09/1882	Atlantic Mine, Houghton County Michigan		12/09/1901
Bloch Jacques	15	Idem	Wintzenheim, 13/11/1878	Newark NY	Parents in industry	1893
Bloch Jules-Simon dit Sylvain	17	?	Haguenau, 14/10/1894 Stbg-Colmar 1910	Nicaragua		1911
Bloch Léon	17	Tradesman	Wintzenheim 20/03/1885	America	Visit with uncle	1901
Bloch Lucien	15	Tradesman	Colmar	Mexico		1885
Bloch Maurice	10	Tradesman	Wintzenheim 31/08/1879 plus parents	Galveston TX		July 1889
Bloch Gustave	15	idem	Colmar 14/07/1876 and brother Jules 20/02/1878	North America		1891
Bloch Samuel	15	idem	Krautergersheim 20/02/1877	America		1893
Bloch Robert	23	idem	Grüssenheim	America		1/10/97
Bloch			Grüssenheim	New		

Name	Age	Occupation	Origin	Destination	Notes	Date
Pauline				York		
Bollack Alphonse	21	Tradesman	Sierentz	America		June 1896
Brunschwig Joseph	?	Butcher	Mulhouse with wife	New York	Visit with son	13/04/189 ?
Brunschwig Jules	16	Clerk	Habsheim, 26/02/1877	Texas	Joining paternal uncle Tradesman	October 1893
Brunsch-wig Louise	38	Widow	Habsheim-Mulhouse 5/01/1851 plus 6 children	New York	Joining father	1889
Cahen Arthur	19	Tradesman's son	Colmar	New York	Anvers Red Starter	22/02/1908
Dreyfuss Aron	15		Cernay 5/6/1878	USA	Joining uncle	1893
Dreyfus Berthe	23		Uffholtz	NY	Joining sister	8/12/1893
Dreyfus Caroline	15	Seamstress	Uffholtz	NY	Joining parent	25/09/1890
Dreyfus Cécile	18	Seamstress	Habsheim	NY		1891
Dreyfus Daniel plus Dreyfus Flor	18 17	Tailor	Blotzheim	NY	Joining parents	17/11/1892
Dreyfus David	?	?	Uffholtz	America		1889
Dreyfus David	18	?	Blotzheim	America	Joining parents	1891
Dreyfus Edgar	?	?	Soultzmatt 26/10/1871	America		
Dreyfus Elias, son épouse et leurs 3 enfants	52	Butcher	Blozheim	NY	Joining two sons	31/10/1894
Dreyfus Henriette	15	Seamstress	Blotzheim	NY	Joining brothers	14/07/1894
Dreyfus Georges	16	School	Mulhouse 30/011878	San Salvador		1894
Dreyfuss Ida	17	Seamstress	Sierentz	America	Joining parents	Nov 1894
Dreyfus Joseph	17	Tailor	Habsheim, 28/04/1875	America		17/11/1892
Dreyfus Jules	14		Wintzenheim, 7/01/1879	Buffalo	Joining uncles, brothers	1893/94

						tradesman	
Dreyfuss Jules	17	School	Mulhouse, 8/10/1879	Salvador Antiqueza			1890
Dreyfuss Mathilde	17	Seamstress	Habsheim	Oakland		Employed by the Wertheimer company	1891
Dreyfus Nephtali	16	?	Cernay, 15/06/1875	America		Joining parents	Sept 1896
Dreyfus Pauline Aron's widow	49		Sierentz, 26/03/1847				
Dreyfus Robert	15		Benfeld/Colmar 28/04/1896	America			1911
Dreyfus Salomon	20	Butcher	Sierentz Mulhouse	NY			1890
Dreyfus Sara plus 2 children	63		Uffholtz	Brooklyn		Joining children and relatives	9/11/1893
Dreyfuss Jacques	?	?	Altkirch 17/02/1852	Chicago		one relative	1873
Ehrlich Eugénie	20	Weaver	Munster	America			Bet.Oct. 1897, Oct 1898
Ginztburger Heumann Fanny	17						
Geintzburger Gaspar	18		Uffholtz	America			End 1889/1890
Gintzburger Isac Femme	60	Horse-dealer	Uffholtz 1831 24/03/1833	NY		Joining 2 sons	Sept 1891
Ginzburger Sylvain	16	Assistant horse-dealer	Uffholtz 4/12/1895	Georgia, Fulton Co.			1911
Goetschel Aline	22	?	Hagenthal le Bas	America		Joining parents	1893
Hirsh Caroline born Ullmo	Widow		Sierentz	NY			4/08/92
Kahn Félix	12		Durmenach, 6/07/1878	Mexico		Joining uncle	1890
Kahn Gustav Cf. Bloch Jacques							

Kahn Isaac Arnold	17	Tradesman	Mulhouse 13/12/1889	Chicago	Joining brother	1897
Kahn Valentin			Durmenach with sons Robert, 4/06/1879 Lucien	Mexico		1891
Kahn René	20		Wintzenheim	America		1904/1905
Kahn Félix	19	?	Durmenach 29/02/1852	America		1871
Lang Jacques	26	Locksmith	Riedesheim 19/08/1865	California		1891
Lang Jacques		Apprentice shoemaker	Morschwiller le Bas	North America		1892
Lévy Caroline	27	Seamstress	Blotzheim 25/08/1869	NY	Joining brother	25/05/1896
Lévy Fanny		Seamstress	Blotzheim	NY	Joining parents	17/11/1892
Lévy Henri	?	?		America		1891
Meyer Félix	15	Horse dealer	Wintzenheim 25/09/1880	America		1895
Meyer Félix	25	Tradesman	Wintzenheim	America		1903-1904
Meyer Flore and Meyer Emma	14 24	Seam-Stresss	Wintzenheim			1895
Meyer Henri	15		Wintzenheim	America		19/04/1905
Meyer Henri	25 ?		Wintzenheim 28/08/1878	Chicago	Joining uncle Tradesman	1893
Meyer Isaac, son père Isaïe, Bollack, la soeur	17 59	Tradesman horse dealer	Wintzenheim 4/08/1884	America		Mai 1901
Meyer Mélanie née Olf, Meyer Ed Leona, Blanche Caroline	13 55 26 21 20		Wintzenheim	America		1904-1905
Schwab Isidore, Berthe Rosalie (née	40 26	Tradesman	Rixheim 6/7/1859 28/2/1874	Brazil	To live with elder brother	1899

243

Name	Age	Occupation	Origin	Destination	Notes	Date
Aron)						
Schwab Justine plus 1	29		Mulhouse 30/01/1861	America		1890
Wurmser Moïse, Schwartz Simon Cf. Armand	22	Tradesman	Mertzwiller Mulhouse 2/02/1869	San Salvador		1891
Ullmann Charles	16		Seppois le Bas 1/08/1876	America		1892
Ullmannn Salomon	22	Dyer	Huningue	Paterson near NY	With Heymann family	12/09/1869
Heymann Moise	24		Sierentz 9/04/1889	Birmingham		
Ullmo Edouard, Samuel	21	Tradesman	Mulhouse 24/07/1870	Nicaragua		1891
Ullmann Maurice	16	Student	Durmenach 26/12/1891	Mexico		1908
Weiler Michel	?	Butcher	Mulhouse	America		1893
Weill Meyer	24		Mulhouse	America		15/05/1892
Weill Palmyre	24		Mulhouse 6/08/1862	America		1/05/1892
Wolf Jacques	19	Butcher	Blotzheim	NY	Escaping sentencing	4/06/1889
Wurmser Aron	24	Tradesman	Mulhouse	NY		1904
Wurmser Joseph	21	Tradesman	Brisach 31/12/1886	NY		9/01/1908
Additional List						
Levy Gaspard	16		Thann 28/10/1855	?		1871
Spira Albert	19		11/05/1854	?		11/05/1873
Levy Théodor	18		Uffholtz 24/08/51	?		Aug. 1869
Meyer Isaac	18		Uffholtz 15/01/1854	?		1/07/1872
Meyer Jacob	17		26/12/1855	?		1/7/1872
Schabad Jacob	18		Weiler 26/12/1853	?		Sept. 1871

APPENDIX II- LETTER

Communication from Louis Geismar dated 13 March 1906 in Hebrew with the Picard & Geismar Store letterhead

Translation into Judeo-Alsatian on following page

```
                    Picard et Geismar    ,Ltd        PICARD STOR  Dutchtown Ld
   Telephon Call    General Merchants                GEISMAR StoreGeismar Ld
   Cable Adress                                      RESCUE Store Gonzales Ld
   Shipping Statiob
   Postal Telegraph                     GEISMAR,LA  Mch 13 1906
   American Express
```

       Lieber Kusin
Warscheinlich bist du sürpreiset von mir einen Brief zu erhalden und
warscheinlich hast Du fon meinem Vader gehört als ich deinen Bruder
seine Adresse erhalten habe und ich habe ihm einen langen Brief
keschrieben und habe ihm alles gesagt .. an dem kelt was er
erhalden soll von seine Eldern ich habe einen schönen prief fon ihm
erhalten ich habe seinprief in deitsch überschreiben lassen und habe ihn
zu meinen eldern geschikt   Du kanz zu meinen zu schreiben und sie
um diesen prief zu fragen   ich hoffe Du wirst kein Mühe für das
kelt zu erhalten in meinemnächsten mal ich wieder zu Eiropa komme
wenn kottes willen ist in 5 Jahr da werden wihr an dier wider
anrufen lieber kusin ich will dich um ein kefallen zu fragen und
ich hoffe du werst mir es nicht refüsieren wenn ich in deinem
Haus wahre habe ich sein bruder SIMON (Sein n'est pas MXX/ sûr)
peut-être mein)-- sein fodokraf gesehen in deinem albom
        er hat es machen lassen wenn er sehr jung war   ich mochte
einege von dem selben fodografie abmachen lassen und dann werte ich
dir deines wieder zurück schikken   ich habe einen praif von deiner
dochter ROSAJIE kestern erhaltend ich wehr so froh fon iren zu hören
    ist sie wihder kesund meine liebe frau möchte es so kern wissen
ob sie wihder kanz kesund ihst ich habe zu deinem sohn keschriben
wenn wir zurük nach haus kommen aber ich habe keine andwort von ihm
erhlden
         ich hoffe als aich diesen prief in kuder kesundheit andrefen
wirt
          mein bester krus zu dihr und alle die kanze familien meine
liebe frau sent ihren krus zu alle
                       signé: Louis Geismar

(Courtesy of the author's cousins, Lili and Raymond Ullman, Basel, Switzerland)

APPENDIX III- MAPS

Towns and villages of origin of French Jewish immigrants living near the German frontier (*Author's collection*)

Towns and villages of origin of German Jewish immigrants living near the French frontier (*Author's collection*)

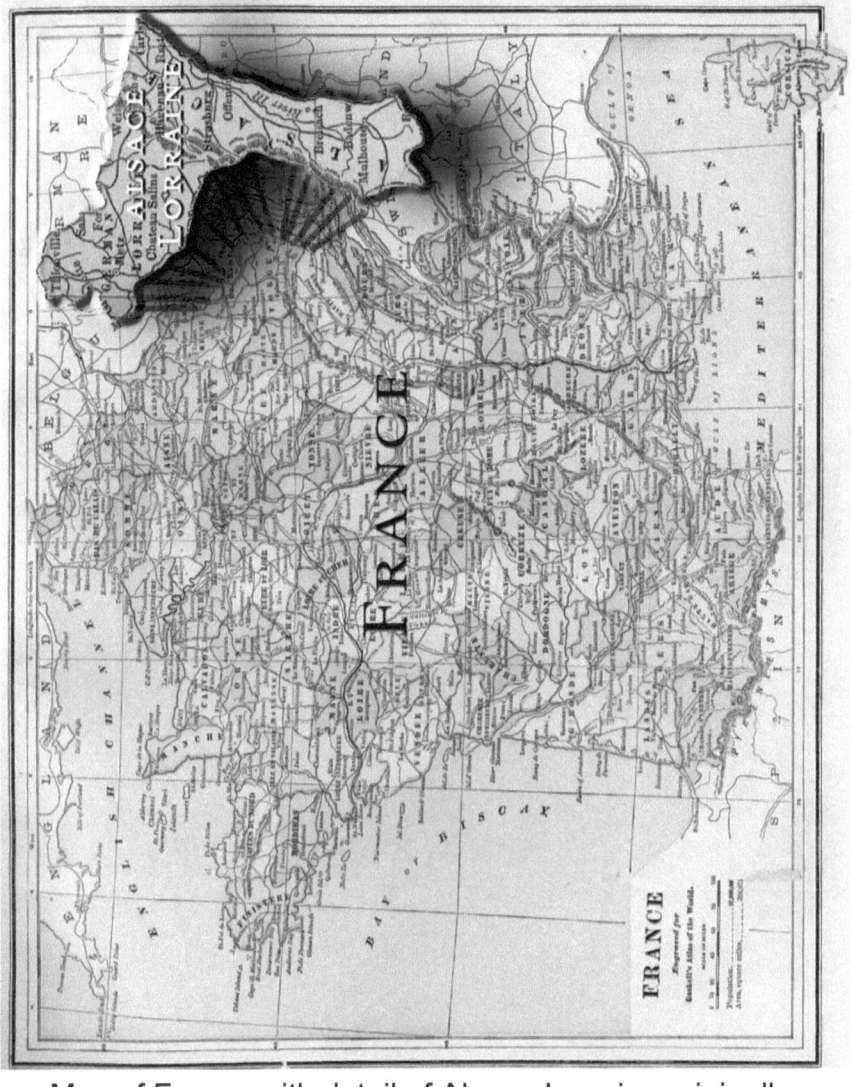

Map of France with detail of Alsace-Lorraine originally engraved for Gaskell's Atlas of the World, 1886

(*Courtesy of the Historic New Orleans Collection, acc. No. 80-545-RL, Gift of Mr. & Mrs. Richard Plater*)

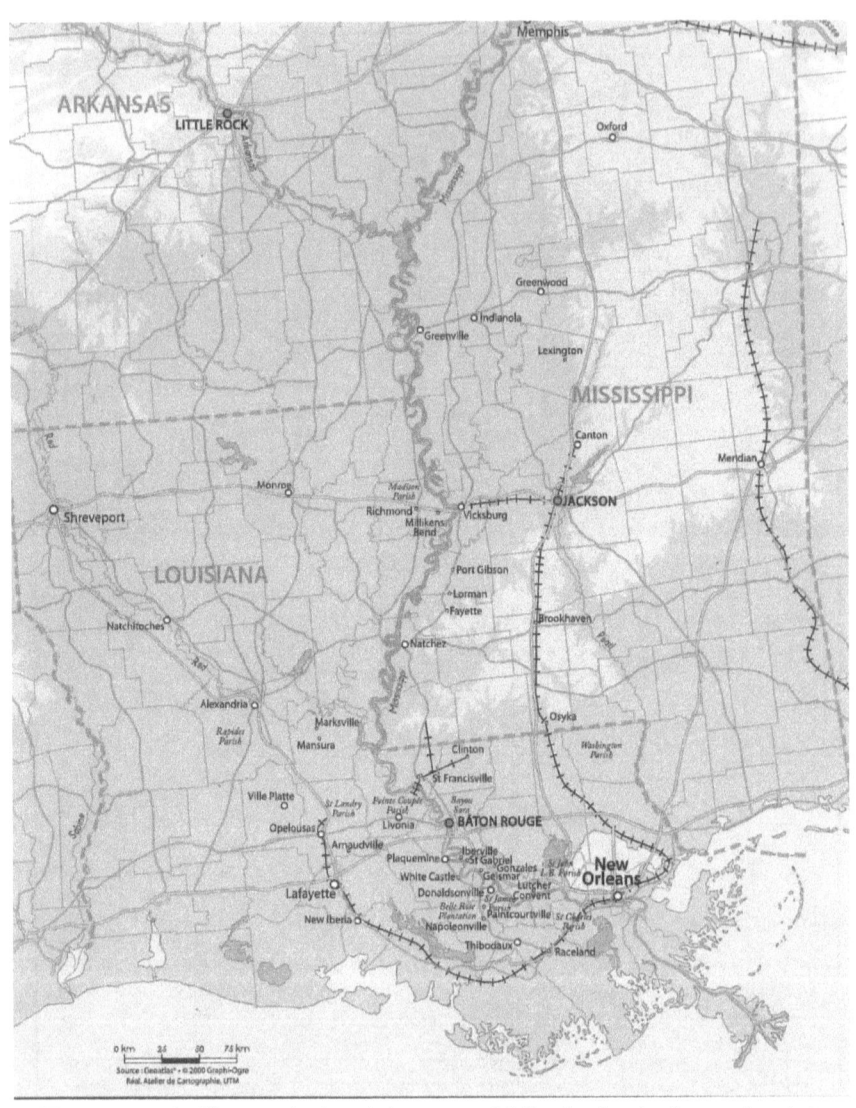

Towns and villages in Louisiana and Mississippi where Jewish immigrants from the Rhine Valley settled in the Nineteenth and Twentieth Centuries (*Author's collection*)

BIBLIOGRAPHY

Archives

Archives départementales du Haut-Rhin (ADHR) **(Departmental Archives of the Haut-Rhin, Alsace)**

Emigrants to America 1800-1870, list established by D. Dreyer, Secretary General of the Archives.

ADHR, list of emigrants from the Haut-Rhin, Alsace, to America, 1871-1918, n° 25 266.

MS714, list of emigrants from the Haut-Rhin, Alsace, between1871 et 1918 established by D. Dreyer.

Archives départementales du Bas-Rhin (ADBR) **(Departmental Archives of the Bas-Rhin)**

Série D

ADBR 414 D, 2154, emigration statistics, 1855-1865. Departure for Le Havre.

ADBR 414 D, 2154, emigration statistics, 1855-1865. Wissembourg district, emigration agency for America and Algeria.

ADBR 414 D, 2154, departure to le Havre- Emigration agencies for America and Algeria, 1855-1870.

Série M

ADBR 3M 668, record of the number of passports delivered for foreign travel, Department of the Bas-Rhin.

ADBR 3M 701, report on the causes of emigration to America (head of police squadron in the Bas-Rhin, prefect of the Bas-Rhin), April 12, 1838.

ADBR 3M 701, Immigration of Bas-Rhin inhabitants to America.

ADBR 3M701, Emigration, Colonization. Circular for mayors concerning requests for passports to America, April 28, 1824.

ADBR 3M 703, Immigration to America, 1828-1837.

ADBR 3M 703-705, Record of the number of inhabitants who emigrated to America, in the years 1828-1837, Saverne, Sélestat, Strasbourg, Wissembourg.

3ADBR M 704, Foreign passengers in America, from the Wissembourg sub-prefecture to the prefecture of the Bas-Rhin, April 22, 1836.

ADBR 3M 704, Passengers to America, Prefecture of the Bas-Rhin, 7-9 November 1854, Prefecture of the Bas-Rhin.

ADBR 3M 704, Foreign passengers in America, Interior Minister to the Prefecture of the Bas-Rhin, 9 June 1854.

3M 704, Passengers in America, Prefecture of the Bas-Rhin, November 7-9 1854, prefecture of the Bas-Rhin to the commanders of police headquarters, Superintendents of the cantons of Brumath, Bischwiller, Haguenau.

3M 704, The sub-prefect of Sélestat to the prefect of the Bas-Rhin, letters dated July 1 and 5, 1832.

Série R

1R 268 33, 1R 662, 1R 695, 1R 696, Provisional inventory of *série R*, military affairs (1791-1870).

Série V

V 565, Creation of schools. Courses in religious instruction at the *école normale*, 1819-1859.

Manuscripts

ARON, Lucille, *The Peddler, American Jewish Archives*, Cincinnati, Ohio, Series small Collection, Abraham Simon.

CAHN, Rosine, *Recollections of the Weil and Cahn Families*, Paris, 1837, San Francisco, 1909.

DREYFOUS, Abel, *Correspondances, 31 janvier 1849-1er mai 1892*. [Correspondence, January 31 1849 to May 1 1892]. Unpublished.

GODCHAUX EMKE, Jane, *Leon Godchaux and the Godchaux Business Enterprises*, narrative, 1995.

Golden Jubilee Temple Sinaï, New Orleans, Tulane University, Manuscript Department, 1922.

FROMENTHAL, Benoît, *147 lettres écrites à ses parents, 28 janvier1854 - 10 janvier 1875*, [147 Letters written to his parents, January 28 1854 to January 1875]. Cincinnati, American Jewish Archives, Manuscript

Collection, n° 461-Diary kept by Isaac Levy, born in Lembach on December 16, 1870. Day of October 24, 1892.

LOWENBURG, MOSES Clara, *My Memories*, Recollections, 1942, Manuscript, Box 1, Special Collection, Mayer Moses Family, Howard-Tifton Library, Tulane University.

SARTORIUS, Philip, *Reminiscences of my Father Philip Sartorius written by him for me, 1910*.

UHRY, Edmund, « Galleries of Memory », Leo Baeck Institute, NYC, Typescript, E. 1946, t.1, t. 2.

Books

ALBERT, Jean-Pierre, «Écritures domestiques», in FABRE Daniel, *Écritures ordinaires*, POL, Centre Georges Pompidou, Paris,1993.

ARENDT, Hanna, *Rahel Varnhagen, the Life of a Jewess*, Johns Hopkins University Press, paperback, 2000.

ASHKENAZI, Elliott, *The Business of Jews in Louisiana, 1840-1875*, Tuscaloosa & London, University of Alabama Press, 1988.

ASHKENAZI, Elliott, *The Civil War Diary of Clara Salomon, Growing Up in New Orleans (1861-1862)*, Baton Rouge and London, Louisiana State University Press, 1995.

BANDRY, Michel, *Le Sud*, Nancy, Presses Universitaires de Nancy, 1992.

BARKAÏ, Avraham, MENDES-FLOHR Paul, *Branching out, German-Jewish History in Modern Times*, New York, Columbia University Press, 1996.

BARKAÏ, Avraham, *German-Jewish Immigration to the United States, 1820-1914*, New York and London, Holmes & Meier, 1993.

BASTIDE, Roger, *Le Prochain et le Lointain*, Paris, L'Harmattan, new edition, 2001.

BAUMAN, Marc K. and BERKELEY Kalin, (ed.), *The Quiet Voices, Southern Rabbis and Black Civil Rights, 1880s to 1990s*, Tuscaloosa, The University of Alabama Press, 1997.

BELLAH, Norbert, *Beyond Belief, Essays on Religion in a Post-traditionalist World*, University of California Press, 1970, 1991.

BELLAH, Robert N., MADSEN Richard, SULLIVAN William M., SWIDLER Ann, TIPTON Steven M., *Habits of the Heart, Individualism and Commitment in American Life*, Berkeley, Los Angeles, London, 1985.

BENJAMIN, Judah P., *The Jewish Confederate*, New York, Free Press, 1988.

BERLIN, Ira, *Slaves Without Masters, The Free Negro in the Antebellum South*, New York, Vintage Books, 1976.

BERMAN (ed.), *Blacks and Jews, Alliances and Arguments*, NY, Delacorte Press, 1994.

BERTAUX, Daniel, *Histoire de vies ou récits de pratiques, méthodologie de l'approche biographique en sociologie*, Cordes, 1971.

BIALE, David (ed.), *Les Cultures, une nouvelle histoire des juifs*, éditions de l'Éclat, 2002, French translation, 2004.

BIRNBAUM, Pierre, *Sur la corde raide, parcours juifs entre exil et citoyenneté*, Paris, Flammarion, 2002.

BIRNBAUM, Pierre, KATZNELSON Ira (ed.), *Paths of Emancipation, Jews, States and Citizenship*, New Jersey, University Press, 1995,

BLASSINGAME, John W., *Black New Orleans, 1860-1880*, Chicago, University of Chicago Press, 1973.

BLOCH-RAYMOND, Anny, « Ce que nos mères et grand-mères nous ont transmis de la cuisine juive alsacienne », *Regards sur la culture judéo-alsacienne, des identités en partage*,(Freddy Raphaël dir.) Strasbourg, ed. La Nuée bleue, 2001.

BLUMBERG, Peggy, *Jewish Roots in Baton Rouge*, unpublished.

BLUMER, Herbert, *Critiques of Research in the Social Sciences. An Appraisal of Thomas and Znaniecki's « The Polish Peasant in Europe and America »*, New York, Social Science Research Council, 1939, new edition, Transaction Books, New Brunswick, NJ, 1979.

BODNAR, John, *The Transplanted. A History of Immigrants in Urban America*, Bloomington University Press, 1985.

BORDES-BENAYOUN, Chantal, SCHNAPPER Dominique, *Diasporas et Nations*, Paris, Odile Jacob, 2006.

BOWER, Anne L., *Recipes for Reading: Community Cookbooks, Stories, Histories*, Amherst, 1997.

BRASSEAUX, Carl A., *The Foreign French, 19th Century French Immigration to Louisiana, 1840-1848*, Louisiana Studies University, 1992.

BRENNER, Michael, CARON Vicki, KAUFMANN Uri R. (ed.), *Jewish Emancipation Reconsidered*, Tubingen, London, Leo Baeck Institut/J.C.B. Mohr (Paul Siebeck), 2003.

BROWNELL, Blaine, A., GOLDFIELD David R., *The City in Southern History, The Growth of Urban Civilization in the South*, Port Washington, N.Y., London, National University Publications, Kennikat Press, 1977.

BULTMAN, Bethany Ewald, *Compass American Guides. New-Orleans*, Fodor's Travel Publications, 1996.

CABANEL, Patrick, BORDES-BENAYOUN Chantal, *Un modèle d'intégration, Juifs ou Israélites en France et en Europe aux XIXe et XXe siècles*, Paris, Berg International, 2004.

CANDAU, Joël, *Anthropologie de la mémoire*, Paris, Armand Colin, 2005.

CARON, Vicki, *Between France and Germany: Jews and National Identity in Alsace Lorraine, 1871-1918*, California, Stanford University Press, 1988.

CASH, Wilbur Joseph, *The Mind of the South,* 1941, new edition, with a new introduction by WIATT-BROWN Bertram, New York, Vintage Books, 1991.

CHAPOULIE, Jean-Michel, *La Tradition sociologique de Chicago 1892-1961*, Paris, Seuil, 2001.

CHANDEZE, Gustave, *De l'intervention des pouvoirs publics dans l'émigration et l'immigration au XIXe siècle*, Paris, Imprimerie Paul Dupont, 1898.

CHASE, Leah, *Dooky Chase Cookbook*, New Orleans, Pelican Publishing Company, 1990.

CHERNISS, Ruth, *Meyer, Max Meyer, 1876-1953, Private Papers (1980)* Introduction Max Meyer, novembre 1941, unpublished.

CLEGG, Holly Berkowitz, *From Louisiana Kitchen,* Memphis, Dallas, San Antonio, Wimmer Brothers, 1983, 1991.

COHEN, Albert Phyllis, *The Modernization of French Jewry: Consistory and Community in the 19th century*, Hanover, Brandeis University Press, 1977.

COHEN, David, *La Promotion des Juifs en France à l'époque du second Empire, (1852-1879,* 2 vols, thesis in Aix-en-Provence, 1980.

COHEN, Edward, *The Peddler's Grandson: Growing Up Jewish in Mississippi*, New York, Dell Publishing, 1999.

COHEN, Rubin, *Global Diasporas, An Introduction*, UCL Press, 1997.

COHEN, Steven M. and EISEN, Arnold M., *The Jews, Self, Family and Community in America,* Bloomington and Indianapolis, Indiana University Press, 2000.

COHEN FERRIS, Marcie and GREENBERG, Mark I, *Jewish Roots in Southern Soil, A New History*, Waltham, Mass, Brandeis University Press, 2006.

COLLIN, Rima and Richard, *The New Orleans Cookbook*, 1975, New York, A. Knopf, 2004.

COSSÉ, Caryn Bell, *Revolution, Romanticism and the Afro-Creole Protest tradition in Louisiana*, Baton Rouge and London, Louisiana State University, 1994.

COVERT, Mildred L., GERSON Sylvia P., *Kosher Creole Cookbook*, Pelican, 1989.

CREAGH, Ronald, *Nos cousins d'Amérique, Histoire des français aux États-Unis*, Paris, Payot, 1988.

DELORY-MOMBERGER, *L'Invention de soi au projet de formation*, Anthropos, 2000.

DILLON, Michèle, *Handbook of the Sociology of Religion*, Cambridge, Cambridge University Press, 2003.

DINER, Hasia R., *In the Almost Promised Land, American Jews and Blacks, 1915-1935*, Westport, London, Greenwood Press, 1977.

DINER, Hasia R., *A New Promised Land, a History of Jews in America*, Cambridge, Massachusetts, & London, Harvard University Press, 2001.

DINER, Hasia R., *Hungering for America, Italian, Jewish, Foodways in the Age of Migration*, Cambridge (Mass.), Harvard University Press, 2002.

DINER, Hasia R., BENDERLY Beryl Lieff, *Her Works praise her. A History of Jewish Women in America from Colonial Times to the Present*, Cambridge, Hardback edition, Basic Books, 2002.

DINNERSTEIN, Leonard, *Antisemitism in America*, Oxford University Press, 1994.

DINNERSTEIN, Leonard, PALSSON Mary Dale, *Jews in the South*, Baton Rouge, LSU, 1973.

DOLLARD, John, *Caste and Class in a Southern Town*, Madison, University of Wisconsin Press, 1927.

300 Jahre Pfälzer in Amerika, 300 years, Palatinates in America, efd. Roland Paul, Landau, Pfälzische Verlagsanstalt, 1983.

DREYFOUS, Ruth, *It has been interesting my life*, 1995, unpublished.

DUMONT, Fernand, *Le Lieu de l'homme. La culture comme distance et mémoire*, Montréal, HMH, 1968.

DURKHEIM, Émile, *Les Formes élémentaires de la vie religieuse*, 1912, Presses Universitaires de France, 5e éd., 1968.

DURKHEIM, Émile, *Textes. 1. Éléments d'une théorie sociale*, Paris, Éditions de Minuit, 1975.

ÉTOURNEAU, M., *Livret-guide de l'émigrant, du négociant et du touriste dans les États-Unis et au Canada*, 1855.

EVANS, Eli N., *The Lonely Days were Sundays. Reflections of a Jewish Southerner*, Jackson, University Press of Mississippi, 1992.

EVANS-PRITCHARD, Edward, *Anthropologie sociale*, 1950, Paris, Payot, 1969.

FABRE, Daniel « Vivre, écrire, archiver », *Sociétés et représentations, Histoire et Archives de soi*, CREDHESS, 13, 2003.

FABRE, Daniel, *Les Écritures ordinaires*, Paris, POL-BPI, 1993, Paris, MSH, 1997.

FABRE-VASSAS, Claudine, *La Bête singulière. Les juifs, les chrétiens et le cochon*, Paris, Gallimard, 1993.

FATH, Sébastien, *Militants de la Bible aux États-Unis : Evangélistes et fondamentalistes du Sud*, Paris, Éditions Autrement, 2004.

FEIBELMAN, Julian B. (Rabbi), *L'Histoire de la communauté juive à La Nouvelle-Orléans*, Tulane University, Dixon Hall.

FERRARROTI, Franco, *Histoires et Histoires de vie, La méthode biographique dans les sciences sociales*, Paris, ed. Méridiens Klinsieck, 1990.

FIROR, SCOTT Ann, *The Southern Lady From Pedestal to Politics, 1830-1930*, Chicago, University of Chicago Press, 1970.

FOHLEN, Claude, *Histoire de l'esclavage aux États-Unis*, Paris, Perrin, 1998.

FOUCHE, Nicole, (ed.), *L'émigration française, étude de cas, Algérie, Canada, États-Unis*, Paris, Publications de la Sorbonne, 1985.

FOUCHÉ, Nicole, *L'Émigration alsacienne aux États-Unis, 1815-1870*, Paris, Publications de la Sorbonne, 1992.

FOUCRIER, Annick, *Le Rêve californien. Migrants français sur la côte pacifique, XVIIIe-XXe siècle*, Paris, Belin, 1999.

FUCHS, Lawrence H., *The American Kaleidoscope, Race, Ethnicity, and the Civic Culture*, Hanover and London, University Press of New England, 1990.

GABACCIA, Donna, *From the Other Side, Women, Gender and Immigrant Life in the US, 1820-1990*, Bloomington and Indianapolis, Indian University Press,1994.

GAGNON, Nicole, « On the Analysis of Life Accounts » in *Biography and Society, The Life History Approach in the Social Sciences*, ed. Daniel Bertaux.

GEHMAN, Mary, *Introduction, The Free People of Color of New Orleans*, New Orleans, Margaret Media, 1994.

GLAZER, Nathan, *American Judaïsm*, 1957, University of Chicago Press, new edition, 1989.

GLAZER, Nathan, MOYNIHAN, Daniel P., *Beyond the Melting Pot, The Negroes, Puerto-Ricans, Jews, Italians, and Irish of New York City*, MIT, 1963, 1970, 1990.

GOLDBERG, David J., *A Study of Small Community Jewry in Five Southern Eastern States*, Columbia College, 1974.

GOLDFIELD, David, BROWNELL, Blaine, *Urban America: A History*, 2nd edition, Houghton, Mifflin, 1990.

GRAFMEYER, Y., JOSEPH, I., *L'École de Chicago, naissance de l'écologie urbaine*, Paris, Aubier, 1994.

GREEN, Nancy L., *Repenser les migrations*, PUF, 2002.

GREEN, Nancy L., *Du sentier à la 7e Avenue, la confection et les immigrés, Paris, New York, 1880-1980*, Paris, Seuil, 1997.

GREEN, Nancy, *Et ils peuplèrent l'Amérique, L'odyssée des émigrants*, Paris, Gallimard, 1994.

GREEN, Nancy et WEIL François, (éd.) *Citoyenneté et émigration. Les politiques du départ,* Paris, EHESS, 2006.

GREENBERG, Cheryl Lynn, *Troubling the Waters, Black-Jewish Relations in The American Century*, Princeton and Oxford, Princeton University Press, 2006.

HAARSCHER, André, « Il y a 150 ans : la révolution de 1848 et les mouvements anti-juifs dans la région de Saverne », *Société* d'histoire des israélites d'Alsace et de Lorraine, XX° colloque, 7, 8 février, 1999.

HAGY, William, *Jews of Charleston, This Happy Land, The Jews of Colonial Antebellum*, Charleston, Tuscaloosa, London, University of Alabama Press, 1993.

HALBWACHS, Maurice, *Les Cadres sociaux de la mémoire*, Paris, 1° éd., Librairie Alcan, 1925, Albin Michel, 1994

HALBWACHS, Maurice, *La Mémoire collective*, Paris, Presses Universitaires de France, 1950, nv éd., Albin Michel, 1997.

HALFF, Sylvain, *La Fidélité française des israélites d'Alsace et de Lorraine (1871-1918),* Paris, Librairie Durlacher, 1921.

HAMILTON, Malcolm B., *The Sociology of Religion, Theoretical and Comparative Perspectives*, London and New York, Routledge, 1995.

HANDLIN, Oscar, *A Pictorial History of the Immigration*, New York, Crown Publishers, 1972.

HANDLIN, Oscar, *The Uprooted*, Little Brown Company, 1951, 1973.

HANSEN, Marcus Lee, *The Atlantic Migration, 1607-1860*, New York, Harper Row, 1940, 1961.

Harvard Encydopedia of American Ethnic Groups, THERNSTROM, Stephan, HANDLIN, Oscar.

HAYIM, Yosef Yerushalmi, *Zakhor, histoire juive et mémoire juive*, Paris, La Découverte, 1984.

HERMAN, Isaac, *Memoirs of a Confederate Veteran*, CSA Press, Lakemont Georgia, 1911.

HERVIEU-LEGER, Danièle, *La Religion pour mémoire*, Paris, Le Cerf, 1993.

HERVIEU-LEGER, Danièle, *Le Pèlerin et le converti, la religion en mouvement,* Paris, Flammarion, 1999.

HEFFER, Jean, WEIL François (dir.), *Chantiers d'histoire américaine*, Paris, Belin, 1994.

HERBERG, Will, *Protestant, Catholic, Jew*, New York, Double Day, 1960.

HEARN, Lafcadio, *Inventing New Orleans, writings of Lafcadio Hearn*, Edited by S. Fredrick Starr, Jackson, University Press of Mississippi, 2001.

HERMAN, Isaac, *Memoirs of a Confederate veteran*, CSA Press, Lakemont Georgia, 1911, 1973.

HERTZBERG, Arthur, *The Jews in America, Four Centuries of an Uneasy Encounter*, New York, Simon & Shuster, 1989.

HINCHIN, Martin I (Rabbi), *Four Score and Eleven*, ed. Martin.I. Hinchin, 1984.

HIGHAM, John, *Send These To Me: Immigrants in Urban America*, Baltimore, John Hopkins University Press, 1984.

HIGHAM, John, *Strangers in the Land: Patterns of American Nativism, 1860-1925*, Westport, Conn., Greenwood Press, 1980, 1963.

HIRSCH, Arnold R. and LOGSON Joseph (ed.), *Creole New Orleans, Race and Americanization*, Baton Rouge and London, Louisiana State University Press, 1991.

HOWE, Irving, *World of our Fathers, The Journey of the East European Jews to America and the Life They Found and Made*, New York, Schocken Books, 1976.

HUGHES, Everett C., *Le Regard sociologique, Essais choisis*, Textes rassemblés et présentés par CHAPOULIE Jean-Michel, Paris, École des hautes études en sciences sociales, 1996.

HYMAN, Paula E., « Des Juifs d'Alsace », in BIRNBAUM Pierre, *Histoire politique des Juifs de France*, Paris, Presses de la FNSP, 1990.

HYMAN, Paula E., *The Emancipation of Jews of Alsace: Acculturation and Tradition in the Ninetieth Century*, New Haven and London, Yale University Press, 1991.

Inventory of the Church and Synagogue Archives of Louisiana, Jewish Congregations and organisations, The Louisiana Historical Records Survey, Division of Community Service Programs, Work Projects Administration, Department of Archives, Louisiana State University, 1941.

JACQUIN, Philippe, ROYOT Daniel, WHITFIELD Stephen, *Le Peuple américain, origines, immigration, ethnicité et identité*, Paris, Seuil, 2000.

JOUTARD, Philippe, *Ces voix qui nous viennent du passé*, Paris, Hachette, 1983.

KAGANOFF, Nathan M., UROFSKY Melvin I., (ed.), *Turn to the South, Essays on Southern Jewry*, Charlottesville, University Press of Virginia, 1979.

KANE, Harnett T., *Queen New Orleans, City by the River*, New York, William Morrow & Company, 1949.

KAPLAN, Ben, *The Eternal Stranger*, New York, Bookhaven, 1957.

KASPI, André, *Les Juifs américains. Les Juifs américains ont-ils réellement le pouvoir qu'on leur prête*, Paris, Plon, 2008.

KAUFFMANN, Uri R., « Das Judische Schulwesen auf dem Lande Baden aund Elsass im Vergleich 1770-1848 » in RICHARZ Monika, RÜRUP Reinhard, (hereausgeben) *Judisches Leben auf dem Lande, Studien zur deutsch-judischen Geshischte*, Tübingen, Mohr Siebeck, 1993.

KINTZ, Jean-Pierre, « Une enquête administrative sur l'émigration en Amérique sous la monarchie de Juillet, le cas des Alsaciens », *Mélanges offerts à DUPAQUIER Jacques, Mesurer et comprendre*, PUF, 1993.

KIRSHENBLATT-GIMBLETT, Barbara. « Kitchen Judaism », *Getting Comfortable in New York: The American Jewish Home, 1880-1950*, ed. Susan L. Braunstein and Jenna Weissman, New York, The Jewish Museum, 1990.

KLEIN, Sybil (ed.), *Creole, The History and Legacy of Louisiana's Free People of Color*, Baton Rouge, Louisiana State University Press, 2000.

KOENISGSMARK, Anne Rochell, *Isidore Newman School one Hundred Years*, New Orleans 2004.

KOHLER Kaufman, *Jewish Theology*, New York, 1928.

KORN, Bertram William, *The Early Jews of New Orleans*, American Jewish' Historical Society, Waltham Mass., 1969.

KORN, Bertram William, *Jews and Negro Slavery in the old South*, 1789-1865, Elkin Park, Pa, 1961.

KORN, Bertram William, *American Jewry and the Civil War*, Marietta, Georgia, Bellum Edition, 1995.

KRAMER, Bertha F. , «*Aunt Babette's* » *Cook Book. Foreign and Domestic Receipts for the Household. A valuable collection of receipts and hints for the housewife, many of which are not to be found elsewhere*, Cincinnati and Chicago, The Bloch Publishing and Printing Co, 1897.

KRAUSE, Allen, « Rabbis and the Negro, Rights in the South », 1954-1967 in *Jews in the South*, Leonard Dinnerstein and Mary Dale Palsson, Baton Rouge, LSU, 1973.

LACHOFF, Irwin, KAHN Catherine C., *The Jewish Community of New Orleans*, Arcadia, 2005.

LACORNE, Denis, *La Crise de l'identité américaine, du melting pot au multiculturalisme*, Paris, Fayard, 1997.

LACORNE, Denis, *De La Religion en Amérique Essai d'histoire politique,* Paris, Gallimard, 2007.

LAPIERRE, Nicole, *Pensons ailleurs*, Paris, Stock, 2004.

LAVENDER, Abraham D., « Jewish Values in the Southern Milieu », in *Turn to the South*, ed. Nathan M. Kaganoff and Melvin I. Urofsky, Charlottesville, University Press of Virginia, 1979.

LAYBOURN, Norman, *Contribution à l'histoire des Alsaciens et des Lorrains du XVIIIe au XXe siècles et les Strasbourg à travers le monde*, thèse de 3e cycle [doctoral history thesis], Strasbourg, 1983, 3 vols., published by the *Association des publications auprès des universités de Strasbourg*, 1986, 2 volumes.

LE GOFF, Jacques, *Histoire et Mémoire*, Paris, Gallimard, 1988.

LERDA, Valeria (dir.), *From melting Pot to Multiculturalism: the Evolution of Ethnic Relations in the United States and Canada*, Rome, Bulzonni Editore, 1990.

LEMANN, Nicholas, *The Promised Land, The Great Black Migration and how it Changed America*, New York, Random House, 1992.

LEUILLIOT, Paul, *Essais d'histoire politique, économique et religieuse, l'Alsace au début du 19e siècle*, t. II, *Les Transformations économiques*, Paris, SEVPEN, 1959.

LOCOUL-GORE, Laura, *Mémoires de la vieille plantation familiale*, Vacherie Louisiane, Zoe Company, 1936, 2000.

LUEBKE, Frederich C., « Alsatians » in THERNSTROM Stephan, ORLOV Ann, HANDLIN Oscar, (ed.), *Harvard, Encyclopedia of American Ethnic Groups*, Cambridge (Mass.), Harvard University Press, 1980.

MACMILLEN, Sally G., *Southern Women, Black and White in the Old South*, Wheeling, Harlan Davidson, 1992.

MAIRE, Camille, *L'Émigration des Lorrains en Amérique*, Metz, Centre de recherches internationales de l'université de Metz, 1980.

MALONE, Bobbie, *Rabbi Max Heller, Reformer, Zionist, Southerner, (1860-1929)*, Tuscaloosa and London, University of Alabama Press, 1997.

MARCUS, Jacob Rader, *United States Jewry, 1776-1985*, Detroit, Wayne State University Press, 1989.

MARCUS, Jacob Rader, *To Count People, American Jewish Population, data 1584-1984*, United Press of America, New York, London, 1989.

MARCUS, Jacob Rader, *The American Jew (1585-1990)*, Brooklyn, NY, Carlson, 1995.

MARIENSTRAS, Richard, *Être un peuple en diaspora*, Maspéro, Paris, 1975.

MEIER, August and RUDWICK, Eliott, *From Plantation to Ghetto*, New York, Hill and Wang, 1966.

MEYER, Michael A., *Response to Modernity, A History of The Reform Movement in Judaism*, Wayne State University Press, 1995.

MILLS-NICHOL, Carol, *The Forgotten Jews of Avoyelles Parish, Louisiana*, Santa Maria, CA: Janaway Publishing, 2012.

MORAWASKA, Ewa, *Insecure Prosperity, Small-Town Jews in Industrial America, 1890-1940*, Princeton, N.J., Princeton University Press, 1996.

MORIN, Edgar, *Le Monde moderne et la question juive*, Paris,Le Seuil, 2006.

MORIN, Louis, *La Méthodologie de l'histoire de vie, sa spécificité, son analyse*, Québec, Université Laval, 1973.

MUXEL, Anne, *L'Individu et la mémoire familiale*, Paris, Nathan, 2002.

MYERS, W.E. *The Israelites of Louisiana: their Religious, Civic, Charitable, and Patriotic Life*, New Orleans, Myers, 1904.

NAU, John F., *The German People of New Orleans, 1850-1900*, University of Southern Mississippi, Hattisbourg, n.d.

NETTER, Nathan, *La Patrie absente et la patrie retrouvée. Sermons patriotiques et allocutions patriotiques*, Metz, 1929.

PASCOE, Craig S., LEATHEM TRAHAN Karen and AMBROSE Andy (ed.), *The American South in the Twentieth Century,* Athens, Georgia, 2005.

PECK, Abraham J., *Sharing the Agenda? African-Americans and Jews in the post-Civil Rights: an American Historical Perspective*, Washington University, Saint Louis, Missouri, 1993.

PICHON, Muriel, *Les Français israélites de 1918 au milieu des années cinquante, Histoire, mémoires, représentations, études d'itinéraires*, thèse de 3e cycle [doctoral thesis], Toulouse, 2 vols, 2003.

POIRIER, Jean, CLAPIER-VALLADON Simone, RAYBAUT Paul, *Les Récits de vie. Théorie et pratique*, Paris, PUF, 1983.

POUTIGNAT, Philippe, STREIFF-FENART Jocelyne, *Théories de l'ethnicité*, suivi de BARTH Frédérik, *Les groupes ethniques et leurs frontières*, Paris, Presses Universitaires de France, 1995.

ROUGÉ, Robert, *Les Immigrations européennes aux États-Unis (1880-1910)*, Paris, 1987.

RABINOWITZ, Howard N., *Continuity and Change, Southern Urban Development, 1880-1900, The City in Southern History, The Growth of Urban Civilization in the South,* Blaine A. Brownell and David R. Goldfield (ed.), Port Washington N Y, Keniyat Press, 1977.

RAPHAËL, Freddy, WEYL, Robert, *Juifs en Alsace*, Toulouse, Privat, 1977.

RAPHAËL, Freddy and LERCH Dominique, « Enracinement et Errance : le colportage juif en Alsace au XIXe siècle », in Freddy Raphaël et Robert Weyl, *Regards nouveaux sur les juifs d'Alsace*, Strasbourg, Istra, 1980,

RAPHAËL, Freddy, *Judaïsme et capitalisme, essai sur la controverse entre Max Weber et Werner Sombart*, Presses universitaires de France, 1982.

RAPHAËL, Freddy, « Rôdeur de frontières ou l'entre deux », Toulouse, Proceedings of the Colloquium *Passer, dépasser les frontières*, May 2004, ed. by Colette Zytnicki, Anny Bloch-Raymond, Jean François Berdah), and the book *D'une Frontière à l'autre: migrations, passages, imaginaires*, (ed. by Colette Zytnicki, Anny Bloch-Raymond, Jean François Berdah,),Toulouse, éditions méridiennes, 2007.

REINHARZ, J., and SCHATZBERG, W., *The Jewish Response to German Culture. From the Enlightenment to the Second World War*, Hannover, London, University Press of New England 1985.

RICHARZ, Monika, RÜRUP Reinhard (Hereausgeben), *Jüdisches Leben auf dem Lande, Studien zur deutsch-judischen Geschischte*, Tübingen, Mohr-Siebeck, 1993.

RICHET, Isabelle, *La Religion aux États-Unis*, Presses universitaires de France, 2001.

RICŒUR, Paul, *La Mémoire, l'histoire, l'oubli*, Paris, Seuil, 2000.

ROSENGARTEN, Theodore, ROSENGARTEN Dale, *A portion of the People, Three Hundred Years of Southern Jewish life*, Carolina, University of South Carolina Press, 2002.

ROTH, Henry, *L'Or de la terre promise*, Paris, Grasset, 1989.

RÜRUP, Reinhard, « The European revolution of 1848 and Jewish Emancipation » , *in Revolution and Evolution 1848 in German-Jewish History*, Werner, A. Mosse, Arnold Paucker, Reihard Rürup (ed.), Tübingen, Mohr, 1981.

SACHTEL, Bernard, *Jewish Life in Natchez, 1934-1966*, Cincinnati, Ohio, HUC, 1971.

SCHNAPPER, Dominique, *La Relation à l'autre. Au cœur de la pensée sociologique*, Paris, Gallimard, 1998.

SCHNAPPER, Dominique, *La Compréhension sociologique. Démarche de l'analyse typologique*, Paris, Presses universitaires de France, 1999.

SCHNAPPER, Dominique, « Modèle des israélites ou modèle démocratique », in *Juifs ou Israélites en France et en Europe aux XIXe et XXe siècles* (Patrick CABANEL, Chantal BORDES-BENAYOUN), Paris, Berg International, 2004.

SCHNURMANN, Erwin, *La Statistique de la population juive de Strasbourg*, Strasbourg, 1933.

SCHWARZFUCHS, Simon, *Du Juif à l'israélite, histoire d'une mutation, 1770-1870*, Paris, Fayard, 1989.

SEGALEN, Martine and LE WITA Béatrix (dir.), *Chez soi, objets et décors: des créations familiales*, Paris, ed. Autrement, 1993.

SIMONS, Andrew and The Greater New Orleans Archivists, Introd. Irwin LACHOFF, Lester SULLIVAN, New Orleans, *Jews of New Orleans, An Archival Guide*, 1998.

SIMMEL, Georg, « Le Pont et la porte » in *Tragédie de la culture*, 1908, Paris, Rivages, 1988.

SIMMEL, Georg, *La Philosophie de l'aventure, principe de philosophie relativiste*, Félix Alcan, 1912, Paris, L'Arche, 2002, (previously published as «Mélanges de philosophie relativiste »).

SINGAL, Daniel Joseph, *The War Within. From Victorian to Modernist Thought in the South, 1919-1945*, Chapel Hill, 1982.

SOLLORS, Werner, *Beyond Ethnicity, Consent and Descent in American Culture*, New York, Oxford, Oxford University Press, 1986.

SONIAT, Leon E. Jr., *La Bouche créole*, Gretna Louisiane, Pelican, 1981.

SOYER, Daniel, *Jewish Immigrant Associations and American Identity in New York, 1880-1939*, Cambridge, Massachusetts, London, England, Harvard University Press, 1997.

STARR, S. Frederick, *Inventing New Orleans: Writings of Lafcadio Hearn*, Jackson, University Press of Mississippi, 2001.

STEINBERG, Stephen, *The Ethnic Myth: Race Ethnicity and Class in America,* Boston, Bacon Press, 1981, *Louisiana Historical Quarterly*, 1942.

SUBERMAN, Stella, *The Jew Store, a Family Memoir*, North Carolyn, Algonquin Books of Chapel Hill, 1998.

TARRIUS, Alain, *Les Nouveaux Cosmopolitismes, mobilité, identités, territoires*, Paris, L'aube, 2000.

TARRIUS, Alain, *La Mondialisation par le bas, les nouveaux nomades de l'économie souterraine*, Paris, Balland, 2002.

THERNSTROM, Stephan, *Poverty and Progress : Social Mobility in the Nineteenth Centuries City*, Waltham (Mass.), Harvard University Press, 1981.

THERNSTROM, Stephan, *Other Bostonians : Poverty and Progress in the American Metropolis*, Waltham (Mass.), Harvard University Press, 1976.

THOMAS, W.I., and ZNANIECKI, F., *Le Paysan polonais en Amérique, récit de vie d'un migrant*, Introd. Pierre Tripier, Paris, Nathan, 1998.

THOMAS, W.I., and ZNANIECKI, F., *The Polish Peasant in Europe and America*, 1918, nv. ed. 1988.

TOCQUEVILLE, Alexis de, *De La Démocratie en Amérique*, UGE, 1963.

TRAVERSO, Enzo, *Les Juifs et l'Allemagne, de la symbiose judéo allemande à la mémoire d'Auschwitz*, Paris, La Découverte, 1993.

UBERFILL, François, *La Société strasbourgeoise entre France et Allemagne (1871-1924)*, Publications de la société savante d'Alsace, 2001.

UROFSKY, Melvin F., KAGANOFF Melvin I., *Turn to the South, Essays on Southern Jewry*, University Press of Virginia, 1979.

VECOLI, Rudolph J., « From the Uprooted to the Transplanted: the Writing of American Immigration History, 1951-1989 » in Valeria Lerda ed. *From Melting Pot to Multiculturalism: the*

Evolution of Ethnic Relations in the United States and Canada, Rome, Bulzoni Editore, 1990.

VOGLER, Bernard, HAU Michel, *Histoire économique de l'Alsace, Strasbourg*, La nuée bleue, 1997.

WAHL, Alfred, *Confession et comportement dans les campagnes d'Alsace et de Bade, 1871-1939*, thesis, Université de Metz, COPRUR, 1980.

WAHL, Alfred, *Les Problèmes de l'option des Alsaciens-Lorrains (1871-1872)*, thèse de 3e cycle [doctoral thesis], Strasbourg, 1972.

WEBER, Max, *L'Éthique protestante et l'esprit du capitalisme*, 1905, Plon, 1967.

WEBER, Max, *Essais sur la théorie de la science*, collection of articles published between 1904 and 1917, Paris, Plon, 1965.

WEBER, Max, *Economie et société*, 1921, Paris, Plon, 1971.

WEBER, Max, *Le Judaïsme antique*, Mohr, 1920, new edition. Pocket, 1998, trans.. into French by Freddy Raphaël.

WEIL, François, *Naissance d'une Amérique urbaine, 1820-1920*, Paris, SEDES,1992.

WEIL, François, and HEFFER, Jean, *Chantiers d'histoire américaine*, Paris, Belin, 1994.

WEIS, Julius, *Autobiography of Julius Weis*, New Orleans, Goldmans Printing Office, 1903.

WEISSBACH, Lee Shai, *Jewish Life in Small-Town America*, A History, New Haven and London, Yale University Press, 2005.

WEISSER, R. Michael, *Jewish Landmanshaften in the New World, A Brotherhood of Memory*, New York, Basic Books, 1985.

WYATT-BROWN, Bertram, *Honor and Violence in the Old South*, Oxford University Press, 1986.

WHYTE, William Foote, *Street Corner Society, la structure sociale d'un quartier italo-américain*, Paris, La Découverte, 1995.

WIEWORKA, Michel, *Vers un multiculturalisme français*, 2003, Éditions de la Différence, 2001.

WINTER, Elke, *Max Weber et les relations ethniques, du refus du biologisme racial à l'Etat multinational*, Presse universitaires de Laval, 2004.

WIRTH, Louis, *The Ghetto*, Chicago, University of Chicago Press, 1928, new edition with a new introduction by Hasia R. Diner, Brunswick and London, Transaction publishers, 1998, French version, *Le Ghetto*, 2nd ed., with an introduction by ROJTMAN J., Grenoble, PUF, 1980.

WOLCHANSKY, Maxine and LEDNER Beulah, « *Let's bake* » *with Beulah Ledner: a legendary New Orleans Lady*, s.l., s.d.

YERUSHALMI, Yoseph Hayim, *Zakhor, Histoire juive et mémoire juive*, Paris, Gallimard, 1991.

ZANGWILL, Israël, *The Melting Pot, a Drama in Four Acts*, 1908, 6th edition, revised, New York, Macmillan, 1917.

Articles

BENJAMIN, Judah P., *Louisiana Historical Quarterly*, 1936, vol. 19, Free Press, New York, 1988.

BLOCH-RAYMOND, Anny :

-« Green Card, sur les traces des communautés juives alsaciennes à New York », in *Saisons d'Alsace, printemps 1992, Nos cousins d'Amérique.*

- (in collab. with Marie-Noële Denis, Alain Ercker), « Une région dans ses meubles », (ed. Segalen Martine, Le Wita, Beatrix), *Chez soi. Objets et décors : des créations familiales* ?, Paris , ed. Autrement, 1993.

- (in collaboration with ERCKER Alain), « Une culture des frontières ? État cruel des lieux », *Revue des sciences sociales de la France de l'Est*, 23, 1996.

- « Mobilité des familles juives émigrées d'Alsace aux États-Unis à la fin du XIXe siècle », Proceedings of the 5th International Congress of Jewish Genealogy, July 13-17, 1997.

- « L'Émigration juive alsacienne aux États-Unis (1830-1930) », *Archives juives*, Les Belles lettres, 32, 2, 1999.

- "Mercy on rude streams: Jewish Emigrants from Alsace-Lorraine to the Lower Mississippi Region and the Concept of fidelity," *Southern Jewish History,* Miami, 2, 1999.

- "Enemies abroad, Friends in the United States: Jewish Diaspora from Alsace-Lorraine vs. Jewish Diaspora from Germany, 19th, 20th century," November 16, 17, 2002, Dickinson College, published by the Clarke Center, Contemporary Issue series, Nov. 2004.

- « Les Écoles juives en Alsace », *Archives juives*, 2006 39, 2.

- « Journaux et mémoires de migrants en Amérique : créer un pont entre deux continents » in Proceedings of the International Colloquium, *Passer, dépasser les frontières*, May 27-29, 2004, Toulouse, (Jean François Berdah, Anny Bloch-Raymond, Colette Zytnicki, ed.), Toulouse, Editions méridiennes, 2007.

BORDES-BENAYOUN, Chantal, « Revisiter les diasporas », *Diasporas, Histoire et Sociétés*, 2002.

CARON, Vicki, "The Social and Religious Transformation of Alsace Lorraine Jewry, 1871-1914," *Leo Baeck Institute Yeanbook*, 1985.

CHATELAIN, « Recherches et enquêtes démographiques, les migrations françaises vers le nouveau monde aux XIXe et XXe siècles », *Annales, économie, sociétés, civilisations*, Paris, Armand Colin, 1947.

CHEVALIER, Louis, « L'émigration française au XIXe siècle » in *Études d'histoire moderne et contemporaine*, 1947.

COHEN, Martine, « De l'émancipation à l'intégration : les transformations du judaïsme français au XIXe siècle » in *Archives de sciences sociales des religions*, October, December, 1994, 88.

DALTROFF J., « L'émigration en Amérique des Juifs d'Alsace-Lorraine », *Liaisons, n°11, Bulletin du Consistoire israélite de la Moselle*.

DAVID, Thelen, "Memory and American History", *Journal of American Ethnic History*, 1989, p. 1120-1129.

DINER, Hasia R., "Entering the Mainstream of Modern Jewish History: Peddlers and the American Jewish South," *Southern Jewish History*, 8, 2005.

DURKHEIM, Émile, « Communauté et société selon Tönnies », *Revue philosophique*, 27, 1889, 416-422.

FERRIS COHEN, Marcie, "From the Recipe File of Luba Cohen: a study of Southern Jewish Foodways and Cultural Identity," *Southern Jewish History*, 2, 1990.

FOHLEN, Claude, « Perspectives historiques sur l'immigration française aux États-Unis », *Revue européenne des migrations internationales*, REMI, 6, 1, 28-41.

GAGNON, Nicole, « Les vies dans la pratique culturelle » in *Cahiers internationaux de sociologie*, Vol. LXIX, 1980.

GINSBURGER, Moses, « Les troubles contre les Juifs d'Alsace en 1848 », *Revue des Etudes juives*, 1903.

GLANZ, Rudolf, "The Immigration of German Jews up to 1880,"*Yivo Annual of Jewish Social Science*, 7,2.

GLANZ, Rudolf, "Early Jewish Peddling in America," *Studies in Judaica Americana*, Krav Publishing House, 1970.

GREEN, Nancy L. "Jewish Migrations to France in the Nineteenth Century and Twentieth Centuries: Communities or Communities?" *Studia Rosenthalina*, ed. M.P. Beukers J.J. Cahen, XXIII, 2.

GREENBERG, Cheryl Lynn, *Troubling the Waters, Black-Jewish Relations in The American Century,* Princeton and Oxford, Princeton University Press, 2006.

GREENBERG, Mark I, "Becoming Southern: The Jews of Savannah, Georgia, 1830-1870," *American Jewish History*, 62-63.

HERVIEU-LEGER, Danièle, « Le converti, une figure de description de l'ultra-modernité religieuse », *Diasporas, Histoire et Sociétés*, n° 3, 2003.

KLAPPER, Melissa, "A Long and Broad Education: Jewish Girls and the Problem of Education in America 1860-1920," *Journal of American Ethnic History*, 22, 1, 2002.

LEUILLIOT, Paul, « L'émigration alsacienne sous l'Empire », *Revue historique*, sept.-déc. 1930.

LIPSON–WALKER, Carolyn, "The relativity of Southern Jewish Identity and Folklore, Northern and Southern Comparisons," unpublished.

MAIRE, Camille, «Erckmann-Chatrian, l'Amérique et les émigrants », *Revue lorraine populaire*, avril 1985.

MAIRE, Camille, «L'émigration en Amérique des juifs du pays de Phalsbourg », *Les Cahiers lorrains*, 1986, n°1-2.

MALONE, Bobbie, "New Orleans Uptown Jewish Immigrants: the Community of Congregation Gates of Prayer, 1850-1860," *Louisiana History*, 1992, 32, 3.

MARCUS, Jacob R., "A Selected Bibliography of American Jewish History," New York.

MORIN, Françoise, « Anthropologie et histoire de vie », *Cahiers internationaux de sociologie*, vol. LXIX , 1980.

PARK, Robert Ezra, "Human Migration and the Marginal Man," *American Journal of Sociology*, vol. 33, 1928.

RAPHAËL, Freddy, « Le travail de la mémoire et les limites de l'histoire orale », *Annales, Economie, Sociétés, Civilisations*, 38e année, 1, January - February. 1980.

RAPHAEL, Freddy, « Stéréotype du juif dans un village d'Alsace en 1876 », *l'Alsace rurale, Revue des sciences sociales de la France de l'Est*, 1978, 142-153.

REISSNER, Hans G., "The German-American Jews (1800-1850)," *Leo Baeck Institute Yearboook*, 10,1965.

RICHET, Isabelle, « Religion et politique, une pas si sainte alliance », *Hérodote*, 106, 3, 2002.

RICHEZ, Jean-Claude, « Le Juif, le Forestier, l'État », *Ethnologie française*, 21, 1991, n° 3.

RIFF, Michael, "The Anti-Jewish Aspect of 1848 in Baden and its Impact on Emancipation," *Leo Baeck Institute Yearbook*, 1976.

ROGOFF, Leonard, "Is the Jew White? The Racial Place of the Southern Jew," *American Jewish History*, 85, 5, 1997.

ROHRBACHER, Stephen, "From Würtemberg to America," *American Jewish Archives*, 41, 1989.

ROSENTHAL, Erich, "Acculturation without Assimilation? The Jewish Community of Chicago, Illinois," *American Journal of Sociology*, 66, 1960, 275-288.

RÜRUP, Reinhard, "The Tortuous and Thorny Path to Legal Equality, Jew Laws and Emancipatory Legislation in Germany from the Late Eighteenth Century," *Leo Baeck Institute Yearbook*, 31, 1986.

STADTLER, Edouard, « Die Judenkraawalle von 1848 im Elsass », *Elsassiche Monatschrift für Geshichte und Volkskunde*, 2, 1911.

SCHWARTZ, John, "Repaired Shield for New Orleans," *The New York Times*, May, 25, 2006.

SCHNAPPER, Dominique « De l'État-nation au monde transnational, du sens et de l'utilité du concept de diaspora », *Revue européenne des migrations internationales*, 17, 2, 2001.

THELEN, David, "Memory and American History," *Journal of American Ethnic History*, 1989, 1120-1129.

TÖLÖLYAN, Khachig, "Rethinking Diaspora(s): Stateless Power in the Transnational Moment," *Diasporas, Histoire et Sociétés* (5), 1, 3-64. 1996.

WALL, Bennet H., "Leon Godchaux, and the Godchaux Business Enterprises," *American Jewish Historical Quarterly*, 16, 1, 1976.

WEIL, François, « Les migrants français aux Amériques (XIXe-XXe siècle), nouvel objet d'histoire », *Annales de démographie historique*, 2000.

WEINTRATER, Meir, « USA : les Blacks contre les Jews », *l'Arche*, September 1999, 75-111.

WEISSBACH, Lee Shai; "East European Immigrants and the Image of Jews in the Small-Town South," *American Jewish History*, Vol. 85, 1997.

GENERAL INDEX

Abraham, Julia, 78

Acadiana, 43, 102, 106

Accommodation, x, 151, 208

Acculturation, xxi, 24, 54, 56, 201

Adaptation by immigrants, 20, 22, 23, 25, 75, 157, 208

Adler, Rabbi David, 54

Alabama, xiv, xxv, 17, 24, 26, 36, 41, 108, 120, 177, 182, 183, 185, 188, 202, 204

Alexandria, LA, 21, 26, 30, 42, 57, 76, 77, 107, 142, 165, 204

Algeria, 2, 8

Alsace-Lorraine, xviii, xix, 1, 2, 52, 122,

American Jewish Archives, xiv, 15

Americanization, 23-25, 53, 55, 57, 59, 60, 68, 89, 108, 109, 141, 154, 155, 169, 201, 208

Anti-poverty programs, 147, 172

Anti-Semitism 1, 2, 60, 83, 119, 149, 150-153, 156, 173, 186, 190, 200, 206

Aron, Lucile, née Lazare 30, 31

Ascension Parish, 16, 38, 48, 107, 132, 134

Ashkenazi, Elliott, 26, 36, 38, 41, 48, 101, 181

Ashkenazi Jews, xxi, 56, 140

Asmonean, 55

Assimilation, xxvi, 22-24, 55, 56, 58-60, 68-71, 89, 151 165-168, 171, 173, 201, 205, 208

Association pour le Rétablissement des Institutions et des Œuvres israélites en France, 162, 163

Atkin, Bettie, 191, 194, 195

Atlanta, GA, 43, 47, 86, 159, 188

Aunt Babette's Cookbook, 118, 119

Avoyelles Parish, 77, 175

Babin, Brenda S., 37

Baden, xv, 2, 3, 8, 41, 115, 156

Balfour Declaration, 83

Balogh, Malvina, 173, 174

Bandry, Michel, 42, 43

Baptist, 65, 73, 76, 78, 79, 165, 170-173, 175, 179

Barkaï, Avraham, xix, 1, 2, 14,

Bar mitzvah, 62, 73, 80, 81, 88, 114, 178

Barriers between Jews and Christians, 18, 150, 172-175

Bas-Rhin, Alsace, xii, 2-4, 8, 10-13, 41, 78, 101, 119, 125, 126, 142, 183,

Bat mitzvah, 62, 81

Baton Rouge, LA, vii, xi, xiv, 13, 21, 27, 34, 58, 73, 84-86, 88, 99, 107-109, 115, 117, 119, 126, 138, 142, 145, 146, 153, 157, 165, 171, 176, 184, 186, 191, 194-196,

Baumann, Émile, 7

Bayous, xiii, 20, 21, 26, 106, 115, 117, 119

Bayou Sainte-Marie, 21

Bayou Sara, LA, 21, 26

Beignets, xiii, 113

Belfort (Franche-Comté), 19, 116, 127

Bellah, Norbert, 51, 52

Benjamin, Samuel Louis, 159

Berlin (Germany), 6, 53

Bernstein, L.J., 151

Bersheva (Israel), 73

Berson, Leonora, 150

Bikur Cholim Cemetery, 48

Bischwiller, (Bas-Rhin, Alsace), xiv

Birmingham, AL, 43, 177, 178, 204

Block, Matthias, 187

Bloom, Lazare, 138

Blumberg, Peggy, 138, 145, 146

B'nai B'rith, 61, 141, 192

Bon Séjour Plantation, 35

Book of Israelites, 55, 138, 140, 146

Boston Club, 71, 150, 151, 174

Boudousquié family, 32

Bouxwiller (Bas-Rhin, Alsace), 159

Brasseaux, Carl A., 17

Bremen (Germany), 9

Bronson, Aaron, 187
----------, James Dunwoddy, 18

Brookhaven, MS, 21

Brumath (Bas-Rhin, Alsace), 8, 101

Bunche, Ralph, 189, 190

Burkenroad family, 97

Cabildo, xii, 115

Cable, George Washington, 113

Café brûlot, 114

Cahn, Bertha, née Jacobsen, 128
-------, Léo Solis, 10, 15, 128
-------, Rosine Weil, xiv, 15, 20, 21, 33, 34, 92, 93

California, xv, 11, 32, 120, 183,

Canada, 11

Canal Street, xiii, 19, 32, 47, 168, 194

Caron, Vicki, xviii

Carvalho, David Nunez, 54

Catholics, Catholicism, xx, xxv, 5, 15, 56, 65, 70, 71, 74, 76, 77-79, 104, 149, 165, 166, 168-172, 174, 176, 179, 191, 197,

Central Conference of American Rabbis (CCAR), 64, 68, 83

Chandèze, Gustave, 8

Charleston, SC, 11, 54, 176

Chase, Leah, 118

Chevalier, Louis, 15

Chicago School of Sociology, xx, 23, 208

Cholera, 15, 20

Christianization of Jews, 65, 67, 68

Cincinnati, OH, xiv, 12, 15, 49, 56, 84, 104, 118, 178

Citizenship, 55, 100, 112, 155-158

Civic action, 137, 138, 144

Civil Rights, 44, 157, 172, 189-195, 199

Civil War,18, 20, 29, 32, 36, 41, 45, 49, 52, 94, 98, 100, 103, 104, 151, 158, 161,179,181-183, 186, 187

Classifications, Social, xii, xxiv, 4, 18, 23, 30, 95, 97, 103, 105, 113, 118, 119, 167, 173, 186, 197, 203, 206

Clegg, Holly Berkowitz, 119

Clinton, LA, 21, 26

Code Noir, 183

Codofil, 102, 107

Cohen, Edward, 33, 86
--------, Marcie, ix, 118
--------, Rosalie, née Palter, 84, 101, 147, 148

Cohn, Rabbi Edward Paul, 69

Coleman Adler, jewelers, 98

Communal Hebrew School, 147

Concordia, TN, 33

Confirmation, 56, 61-64,

Congregation Shaare Chesed, 145, 146

Conversion, 64, 69-72, 74, 205

Cooper, Minette, née Switzer, 158

CORE, 189

Cotton brokers/factors, 39-41, 45, 139, 140, 156,

Court-bouillon, 113, 114

Covert, Mildred L., 101, 120

Creagh, Ronald, 19

Crescent City (See New Orleans), x

Creoles of Louisiana, 18, 33, 48, 112

Dallas, TX, 17, 47, 62, 82,

Danziger, Emilie, née Dreyfous, 128
------------, Isidore, 179,
------------, 183

Davis, Edwin Adams, 32

DCA Food Industries, 47

Debutantes, 71, 154, 174

Degas, Edgar, xiii

Demopolis, MS, 26, 185

Dennery family, 47, 48
------------,Charles, 10, 47, 96
------------,Charles, II, 47
------------,Fanny, née Salomon, 10, 96
-----------,Jeannette, née Frank, 96
------------,Marguerite, 10
-----------, Moïse, 103
-----------, Sarah, née Salmon, 96
-----------,Theodore, 10, 96

Desegregation, 149, 185, 188, 189-196, 199

Destrehan Plantation, 31

Detroit, MI, 168

Deutsche Company, 143, 144

Diaspora, xviii, xxi-xxiii, 35, 52, 81, 88, 137, 178, 201-203

Diner, Hasia, 33, 35

Dinnerstein, Leonard, 152

Doberge cake, 119

Donaldsonville, LA, 21, 26, 27, 31, 35, 36, 40, 42, 48, 49, 78, 134, 170, 204

Dooky Chase Cookbook, 118

Dreyer, Daniel, 2

Dreyfous, Abel, 19, 57, 103, 127, 144, 181
------------,Caroline, née Kaufman, 146
------------,Émile, 127
------------,Félix Jonathan, 96, 103, 127, 128, 144, 182
------------,George Abel, 189
------------,Jules, 127
------------,Mathilde née Mendelsohn, 149, 189
------------,Ruth, xiv, 57, 70, 96, 98, 103, 116, 117, 144, 146, 147,149

Dreyfus Affair, 152

Dreyfus Frères, 8

Dreyfus Store, 34

Dreyfus, Emma, née Jonas, 70
-------, Rabbi Stanley, 6, 84, 143,
-------, Rhoda Abraham, 70
-------, Robert, 70

Duke, David, 152, 153, 173

Duppigheim, (Bas-Rhin, Alsace), xii, 119

Eastern European Immigrants, xxv, 3, 59, 159, 202

École Classique, 104

Education of French & German immigrants, xix, xx, 95,
—————, plantation, 95
————— in New Orleans, 43, 45, 148, 166, 185, 189, 192, 193, 196-199, 206

Edwards, Edwin W., 152

Einhorn, David, 54, 68

Emigration, agencies, xviii, 7, 8
———————, French, 156, 157
———————, German 155, 156
———————, Regulation of, 6-11

Emke, Jane Godchaux, 25, 31

English language, 25, 32, 53, 54, 56, 89, 99, 101-109, 121, 208

Episcopalians, 69-71, 165, 169, 170

Ethnicity, xviii-xxi

Evangelical Church, 65, 79, 80, 152, 174

Evans, Eli N., 17, 186

Farrakhan, Louis, 173

Fayette, MS, 32, 33, 139

Feibelman, Rabbi Julian, 151, 190

Fidelity, xxvii, 73, 137, 154-158

Filé (ground sassafras), 113, 115

First, Ruth, 70, 163

Fischel, Bert, 82, 129, 158
—————, Léon, 129, 158
—————, Myra, 82

Forbach (Moselle), 7

Fouché, Nicole, xviii

Fraenkel, Albert, 126, 142, 184
——————, Carrie, née Switzer, 184
——————, Ellie, 86
——————, Emilie, 126, 174
——————, Félix, 30, 126, 142
——————, Harriette, 126

Franco-Prussian War, 96, 158

Frank, Michael, 57

Frankenbourg, Germany, 106

Frankfort, Treaty of, 2

Free African Americans, 32, 112

Freemasonry, 112, 141-143

French, Cajun, 106, 109

French Civil Code (Napoleonic Code), 7, 103, 107

French language, 13, 17, 25 35,

------, use of in Louisiana, 30, 31, 46, 47, 55, 90, 100, 102-110, 112, 144

French Quarter (Vieux Carré), xii, xiii, 19, 92, 96, 98, 100, 112, 168

Friedman, Murray, 191

Friedmann, Karl B., 178
--------------, Max, 177, 178

Friend, Ida, née Weis, 149
--------, Joseph Emanuel, 140

Fromenthal, Benoît, xiv, 92, 101

Galveston, TX, 11

Garden District, xi, xiii, 19, 47, 95, 167

Geismar, LA, xi, 16, 36, 38, 94, 133

Geismar Plantation at Ascension Parish, LA, 16, 36, 37, 38, 94, 132

Geismar, Alfred, 39
-----------, Benjamin Louis, 16-17, 37, 38, 94, 101, 133
-----------, Evelyn, née Vessier, 106
-----------, Florette "Flo", xi, 16, 17, 36-38, 42, 71, 72, 80, 84, 94, 95, 104, 108, 109, 123, 147, 153, 154, 162, 166, 171-173, 179
-----------, Léon, xi, 10, 38, 109, 144, 157, 162
-----------, Minel, 16, 38, 94
-----------, Seraphine, née Heymann, 16, 94, 133
-----------, Simon, 16

Geismar-Toledano family, 39, 97

Genealogical research, xiii, xiv, 70, 76, 100, 108, 205, 208

Gerim, 69

German cuisine, 118, 119
------------language, xix, xx, 13, 17, 25, 30, 52, 100, 101, 104, 105,

Germersheim (Palatinate), 5, 13, 14, 159

281

Gerson, Sylvia P., 101, 120-122

Glaser, Cathy, 151

Glazer, Nathan, 68

Godchaux, Léon, 25, 31, 32, 39, 183

----------------, Mayer, 32

Godchaux Sugar, Inc. 39

Golden, Harry, 150

-----------, Stephanie, 142, 176

Goldsmith & Haber, 28

Gonzales, LA, xi, 38, 58

Grand chambardement, 108

Greater New Orleans Federation, 88, 89

Greensboro, NC, 59

Greenville, MS, 21

Greenwood, MS, 21

Grits, 116, 117, 121

Group identity, 62, 203

Grussenheim (Haut-Rhin, Alsace), 16, 133

Gumbo, x, xii, 113, 115, 116

Haas, Dr. John, 43

Haas, Samuel, 43

Hadassah, 86, 87, 147-149

Hamburg (Germany), 9, 53

Handlin, Oscar, xxvi, 156,

Harby, Isaac, 54

Harmony Club, 143

Haut-Rhin, Alsace, 2, 4, 11, 15, 133,

Hazan (cantor), 51, 62

Hazelhurst, MS, 100

Hearn, Lafcadio, 113

Hebrew Benevolent Association, xx, 20, 56, 138

Hebrew Immigrant Aid Society (HIAS), xx

Hebrew Union College, 56, 68

Heine, Armand, 151

Heller, Rabbi Max, 84-85

Herbeviller (Lorraine), 31

Hermann, Isaac, 158

Herberg, Will, 169

Hertzberg, Arthur, 52, 53

Hervieu-Léger, Danièle, 72

Heymann, Abraham, 17
-------------, Michel, 145
-------------, Seraphine (See Geismar, Seraphine)

High Society (New Orleans), 71, 150, 174

Hiller, Jonas, 139

Hirsch, Pauline, née Weil, 100

Hochstein, Salomon, 158

Holocaust, xviii, 77. 82, 179, 202

Howard Association, xx, 20, 139

Hughes, Everett C., xx

Indianola, MS, 21

Ingwiller (Bas-Rhin, Alsace), 13, 101

Interfaith marriage, 64, 65, 68-70, 73, 74

Interfaith relations, 168-172

Inter-racial marriage, 76, 179

Israel, State of, xxii, 73, 82-89, 137, 148, 172, 202, 203,

Israëlite, The, 55

Jackson, MS, ix, xiv, 21, 26, 42, 75, 86, 138, 165, 167, 170, 178, 187, 192, 193, 196,

Jackson Square, xii

Jacobson, Jennie, née Danziger, 128

Jacobson, Matthew Frye, xxvi

Jambalaya, 113, 117, 118, 121

Jerusalem (Israel), 74, 85, 99

Jerusalem University, 74

Jewish Consistory of the Bas-Rhin, Alsace, 4, 5

Jewish assimilation into a Christian world, 165-168
----------- business acumen, 188
----------- culture, 25, 81, 121, 205
-----------cuisine, 110, 111
-----------dietary laws (kashrut), 110, 111, 114, 119, 120-122
-----------elected officials, 144, 149
---------- exclusion from Carnival Krewes and clubs, 150, 151
-----------"horns," 175, 176
-----------identity, 26, 35, 60 73-75, 89, 119, 121, 122,

154, 199, 202
---------- relations with African Americans, 35, 165, 178-200
----------role of photos & memorabilia, 98, 99
----------Sabbath, 33, 51, 64, 116, 117, 120, 147, 178
----------traditions, 70, 73, 80, 100, 111, 137
----------wives ostracized, 150

Jewish Ledger, 57, 59

Jewish Widows and Orphans Home, 20, 139, 202

Jews, Franco-German, xvii, xxv, 1, 3, 15 ,24, 25, 50, 82, 86, 95, 101, 128, 178, 185, 202

Jews, Southern vs. Northern, 154, 177-180

Judaism, Cultural, 81, 205, 206

Judeo-Alsatian, 100, 101

Julius Weis Home for the Aged, 140

Kahn, Abraham, 167

Kahn, Abraham Metz, 35, 57, 58, 73, 74, 84-86, 88, 99, 107, 108, 142, 153, 157, 170, 175, 176, 180, 184, 187, 191, 194, 195, 196

Kahn, Catherine, née Cahn, 20, 69, 70, 98, 99, 127, 128, 150, 154
-------, Fred II, 46, 47, 96, 97, 105, 128
-------, Lazard, 40, 101
-------, Lazare, 187
-------, Thérèse, née Abraham, 87

Kaiserslautern (Germany), 8, 124, 140

Kander, Lizzie, 118, 119

Kehl (Baden-Württemberg), 8

Kippah, 62, 81, 82

Kirshenblatt-Gimblett, Barbara, 118, 119

Klingen (Palatinate), 14, 30, 139

Klotz, Abraham, 78, 170, 171
------, Salomon, 144
------, Samuel, 99

Kohlmeyer, Hermann, 139
--------------, Herman S., Jr., 41, 104, 105, 124, 125
---------------, Nancy, née Koodish, 99

Kosher Creole Cookbook, 121

Kosher-Creole Cuisine, 110-118, 120-122

Kosher Southern-Style Cookbook, 121

Krewe du Jieux, 151

Krewe du Mishugas, 151

Ku Klux Klan, 152, 153, 193, 194

Kuppermann, Jo-Ellyn, née Levy, 196, 197

Ladies Hebrew Aid Society, xx, 145

Lafayette (now uptown New Orleans), 19, 57

Lafayette, LA, 21, 99, 106, 107, 109, 110

Lake Pontchartrain, LA, xii, 115, 189

Landau (Germany), 8, 14, 139,

Landmannshaften, 17

Lapierre, Nicole, xxii

Laura Plantation, 95

Lauterbourg (Bas-Rhin), 92

Lazarus, Caroline, xii 68, 70
----------- family, 45-47

-----------, Jules Jacob, 46
-----------, Vicki, 71
-----------, Will, xii, 45, 46, 67, 68

Leathem, Karen, 151

Ledner, Beulah, née Levy, 119

Lehmann, Beatrice, 192, 193
------------, Celeste, 192, 193
------------, Elaine Ullman, 116
------------, Flo, 80, 170, 192-193-
------------, Gustave, 144

Lemann General Store, 49, 134, 166

Lemann sugar plantations, 40, 48-50

Lemann, Bernard, 48
-----------, Jacob, 48, 49, 101

Lembach (Bas-Rhin, Alsace), 12, 41, 76, 125,

Le Havre (France), 3, 8, 9, 13-15

Léon, Léopold, 49

Lesser, Isaac, 55

Leuilliot, Paul, 3

Levy, Abraham, 30, 119
-------, Isaac, xiv, 12, 13

-------, Michel, 92
-------, Oscar, xii, 151
-------, Capt. Simon, Jr., 158

Lewis, Read, 23

Lexington, MS, 21, 74, 75, 166

Lisitzky, Ephraim P, 101, 147

Liverpool, England, 41

Livonia, LA, 34

Locoul, Laura, 95

Loeb, Joseph, 139

Lorman General Store, 34, 166

Louisiana, xiii, xv, xix, xx, 17, 18, 20, 24-27, 30, 33-36, 39, 41-43, 48, 49, 57, 58, 76, 77, 85, 102-104, 106-12, 115, 133, 140, 141, 144, 152, 153, 158, 165, 175, 176, 180-183, 191, 202, 204

Louisiana League for the Preservation of Civil Rights, 189

Loyalty, xxii, 24, 55, 61, 89, 154, 155, 158, 159, 182, 187, 201

Luchinger, Philip, 78-80

Lutcher, LA, 21

Lyons, Robert, 55

Mainz (Germany), 9, 14, 57

Maire, Camille, 1

Manouvrier, Rebecca, 43

Mansura, LA, 76, 77

Marcus, Jacob Rader, xiv, xv, 26
---------, Julia, 62, 205
---------, Sylvia, 80, 81

Marksville, La, 76

Marienstras, Richard, xxi

Marrano effect (See Christianization of Jews)

Marx, David, 64
-------, Salomon, 57, 85, 139, 142, 143

Matzo balls, 111, 114, 115, 117, 118, 121

Mayer, Weis & Deutsch, 139

McLaughlin, Leslie Geismar DeBardeleben, 71

Memphis, TN, 17, 21, 28, 37,

Metairie, LA, x, 78, 168

Metairie Cemetery, 140

Methodism, ix, 65, 71, 73, 165, 170, 171

Meyer, Julie Grant, 63, 88, 89, 168

Meyer, Michael, 83

Mezuzah, 99

Michelangelo, 176

Middle class, 4, 105, 118, 119, 167, 206

Milliken's Bend, LA, 28, 29, 131

Mills, Carol, 76-78, 175

Minnesota, 11

Mirliton (christophene, chayote), 114

Mississippi, ix, xv, 17, 19, 20, 21, 24, 26, 27, 32, 35, 41, 42, 78, 153, 158, 161, 175, 202, 204

Mississippi River, x, xi, xiii, xxvii, 14, 16, 19, 20, 21, 24, 28, 31, 95, 101, 104, 115, 158, 175, 203,

Mitzvot, 64

Mobile, AL, 17, 36, 188

Mobility, xxii, xxvi, 25-27, 30, 43, 95, 204,

Moise, Abraham, 54

Mommenheim (Bas-Rhin, Alsace), 187

Monroe, LA, 26, 204

Montgomery, AL, xiv, xxv, 17, 26, 36, 41, 57, 70, 149, 151, 156, 159, 165, 167, 168, 170, 172, 179, 182, 185, 186, 190, 191, 202, 204

Mormon Church, 73

Mulatto, xiii, 76, 77, 175, 179,

Mulhouse (Haut-Rhin, Alsace), 2

Museum of the Southern Jewish Experience, ix, 42, 75, 116, 178

Myers, Joel Bert, 58, 67,68, 86-88, 105, 143, 167

NAACP, 188, 190, 192, 195, 200

Nannies, African American, 180, 184-186

Napoleonic Code, (See French Civil Code)

Napoleonville, LA, 99, 144, 150, 171

Natchez, MS, xiv, 13, 17, 21, 26, 30, 31-33, 42, 77, 92, 116, 139, 150, 159, 165, 170, 204

New Orleans, LA, x-xiv, xix, xx, xxv, 2,10-21, 26-28, 30-34, 36-49, 51, 55-58, 62, 63, 67-73, 77-81, 84, 86-89, 91, 92, 94-98, 101, 103-107, 109-117, 119-121, 123, 126, 127, 133, 139, 140, 143, 145, 147-151, 153, 154, 156, 162, 166-168, 170, 172-175, 179, 181, 183, 184, 186, 189, 194, 196-198, 202, 204, 205

-------dining en famille, 97
-------education in, 196-198
-------furnishings and antiques, 98-100
-------restaurants, xii, 113, 114, 115, 117, 120, 188, 190
------- servants, 93- 97, 160, 181, 183, 186, 194
-------University of, 198

New River Landing, LA,(See also Geismar, LA) xi, 16, 132, 133

New York, ix, xiv, xv, 6, 10, 11-15, 17, 18, 32, 33, 35, 40, 41, 49, 54, 55, 70, 73, 74, 91, 92, 97, 101, 104, 142, 143, 146, 153, 158, 163, 171, 173, 174, 176, 177, 185, 187, 189, 192,

Newman, Isidore, 105, 124, 139, 140

Newman, Rebecca, née Kiefer, 125

Newman School, 104, 105, 140, 174, 197, 198

Niederbronn (Bas-Rhin, Alsace), 10

Nitzkin, Joel, 151

Nussbaum, Rabbi Perry, 192, 193

Oberlauterbach (Bas-Rhin, Alsace), 142

Oberlustadt (Palatinate), 182

Occident, 55

Oftzedaka, 51, 61, 137

Okra, xii, 114, 115

Opelika, AL, 159, 182

Opelousas, LA, 21, 26, 42-44, 58, 106-108, 204

Orthodox Judaism, 6, 53, 55, 57-59, 62, 73, 80, 83-86 88, 120, 122, 147, 201

Osyka, MS, 21

Otterstadt (Palatinate), 159

Oysters, xi, 113, 115-118, 121

Pain perdu, 114

Paincourtville, LA, 139

Palatinate, xv, 2, 3, 5, 8, 10, 13, 30, 124, 133, 139, 140, 156, 158, 159, 182, 183,

Palestine, 83, 84, 86, 87, 147, 148, 189

Palo Alto Plantation, 49

Pannequets, 113

Paracha, 63

Park, Robert Ezra, 23

Parker, Jonathan, xiv

Paris, France, xiv, 9, 13, 14, 16, 39, 40, 103-105, 107, 140, 145, 158

Paris, Leroy H., 75, 76, 166, 167, 195, 196

Pascagoula, MS, 21, 92, 181

Peddler aristocracy, 138

Peddlers, Jewish, xxiv, 4, 20, 26, 27, 29-35, 39, 48, 139, 147, 175, 176, 180, 186, 187, 203

Pennsylvania, 11

Peytavin Plantation, 49

Pfaffenbronn (Bas-Rhin, Alsace), 8

Phagan, Mary, 152

Picard & Geismar General Store, 132, 244

Picard, Joseph "Jo", 16, 17, 36-38, 162

Pickwick Club, 151

Pineville, LA, 77, 142

Pirmasens (Germany), 8

Pittsburgh, PA, 12, 53, 120, 169

Plaçage, 18

Plantations, xi, xiii, xxiv, 16, 18, 19, 29, 31-33, 35-43, 48-50, 93-95, 97, 101, 115, 117, 132, 139, 177, 180, 182, 186, 203

Plaquemine, LA, 21, 30, 139, 149, 204

Plotchnikoff family, 33

Pontchartrain Beach, 189

Port Gibson, MS, ix, 17, 21, 26, 31, 34, 38, 52, 59, 60, 125, 146, 159, 204

Posner, Dr. Gerald, 43, 44, 106

Posner, Isabelle, 43

Postmodernism, 72, 80

Presbyterian Church, 70, 78-80, 165, 170

Princeton, MS, 28

Progressive Union, 144

Rabinowitz, Howard N., 20

Raceland, LA, 21, 67, 167

Rachel Benevolent Association, 146, 147

Ratisbonne, Louis, 4

Reform Judaism, 53-57, 59-61, 63, 64, 68, 69, 73, 79, 80-86, 88, 89, 115, 116, 120, 122, 140, 147,148, 169, 171, 189, 190, 201, 202

Reichshoffen (Bas-Rhin, Alsace), 41, 78, 144

Reissner, Hans G., 1

Reserve, LA, 39

Reserve Plantation, 39

Reveille, The, 59, 60

Rhenish Bavaria, 10

Rhine frontier, xviii

Rhine valley, xvii, xxii, 3, 25, 52, 101, 201, 202

Rhode Island, 58

Richet, Isabelle, 44, 78

Richmond, LA, 28

Richmond, VA, 176

Rio de Janeiro, Brazil, 12

Roediger, David R., xxvi

Rogoff, Leonard, xxvi, 181

Rosenthal, Isaac, 142
-------------, Moses, 142

Rothbach (Bas-Rhin, Alsace), 126

Rothschild, Janet, 101

Rotterdam (Netherlands), 9, 14

Sabbath Schools, 64, 147

Saint Louis (Haut-Rhin, Alsace), 8

Salomon, Clara, 181

San Francisco, CA, xiv, 11, 40, 62, 74, 104, 156, 158

Sartorius, Caroline, 91, 92
------------, Isaac 27
------------, Jacob, 28
------------, Joel, 51, 130
------------, Philip, xiv, 5, 13-15, 21, 27-30, 91, 92, 130, 131, 159, 161, 183
------------, Sophie, née Roos, 130, 161

Savannah, GA, 11, 187

Saverne (Bas-Rhin, Alsace), 8, 10, 15, 52, 182

Schmier, Louis, 177, 187, 188

Schnapper, xxi, xxv

Schwartz, Alfred, 47

Second Empire, 7

Sefer Torah, 51

Segregation in Jewish and Christian neighborhoods, 167, 168

Segregation, racial order, in the South, xxv, xxvi, 93, 94, 149, 150, 182, 186, 188, 192, 193, 194, 199

Sephardic Jews, xxi, 54, 56, 58, 111, 181

Serial immigration, 9

Settlement, xxi, 23

Settlement Cookbook, 118

Shohet, 51

Shotgun cottages, xiii

Shreveport, LA, 21, 26, 27, 30, 36, 57, 68, 84, 143, 165, 184, 204

Siess, Auger, 77
-------, Josephine, née Chatelain, 77
-------, Leopold, 76

Simonnot, Georges, 99, 106, 107, 170, 171

Six-Day War, 82, 88, 202

Slavery and slaves, xiii, xxvi, 18, 27, 29, 31, 32, 41, 48, 93, 94, 100, 112, 115, 126, 157, 159, 160, 177-184, 186, 199, 206

Société israélite française, ix, 101, 163

Solidarity, Franco-German, 201-203

Solis, Jacob, 56

Solomon, Louis, 150

Sons, Abraham, 40

Soulé Business School, 46

South America, x, xiii, 11

Southern Mattress Co., 46

Stamler, Vicki, 97, 193, 194

Staten Island, NY, 97

Stern, Edgar B., 148
-------, Henry, 98

St. Charles Ave., xiii, 19, 47, 97, 112, 113

St. Charles Parish, 31

St. Francisville, LA, 21, 117

St. Gabriel, LA, 21, 108

St. Louis, MO, 11, 28, 47, 157, 161, 183

St. Paul's Cemetery (Mansura, LA), 77

St. Peter the Apostle RC Church, 179, 180

Steeg, Aaron, 57

Strasbourg (Bas-Rhin, Alsace), 5, 9, 10, 15, 100, 101, 139, 158, 194,

Straus, Oscar Solomon, 182

Strauss, Berney, 188

Sugar production, xi, xxiv, 19, 25, 27, 30, 32, 36-41, 48-50, 97, 115, 180, 203

Switzerland, 3, 8, 18

Synagogue, Gates of Mercy (Shangarai Chassed), 51, 56, 140

Synagogue, Gates of Prayer, 19, 57, 78, 170, 179

Synagogue Gemiluth Chessed, Port Gibson, MS, 52, 146

Synagogue, Tememe Derech (New Orleans), 57

Synagogue, Touro, 58, 80, 172, 174, 179

Taglioni, 14

Tallit, 62, 81, 82

Temple Beth Or, 179

Temple Emanu-El (Dallas, TX), 82

Temple Emanu-El, (New York), 54, 146

Temple Sinai (New Orleans), 57, 58, 69, 73, 85, 140, 142, 167, 190

Tête Coupée Bayou, LA, 34

Thibodaux, LA, 21

Toledano, Jackie, 40, 174, 175

Touro Infirmary, 20, 34, 139, 140, 146

Touro, Isaiah, 58

-------, Judah, 58

Transnational, xxi, xxii, 201

Tremolet Hotel, 112,

Tulane University, 148, 198

Tzedaka, 51, 61, 137

Uhrwiller (Bas-Rhin, Alsace), 10

Uhry, Edmond, 13

Union of American Hebrew Congregations, 59, 83

Union française, 144

Varnhaghen, Rahel, 72

Vésoul (Haut-Saône), 10, 47, 96, 103

Vicksburg, MS, xiv, 17, 21, 28, 31, 42, 170

Vieux Brisach (Germany), 41

Vieux Carré (See French Quarter)

Voodoo, Jews seen as, 175, 176

Voorhies family, 77

Vorspan, Albert, 191

Waldhorn, Albertine, née Lob, 135

Waldhorn, Moïse, 98, 135

Waldorf School, 174, 175

Walker, Carolyn, née Lipson, 152, 177

Wampold, Babette, xxv, 149, 185, 186, 190, 191

------------, Charles, 149

Waterloo, Ascension Parish, LA, 38,

Waterloo Plantation, 94

Webb, Clive, 186-188

Weber, Max, 51, 52

Weil, Alexandre, 158

------, Jacob, 159, 160

------, Josiah, 159, 160

Weis, Julius, 13, 14, 30, 32, 39, 44, 92, 139, 140, 183

Weis & Sons, 140

Weissbach, Lee Shai, 59

Wiener, Jay L., 74, 75

Wilson, Alice, 126, 184, 185

Wise, Isaac Meyer, 53-55

Wissembourg (Bas-Rhin), 2, 6, 8, 10, 11, 13, 47, 96

Wittcowsky, Morris, 35

Wolbrette, David, 30, 139

Women's charitable associations, 145-149

Woodville, MS, 21

World War I, 162, 201

World War II, xviii, 44, 60, 85, 86, 161-163

Württemberg (Germany), 4, 156

Wyandotte Chemical Co., 38

Yellow fever, 13, 20, 92, 138, 144

Yiddish, xviii, 25, 100, 101, 111, 121, 147, 202

Yiddish-Daitsch, 100

Youngstown, OH, 84

Zelman, Grace, 171, 173

Zionism, 83-88

www.ingramcontent.com/pod-product-compliance
Lightning Source LLC
Chambersburg PA
CBHW031706230426
43668CB00006B/122